The Master Musicians Series

VAUGHAN WILLIAMS

Series edited by
Sir Jack Westrup, M.A., Hon.D.Mus.(Oxon.), F.R.C.O.
Professor Emeritus of Music, Oxford University

ALDINE PAPERBACKS

RALPH VAUGHAN WILLIAMS
(*Copyright: Karsh of Ottawa*)

THE MASTER MUSICIANS SERIES

VAUGHAN WILLIAMS

by
James Day

With eight pages of plates
and music examples in the text

London
J M DENT & SONS LTD

© Text, J. M. Dent & Sons Ltd, 1961
All rights reserved
Made in Great Britain
at the
Aldine Press · Letchworth · Herts
for
J. M. DENT & SONS LTD
Aldine House · Bedford Street · London
First published 1961
Reprinted 1964
Paperback edition 1972

ISBN: 0 460 02112 5

TO

IAN
AND
UNCLE HENRY

PREFACE

I DO NOT claim that the biographical chapters of this book are in any way complete, but they are an outline of a long life in so far as the events of that life seem to me to be relevant to the music. I should like to thank Mrs Vaughan Williams, who is writing a full-length biography of her husband, for her help in correcting errors in the original draft, for supplying me with photographs, and for giving me permission to reproduce the manuscript of *Bushes and Briars*. This acknowledgment should not be taken to indicate that she is responsible for any interpretation of facts or events set down here; any errors or misjudgments are my own.

Besides Mrs Vaughan Williams, I have been greatly helped by many others. The staff of the B.B.C. gramophone library, and particularly Miss Britten, kindly allowed me to listen to records not commercially available to the public, and the staff of the Music Room in the Cambridge University Library have been most helpful on all the many occasions when I sought their assistance. The present editor of the *R.C.M. Magazine* and his predecessor have allowed me to quote passages from the memorial issue on Vaughan Williams, and thanks to the good offices of my father-in-law, Major-General H. J. Parham, and the editor of the *Mosquito*, a number of ex-Salonika veterans provided useful information concerning Vaughan Williams's army career. Messrs Novello, Curwen, Stainer & Bell, Boosey & Hawkes and the Oxford University Press have kindly granted me permission to quote from works which they publish (in the case of the last-named, this extends also to quotations from Vaughan Williams's critical writings and to his published letters; here again, I am most grateful to Mrs Vaughan Williams and to Miss Imogen Holst for permission to quote from *Heirs and Rebels*). The Times Publishing Company have allowed me to quote from letters written by Vaughan Williams to *The Times*, and Lady Epstein has given me permission to quote from her husband's autobiography, published by the Hulton

vii

Press. Messrs Harrap have also given permission for quotations from the late Hubert Foss's study of Vaughan Williams's music, published by them, and Mr Frank Howes and Dr Percy Young have also allowed me to quote certain interpretations and comments from their studies of the composer's music. I should like too to mention one more useful 'crib': that is the phrase 'The Simple Kleptomaniac', which I have appropriated from Professor Herbert Howells—with permission.

My first revelation of Vaughan Williams's greatness came as a child of five at an Armistice Day memorial service in the Garrison church at Woolwich, when the strength and majesty of *Sine Nomine* created an impression on me that has never faded. Other, deeper qualities have since revealed themselves; not always immediately, but consistently and inevitably as one grew older. To study the music has been a rewarding experience; to submit to its impact, whether as a performer or as a mere listener, an unforgettable one.

JAMES DAY.

Stapleford, Cambridge.
Spring 1961.

NOTE TO SECOND EDITION

I AM most grateful to friends and reviewers for pointing out certain errors and omissions in the first edition—and especially to the Rev. Dr Erik Routley, Mr Michael Kennedy, Mr Keith Falkner, Sir Adrian Boult and Miss Diana McVeagh.

JAMES DAY.

Stapleford, Cambridge.
Autumn 1963.

CONTENTS

ILLUSTRATIONS

CHAPTER I

BACKGROUND AND EARLY LIFE

IF IT is true that children inherit intellectual greatness from their ancestors, Ralph Vaughan Williams was certainly marked out from birth for great achievements in art, scholarship or science. His grandfather, his great-grandfather and one of his paternal uncles were all eminent and gifted lawyers; his mother was both a descendant of Josiah Wedgwood and a niece of Charles Darwin. There seem to be two main characteristics common to both sides of the family—forthrightly expressed originality of outlook and a capacity for sheer hard work.

On the father's side the family was of Welsh extraction. John Williams, Ralph's great-grandfather, was born at Job's Well in Carmarthenshire in 1757 and was educated at the Carmarthen Grammar School, later going up to Jesus College, Oxford, before becoming a scholar of Wadham in 1774 and a fellow in 1780. He enjoyed a distinguished career at the bar—notably as a special pleader —becoming a Serjeant-at-law in 1794 and a King's Serjeant ten years later. As a legal scholar he was famous mainly for his edition of Blackstone's *Commentaries* and of the *Reports and Pleadings in the Court of King's Bench in the Reign of Charles II*, his highly valued, shrewd and lucid notes and references adding greatly to the appeal and value of the latter book in particular.

Serjeant John Williams had three sons and three daughters (one of the latter, Mary, married the sixth Earl of Buckingham). Edward Vaughan Williams, the composer's grandfather, was born in Bayswater in 1797 and educated first at Winchester and then at Westminster, from which he won a scholarship to Trinity College, Cambridge, in 1816. His career as a lawyer was even more distinguished than his father's; after establishing his reputation with an edition of his father's *Notes on Saunders' Reports*, he consolidated it

I

with a treatise *On the Law of Executors and Administrators*, which appeared in 1832 and went into seven editions in its author's lifetime. Knighted in 1847, on becoming a judge, he was renowned as one of the most powerful constituents of the court *in banco*—and well known throughout the profession for his profound learning, common sense and almost infallible judgment. It is recorded that there were fewer retrials on grounds of misdirection attributable to his judgments than to those of any other judge of his time. Those judgments were, his obituary says, 'short, accurate, and concise', a factor to be expected from one who, 'in his choice of words . . . was fastidious, and his delivery somewhat laboured and embarrassed'. He retired from the bench in 1865 and died ten years later.

Sir Edward married in 1828 and had three sons and three daughters. The second of his sons, Arthur Charles Vaughan Williams, was born in London in 1834. Like his father, he went to school at Westminster, which he entered in 1846, and where he became a Queen's Scholar in 1849. He matriculated at Christ Church, Oxford, in June 1853 and took his B.A. in 1857. Three years later he was ordained deacon and was sent as curate to Bemerton, near Salisbury, where George Herbert had been incumbent for many years in the seventeenth century. After serving in parishes in Lancashire and Hampshire, he took priest's orders in 1865. On 22nd February 1868 he married Margaret Susan, the second daughter of Josiah Wedgwood III and of his wife Caroline, *née* Darwin. In the same year he was appointed vicar of the Christ Church living of Down Ampney, in Gloucestershire, near the Wiltshire and Oxfordshire borders. It was here that his three children —two sons and a daughter—were born, and he died here on 9th February 1875.

Ralph, the second son and youngest child of the marriage, had been born just over two years previously, on 12th October 1872. The burden of bringing up the family fell upon Margaret Vaughan Williams, and it is plain that she had her full share of the Wedgwood strength of character. On the death of her husband she returned to live with her sister Sophie at Leith Hill Place, in Surrey, which her father had bought in 1845, and where he continued to live until his death in 1880. It is customary to think of Ralph Vaughan Williams as a west-countryman, and so he was by birth. But his childhood was spent with his mother's relatives in the house surrounded by trees, rhododendrons and azaleas, overlooking the Surrey Downs and the Sussex Weald. His grandfather is believed to have planted many of the trees and bushes himself. The terrace of the house commands a splendid view over the surrounding countryside, and on a clear day the two windmills above Hassocks, in Sussex, some twenty miles away, could be easily seen. Inside, the house was decorated with a number of fine portraits by distinguished artists, including two of Josiah Wedgwood I and his wife painted by Sir Joshua Reynolds, one by Romney of Josiah Wedgwood II's wife, Bessie, and a number of works by George Stubbs. Vaughan Williams thus early acquired a knowledge of and love for other arts besides the one in which he was to excel himself. One of the most interesting topics in early letters from Holst to his friend is his earnest desire to see the beauty in the works of painters whom Vaughan Williams admired, such as Veronese, and to whom Holst was at first unsympathetic. The other interior furnishings of the house at that time were rather drab, and domestic discipline, though kindly, was also strict. Margaret Vaughan Williams was of a kind and serene disposition, but she taught her children respect for the persons and needs of others, whatever their position in life, by precept, example and occasionally by punishment if necessary; in doing so she influenced the character of her younger son so profoundly that kindness and consideration remained indelible features of his character throughout his life.

Two of the cardinal offences were disrespect for the servants and tale-bearing; the virtues encouraged were directness, independence of outlook and industry—with them went a natural dignity and charm that seemed to be a family inheritance—and a kind of austerity which Ralph did not inherit; from his earliest years he appreciated the rich abundance which life offered him, from its everyday tasks to its remotest visions. Whatever calling he might have chosen would have been followed with energy, passion and a respect for duty, buttressed by single-mindedness and resolve. His early interest in music was encouraged by his mother, who erected an organ for him in the hall of Leith Hill Place, an action which he appreciated more than the family servants, whom he persuaded to blow for him. Even as a boy he had developed his lifelong habit of rising early in order to devote some time before breakfast to music, and the servants had to find cogent excuses in order to go about their lawful business so that the routine of the house might remain undisturbed. The butler, Phillips, might protest that he had to lay the breakfast; if one of the maids was called upon she might be late for her work; perhaps the groom or the gardener was chosen. On Sunday mornings Ralph would sometimes continue practising long after the rest of the family had set out for church—the parish church being some two miles from the house—and would arrive just as the service was about to begin.

Perhaps his childhood was—apart from the private organ—not so very different from that of many another boy of the cultured Victorian upper middle class; and yet what he assimilated from the family and the atmosphere at Leith Hill Place was compounded into a very individual personality—strong, and yet gentle and sensitive; full of humour, and yet able to explode—for the moment only—in a flash of wrath; respectful of the virtues that lie in what is ordinary, yet willing and able to explore the unusual. Neither hidebound by convention nor in hysterical revolt against it, the boy was fortunate not only in his relatives and his home but in the way in which he developed what he inherited. His Wedgwood relatives had in previous generations shown a talent for the arts—the drawing-room at Leith Hill Place was hung with graceful water-colours by an aunt of his—and it was from his Aunt Sophie that he received his first music lessons. He himself has given a witty account of these; she not only taught him the rudiments of piano-playing, but also, on the advice of a friend, put him through a course in thorough-bass. This was the result of his first attempt at original composition, a four-bar piano piece written at the age of six and called ('Heaven knows why', as the composer put it) 'The Robin's Nest'. At the age of seven he began to learn the violin, and when he was about eight he went in for a correspondence course organized by the University of Edinburgh, passing both the preliminary and the advanced examinations. His tutor in all these activities was still Aunt Sophie, who introduced him to what was, and what was not, good form in music. From the earliest days his inquiring mind made him think over what he was told and reject it if he disagreed with it. He once wrote how Aunt Sophie told him that Haydn was 'good' and waltzes 'vulgar'; thus he experienced some difficulty in reconciling these two dicta when he found that the second subject of the first movement of Haydn's 'Drum Roll' Symphony was in fact a waltz.

Vulgarity may have been discouraged at Leith Hill Place; snobbery and priggishness were held in even lower esteem. This may have been due to the radical strain in the Wedgwood outlook, which encouraged members of the family always to accept things on their merits and not according to fashionable taste. An aunt of an earlier generation of Wedgwoods had taken her acquaintances severely to task for judging Byron's poetry as bad simply because his private life was loose; this independence of outlook sometimes bubbled over in sheer high spirits in the boy, taking the form of rather ribald observations on his elders. Diana Langton, a childhood playmate, who later became Lady Montgomery-Massingberd, was a frequent guest at Leith Hill Place. In the year 1881 a by-election was to take place at Bournemouth, and it aroused more than local interest. The two candidates were the Liberal, a Mr Davey, and a Conservative, Mr Moss. Diana and Ralph showed the direction of their political sympathies and their opinion of what to do with those who did not share them by fitting the following verse to the tune of the Sankey and Moody hymn 'Hold the fort':

> Hold the fort, for Davey's coming;
> Moss is in the sea;
> Up to his neck in rhubarb pudding,
> That's the place for he!

Very many years later they still sang it with gusto on occasion. It seems from this that the nine-year-old boy was already endowed with that slightly irreverent sense of humour which made him detest the pompous and the insincere. (Not that the unfortunate Mr Moss was necessarily either; he was merely associated with a political party which seemed to the children to warrant their disapproval.)

In 1882 Ralph was sent to a preparatory school at Rottingdean, where he learnt the piano under C. T. West, who introduced him to the music of Bach, and continued his violin lessons under the Irish, man, W. M. Quirke, a well-known Brighton teacher of those days. The high light of his public career as a performer came when Quirke's young charge performed Raff's Cavatina ('double-stops and all', as Vaughan Williams insisted, and on at least one occasion demonstrated, in later life) at a school concert. The only other thing of note in his career at Rottingdean seems to have been a marked proficiency at irregular Greek verbs. In 1887 he joined his brother at Charterhouse, which was then under the headmastership of William Haig Brown—the school's 'second founder'. Both Hervey and Ralph were in Haig Brown's own house. Haig Brown was a man of great willpower and foresight. At the time when he had been appointed headmaster in 1863—the first for many years not to be an Old Carthusian himself; his own school was Christ's Hospital—a vehement controversy was raging about the need for the school to move from Smithfield, where it was then situated. Despite resistance from the governors, Haig Brown succeeded in achieving the transfer to Godalming, where the school reopened with some 150 boys in 1872. By the time Ralph entered it, the enterprise of the headmaster and of the staff he selected had expanded this to over 500, and a limit had to be placed on the size of the school. Haig Brown was neither a great teacher nor a great theorist; in place of these gifts he had the equally valuable one of knowing when formal regulations should be scrupulously observed and when they should be ignored, and he allowed his staff and the boys alike the greatest degree of independence compatible with good order and discipline. A strong loyalty to tradition never blinded him to any necessity for change, and his sternness of character was tempered by a friendly sense of humour.

He may well have needed both his sense of humour and his ability to know when to waive the rules in August 1888, for Ralph and a friend, Hamilton, who played the piano, approached him with some apprehension and asked if they might give a concert of their own compositions. Up till then Ralph had more or less confined his musical activities to playing in the school orchestra and singing in the choir. (The choir practised during the time allotted to extra French and was thus very popular.) In addition, he had taken part in chamber music evenings during the holidays with the family of his mother's friend Colonel Lewin, and had joined with some other boys in tackling *concerti grossi* by Italian composers on Sunday evenings during term-time at the house of one of the masters, Mr Girdlestone. A concert of works performed by schoolboy composers was, however, a novelty; nevertheless, permission was granted, and Vaughan Williams's Trio in G was offered to an audience of masters and their wives—and even some of the boys. Concerned perhaps that such a gathering might be rather more critical of his performance in the Trio in G than an earlier one at Rottingdean had been of his rendering of Raff's Cavatina, the composer took the precaution of getting another boy to help out with the violin part. After the concert the mathematics master, Mr Noon, told the boy that he must continue with his composing.

Possibly as a result of this concert, he was transferred, in 1889, from the headmaster's house to that of the school organist, G. H. Robinson, where he remained for the rest of his school career, becoming a prefect, a position he held for four terms. He continued to play in the school orchestra, learning the viola as well as the violin, and made some progress as an organist, showing a particular likeness for improvising descants on hymn-tunes when he played at home during the holidays. Even if his schooldays were not the happiest days of his life (and there is little evidence that he did not enjoy them) he retained a lifelong affection for Charterhouse and kept up his connections with it and its music-making. In the days when it was only just becoming respectable for a boy with a prosperous middle-class background to take to music as a profession, musical activities at Charterhouse and Leith Hill Place, and the Wedgwood spirit of independence, encouraged him to attempt something that neither a Wedgwood nor a Vaughan Williams had ever attempted before. Few people on either side of the family can have been more than mildly surprised when in 1890 he chose to devote two years to study at the recently established Royal College of Music in London before going up to Trinity College, Cambridge, as his grandfather had done some seventy years before him.

7

CHAPTER II

THE STUDENT (1890–1904)

THE Royal College of Music had been founded under the direction of Sir George Grove in 1883. In the early days there were some fifty or so students, and the teaching staff included, in addition to Grove himself, such men as Sullivan, Parry and Stanford. The college thus maintained a close connection not only with the two older universities (Parry being the professor of music at one and Stanford at the other) but also with the London stage, through Sullivan, and with the musical life of the Church of England. Training a serious composer in the late nineteenth century meant training him to write music for the organ-loft and the festival platform rather than for the stage. Sullivan's operettas—the real beginning of the English musical renaissance in which Vaughan Williams was to be a leading figure—were 'sports', freak creations which it was regarded as neither desirable nor possible for a serious musician to emulate; even Stanford's gallant attempts to write both heroic and comic opera met with consistent failure, not on account of the music, but on account of operatic organization in England, which was regarded as a rather peculiar business best left to foreigners. The young composer of those days often tended, quite naturally and quite unconsciously, to envisage the orchestra as a kind of team version of the organ which accompanied lesser choral works within the framework of the Church's liturgy. If he thought in terms of large-scale compositions, they were usually oratorios and sacred cantatas rather than works for the stage.

Thus it was not strange that Vaughan Williams's first teacher at the college was an organist—F. E. Gladstone, himself a prolific composer of liturgical and organ music. With Gladstone the young student worked through the whole of Macfarren's *Harmony*, a technical discipline which he regarded in later life as salutary and necessary. Gladstone, a first cousin of the great Victorian Liberal statesman,

8

had been the organist at a number of cathedrals before becoming a Roman Catholic convert in 1887. At the time when Vaughan Williams began his studies he was director of the choir of St Mary of the Angels, Bayswater. Ralph had already decided when at school that he wanted to be a composer, and his resolve had been strengthened during the summer vacation before he began his studies at the Royal College, when he had been able to visit Munich and for the first time heard a Wagner music-drama. His reactions, he wrote many years later, were the same as those he was to feel on hearing a folksong or the *Enigma* variations, or on seeing Stonehenge or Michelangelo's 'Day and Night': a feeling of recognition, as of meeting an old friend, an impact 'which comes to us all in the face of great artistic experiences'. While still a student at the Royal College, he was able to repeat the experience at the Royal Opera House, when in 1892, a distinguished cast, under Gustav Mahler, performed the *Ring* and *Tristan*. On one occasion, after a performance of *Tristan*, he was unable to sleep all night.

It had been one of his ambitions to study under Parry. After his two terms under Gladstone he was able to pass Grade 5 in composition, which permitted him to do so. Parry always tried to find out whether the music of his pupils had any individuality, if it contained something 'characteristic'; not merely content, as so many teachers are, with pointing out faults, he also prescribed remedies for them which seemed to him to suit the student's personality. A man of the highest ideals of conduct and in art, he was also a highly independent thinker, politically a radical (one of his *mots* concerning the House of Lords was that its composition would be improved by the admission of a few burglars) and never blind to originality simply because it was unconventional. The very integrity of his artistic ideals, and of those of his colleagues on the staff, did incline towards priggishness in some respects—regarding French opera, for example—but from this Vaughan Williams was saved by the influence of such friends as Richard Walthew, who took him to *Carmen* and introduced him to Verdi's *Requiem*. His conviction that there are no canons in art except those of sincerity and integrity was thus reinforced, and he discovered something which he never forgot, even though it rarely affected his own music, that sentimentality, theatricality, even vulgarity and cheapness, might nevertheless be qualities which were still to be found in a great masterpiece, and in no way diminished its artistic value provided that the composer's vision was sufficiently intense and profound.

After completing two years at the Royal College, he matriculated at Trinity College, Cambridge, in October 1892, having been admitted as a Pensioner the previous June. He read history, his tutor being Dr Glaisher, and his director of studies in music Charles Wood. It is difficult for us to imagine nowadays the importance of the two older universities as musical centres in the late Victorian era. Under the energetic direction of Stanford, Cambridge maintained musical contacts with most of Europe. The University Musical Society's orchestra had, for example, been responsible for the first performance in England of Brahms's first Symphony; performances of sacred music often took place in college chapels—as indeed they still do—and undergraduates and dons alike engaged in numerous musical activities, both formal and informal. Moreover, Stanford had surrounded himself with a number of gifted teachers, among them Charles Wood, who, like Stanford himself and like Vaughan Williams's first violin teacher, Quirke, was an Irishman. Wood was a superb technical instructor, unrivalled, his pupil later wrote, in teaching the craft of composition. He had been one of the first students at the Royal College of Music, entering it as a scholar in 1883, and leaving it five years later for Selwyn College. In 1891 he had been appointed organist at Caius College, and so settled in Cambridge for the rest of his life. Shy and retiring but possessed of a strong sense of humour, his authority was quiet and unobtrusive, and his tastes were for the music of Handel, Haydn, Beethoven and Schubert. He disliked brilliance for its own sake and detested any form of ostentation, either musical or personal, a detestation which his young pupil shared to the full.

Stanford, who was at that time probably the best-known English composer after Sullivan, was a teacher of genius, a conductor of ability and a composer of skill. Prejudiced almost to the point of bigotry, quick-tempered, thin-skinned, but gifted with a born teacher's imagination, he sought to develop his pupils' minds rather than their technique and to counteract their faults by exposing them to new influences. Even in those days Vaughan Williams had a liking for the modes, and Stanford, thinking to counteract this, told him to go away and write a waltz. He did so, neatly turning the tables on his teacher by writing a modal waltz. Stanford later suggested that Vaughan Williams might profit from a stay in Italy. He used almost invariably to refer to his pupil's exercises as 'damnably ugly', yet in later years he did much to gain the young composer a hearing.

Apart from his studies Vaughan Williams was an enthusiastic member of the University Music Club, and also formed and conducted a small choir which rehearsed Schubert masses on Sunday mornings. Whereas the University Musical Society devoted—and still does devote—its attention to the rehearsal and performance of largescale choral and orchestral works, occasionally even staging an opera, the Music Club's interests lay rather in the direction of the study and performance of chamber music; it held weekly concerts on Saturday evenings, as it has done in termtime ever since it was founded. Vaughan Williams himself seems never actually to have appeared as a performer, but he was a regular attendant at the concerts, and was much respected and sought after as a forthright critic. One of those who most sought and benefited from his criticisms was Hugh Allen, the organ scholar of Christ's College, who frequently performed at the concerts and became a close friend.

In those days the club concerts were frequently followed by extempore performances of comic songs, in which, as in the more serious performances, both dons and undergraduates would take part. Vaughan Williams enjoyed and remembered this aspect of the Music Club all his life, and invariably remained for this part of the programme. Here that sense of fun and of the ridiculous which had already been so strong in his boyhood was stimulated by such sights as that of the venerable Trinity College scientist and musician Sedley Taylor parodying Sullivan's *Lost Chord* to words which began 'Batting one day at the Oval'. Cricket, however—least of all the type of cricket that might be musically illustrated by *The Lost Chord*—did not interest Vaughan Williams, though he loved the open air, frequently walking from London to Leith Hill Place at week-ends when he was a student at the Royal College. Tall, handsome, serious-minded, taciturn and somewhat reserved, letting others speak before delivering his own carefully considered opinion, and regarding personal relationships as a more important matter than a mere occasion for social pleasantries, he did not readily make friends. Among his friends, however, was a group centred round Ralph Wedgwood, a kinsman, who was also up at Trinity. They had known one another as children and Vaughan Williams was admitted to what he later called the 'magic circle' of Wedgwood's friends, a circle that contained the philosopher G. E. Moore (later to become famous as the author of *Principia Ethica*), the lawyer and scholar P. M. Sheldon Amos and the great historian George Trevelyan. During the vacations they used to spend weeks together at Seatoller, in Borrowdale, reading and discussing books and philosophy. Some idea of their intellectual calibre can be gained from the fact that three of the five were awarded the O.M. in later life; Wedgwood himself was knighted and became the chief general manager of the London and North Eastern Railway.

Despite his obtaining a good second in the history tripos, Vaughan Williams's actual achievement at Cambridge was not considered impressive; in fact, Charles Wood confessed that he held out no hopes for him as a composer. Certain of his published works date from his days as an undergraduate; two, indeed, of three Elizabethan part-songs, which appeared in 1896, had already been written before he went up to Trinity. The song *Whither must I wander*, though not published till 1902, was written in 1896, two years after Vaughan Williams took the degree of Bachelor of Music, and the title of the song is oddly significant. For all the stimulus of undergraduate life and friendships, for all the imaginative teaching of Stanford and the technical discipline instilled into him by Wood, he was not really sure of the direction in which his talents should be directed. That he was determined to be a composer was certain, but in what manner he could best express the music in him was not. Certainly the conventional academicism, modelled on the style of such composers as Brahms, of some of his teachers did not satisfy him. So in the Michaelmas term of 1894 he returned for a further period of study to the Royal

College of Music, where he studied the organ as well as composition. He had already taken lessons with Alan Gray, Stanford's successor at Trinity as organist and as conductor of the Cambridge University Musical Society; now he attended lessons with Sir Walter Parratt, who had been the first teacher of the organ when the Royal College had been founded and directed the choral class there also.

It was during this second period of study at the Royal College that he met and became friendly with the man whose relationship with him has only one parallel in the whole field of art and literature—that between Goethe and Schiller. Gustav Holst was twenty-one, having won a scholarship to the Royal College in 1895, when he first met Vaughan Williams. The fact that his scholarship was worth only £30 a year was no crippling hardship to one of Holst's frugal nature, though his comparative poverty forced him to supplement his income by playing the trombone in various orchestras during vacations, an activity which he found utterly distasteful. His mind, however, was not of the kind that is deadened by uncongenial activities, and his intimate knowledge of orchestral problems, partly gained during this period, was of invaluable aid to Vaughan Williams when, soon after-wards, they began their celebrated 'field days', on which they would together spend a whole day or part of it, at least once a week, studying and criticizing each other's latest work with a frankness that would have caused offence to acquaintances of less mutual sympathy. Though they were both somewhat reserved by nature they took to one another at once, and Vaughan Williams's help to his friend went beyond advice—it sometimes took the form of financial aid, so that Holst might enjoy a well-deserved holiday from his active life as a teacher and instrumentalist. On other occasions it took the form of banter—such as when Vaughan Williams suggested in a letter that Holst might counteract the effects of the neuralgia from which he had already begun to suffer by writing his music left-handed from a mirror—giving a practical demonstration by quoting a motif from the *Ring*. A good example of the forthright yet tactful way in which Vaughan Williams gave advice to his friend is shown by a letter [1]

[1] *Heirs and Rebels*, ed. by Ursula Vaughan Williams and Imogen Holst (1959), p. 9.

replying to Holst's suggestion that he might have some of his songs printed privately, as no publisher would accept them.

If I see a piece of music published by a man *whom I know nothing else about*, and see those fatal words 'Author's property' at the bottom of the cover, it at once sets me against him, makes me think him a poor fellow, and prevents me wanting to buy his song. Therefore I am afraid that if the rest of the world is like me your purchasers will be limited

   (*a*) to those who know you personally;
   (*b*) to those who know you through your music;

and these owing to your extreme youth are at present, though enthusiastic, unfortunately few.

This letter is typical of their relationship. Whatever the subject under discussion, whether the merits of a libretto, of a composer or of a work, there was the same common sense, the same frankness, the same affection unclouded by sentimentality, the same give and take between equals in ability. The field-days started very early in their friendship and continued until Holst's death nearly forty years later, and there is hardly a work by either composer that the other did not see during that time.

Holst was not Vaughan Williams's only friend and mentor during this period, but he was by far and away the most important. He and Vaughan Williams were the nucleus of a small group of students including John Ireland and Thomas Dunhill which used to meet in a Kensington tea-shop and discuss almost any subject under the sun— an experience which Vaughan Williams remembered with warmth all his life. Another friend whose encouragement was valuable at this time was S. P. Waddington, a first-rate pianist, who used to play through his compositions for him.

Most important of all, however, he had grown to know Adeline, the fifth of the eleven children of Mr and Mrs Herbert Fisher of Brockenhurst. He had met her first as a boy, and she had developed into a girl of singular beauty and charm, slender, gentle, graceful and fair. The Fishers combined intellectual ability and good looks; Adeline's mother had been the model for G. F. Watts's 'Una and the Red Cross Knight', and five of her brothers were to achieve great reputations in fields as varied as those of military and naval warfare, banking, architecture and scholarship. When Adeline became engaged to the shy young musician, who was slightly younger than she was herself, some of the family's acquaintances felt that she was not making a very good match. This did not deter her in the slightest. Allied with her good looks was a discriminating shrewdness, a strong sense of humour and, above all, an unshakable faith in her fiancé's gift. Moreover, she was a talented amateur musician herself; when preparing for their honeymoon visit to Berlin she worked right through the *Ring* with him (one of his reasons for choosing Berlin was that it was at that time the only place where the State Opera performed the whole of the *Ring* without cuts) and later on played the cello in an amateur string quartet known to their friends as the 'Cowley Street Wobblers', in which her husband played the viola.

At the time of their marriage, on 9th October 1897, Vaughan Williams was the organist at St Barnabas's Church, South Lambeth, the only paid appointment he ever held in that capacity. He did not enjoy it at all. In a letter to Holst, asking the latter to deputize for him, he refers to the men in the choir as 'louts' who 'make you mad', and 'slope into choir practice' half an hour after it has begun. After his marriage, he left the 'damned place', as he called it, and decided to spend a further period of several months' study abroad. This consisted of an extension of the honeymoon stay in Berlin by some months, working with Max Bruch. Bruch, like Stanford, was a conservative and somewhat academic composer dilettantishly interested in folk-music, of which he made some use in certain of his own compositions, and, again like Stanford, noted the young composer's predilection for the flat seventh and the modes. Whether the lessons were of much good to Vaughan Williams or not, he always remembered Bruch's kindly encouragement and his warning—despite his assertion that it was wasted on him—that music was written for the ear to enjoy, not the eye.

Some time after his marriage Vaughan Williams took his doctorate in music at Cambridge. This was in 1901, and though it virtually completed his formal musical education (he was to take lessons with Maurice Ravel later in his life), it certainly did not complete his musical education as such. He was, it is true, busy writing songs and more ambitious works, and published some of them. He was not compelled to live from his composing, as he had a private income, but he devoted his time to it in an intensely professional manner, working at it for eight hours a day, and destroying much that he wrote as unsatisfactory. Holst suggested to him in a letter that he ought to rewrite everything some six months after its original completion; whether or not this advice was responsible for the practice, it is certainly true that he revised many of his works on a number of occasions long after their original publication. The *Pastoral Symphony*, for example, written in the 1920's, was revised in the fifties. Some of his works—such as the song *How can the tree but wither*, of 1896—he withheld from publication for as much as thirty years, and the final song of the *Songs of Travel*, written at the beginning of the century, was never published at all in the composer's lifetime. Many of these songs were settings of Pre-Raphaelite poets such as the Rossettis, but Herbert, Tennyson, Shakespeare and Robert Louis Stevenson also find a place. Another significant choice is that of the Dorset dialect poet William Barnes. Here was a poet who wrote in the language and with the inflections of the English peasantry, although himself no peasant.

For although Vaughan Williams was now settled in his vocation, though he was receiving encouragement from those who loved him and had faith in him, though he was in some demand as a scholar (contributing articles on 'Fugue' and 'Conducting' to the 1904 edition of Grove, giving University Extension lectures and performing such tasks as editing two volumes of *Welcome Songs* for the Purcell Society's comprehensive edition), he had still not managed to achieve the characteristic manner of utterance which he knew ought to be his. At times this appeared to worry him. Here Holst was an invaluable support and companion, comforting, advising, criticizing and suggesting methods and techniques for getting the pair of them away from writing 'second-hand music'. Vaughan Williams, continually self-critical, referred to himself as 'stale', 'dried-up' (in inspiration), 'prematurely decayed and getting fat', but Holst discerned the originality of his friend's mind, and never failed to encourage him. At various times in letters, he and Holst ascribed the trouble to lack of

LEITH HILL PLACE FROM THE AIR
(By kind permission of Sir John Wedgwood, Bart)

tradition, lack of roots, lack of industry. Yet the real reason is hinted at in an article published in the *Vocalist* in May 1902: [1]

What we want in England is *real* music, even if it be only a music-hall song. Provided it possesses real feeling and real life, it will be worth all the off-scourings of the classics in the world.

Up till now most of his works had been 'off-scourings of the classics'. A hint from Purcell—he noted with some delight in the preface to the second volume of *Welcome Songs* that Purcell had quoted the Playford dance tune *Hey boys, up go we* almost note for note in one of them—and the influence perhaps of William Morris's ideal of the artist basing his art on that of the cottage craftsman may have influenced him. (Holst was a member of Kelmscott House, the Morris establishment in Hammersmith.) What could be more natural than that musicians should follow in Morris's footsteps, if they wished to free themselves from concocting 'off-scourings of the classics' and academicism alike? Fortunately for Vaughan Williams an instrument had already been forged by means of which he was able to work in this direction: the Folk Song Society. It had been founded in 1898, under most distinguished patronage. But independently of its activities, he had already been out in the field collecting songs. The first of these he had taken down at Ingrave, near Brentwood, in Essex, on 4th December 1903. It was called *Bushes and Briars*.

[1] Reprinted in *Heirs and Rebels*, pp. 27–8.

CHAPTER III

EXPLORING NEW PATHS (1904–14)

DESPITE—or possibly on account of—the distinguished careers of its vice-presidents (one Scotsman, MacKenzie, one Irishman, Stanford, and two Englishmen, Parry and Stainer)—under whose auspices the Folk Song Society had been inaugurated in 1898, certain complaints were being voiced by the time Vaughan Williams became a member in 1904, about the tempo and scope of its activities. Although the society was not responsible for the first efforts at collecting folksongs in England, it was the first fully co-ordinated collecting body of that kind in the country, and it ought to have had a well-directed programme. Some people, however, felt that a total of around one hundred songs collected in six years was a sign of a moribund body rather than a vital one.

In 1904 the Society was perturbed by a declaration from a music-teacher called Cecil Sharp, who had been interested in folksong and folk dance since about the time that the society had been founded. Sharp asserted that it was not the business of members to sit around discussing folksongs in London; they must get out into the field and listen to what the country folk had to sing. He gave point to his argument later by publishing a large collection of songs which he had gathered in the west of England which were a surprise and a revelation. Some idea of the gap between the great men at the top and the people whose music was allegedly their interest may be gained when we remember that Stanford once told Vaughan Williams that it was nonsense to think that a flat seventh was a feature of English folksongs, since they all descended to the tonic anyway. Vaughan Williams remained unconvinced; and, as Sharp's findings and his own were to show, he was correct. In the ensuing controversy as to what constituted a genuine folksong, Vaughan Williams found himself backing Sharp against his former teacher. His findings were based on personal

18

experience; his method of collecting was like Sharp's own—he went among the people. Although he had already met Sharp in 1900 he developed his own collecting methods independently, and they only became friends after he had done a good deal of field work; Sharp and others helped him with the annotations of the sixty-one folksongs which were published in the *Journal of the Folk Song Society*, Volume II, Part 3.

These songs were the fruit of several visits to various parts of England. The first of them—*Bushes and Briars*—was collected at the end of 1903; others were discovered in other parts of Essex, mainly around Brentwood, where he was busy in February, April and October 1904; in Norfolk, particularly around King's Lynn, where he spent a most profitable week from 8th January till 14th January 1905; and in Sussex, mainly from parts not far from Leith Hill, where his visits throughout 1904 were short and frequent. Holiday visits to Yorkshire and Wiltshire in August 1904 also yielded some melodies.

Vaughan Williams is remembered—and rightly remembered—as one of the great folksong collectors. He was also proud of the fact that he was—sometimes in denigration—referred to as a 'folky' composer. The fact that he appreciated the virtues of the English folksong, that he studied it so thoroughly and absorbed its essence into his own music, should not blind us to the fact that the folksong was, as it were, the spring that released his true musical personality, even more than the model on which he built his style. What he gained from it was a tonal freedom and a melodic idiom that fertilized his music; what he made of it was the creation of his own genius. It has sometimes been argued that his conscious effort to fertilize his musical idiom with folksong elements was an anachronism. It is difficult to see why. What matters in any kind of art is not merely the manner in which a thing is expressed, but also the matter which is expressed. The fact that folk music liberated Vaughan Williams's strong and original musical personality is incomparably more important than the fact that the treasures of English folksong were only just being discovered when he came to maturity as an artist, and that he himself was one of the foremost discoverers of them. Like Bartók, Vaughan Williams collected folksongs at a time when the harvest had long since been gathered in the 'less backward' musical countries, but like him—and like Janáček or Mussorgsky for that matter—he did not merely treat folksong as a patch to be sewn on old Teutonic garments. It became a fundamental element of his entire personal idiom—melody, rhythm, form and texture. But it was by no means the only element, and his eventual use of it was that of a creative musician far removed from that of a dilettante or an academic analyst. Anyway, if folksong was, as some people allege, the be-all and end-all of his musical existence, it is difficult to understand why he chose to study with Ravel after he had published a number of 'folky' works.

The recognized method of presenting folksong material in original compositions at the beginning of the twentieth century was the orchestral rhapsody, in which folksongs are woven together in a continuous musical design, the essence of which was colour and con-trast. So Vaughan Williams wrote three *Norfolk Rhapsodies* during 1905–6, which contained some of the fine tunes he had collected from the King's Lynn fisherfolk. He followed them up with an extended orchestral work called *In the Fen Country*, in which he did not actually quote any folk-tunes, but based the shape of the themes on the con-tours of the tunes he had gathered. It was written in 1904, and revised in 1905 and 1907. His interest in folk music dovetailed in an interest-ing manner with a commission he had received in 1904 from a man who had up till then been a complete stranger to him. At that time he used to work in the home which he had rented in Barton Street, Westminster. One day a man announced simply as Mr Dearmer walked in and asked him to edit a hymn-book, saying that it would take about two months. To Vaughan Williams's protests that he knew nothing about hymn-books Dearmer replied that he had been re-commended as musical editor by Cecil Sharp and Canon Scott Holland. This made him feel inclined to accept, and he was finally convinced when Dearmer shrewdly mentioned that if he refused, a musician would be approached with whose musical sympathies Vaughan Williams emphatically did not agree.

When the revised edition of *Hymns Ancient and Modern* had been published in 1904, a group of like-minded friends, mostly High

VAUGHAN WILLIAMS, AGED ABOUT TWENTY-FIVE
(By kind permission of Mrs Ursula Vaughan Williams)

Churchmen, of whom Dearmer was one, had been rather disappointed with the result, even though they thought that it was a great improvement on what had gone before. They had therefore set about compiling a supplement, and had soon found that they had enough verse material for a complete hymn-book. It was Vaughan Williams's job to provide music for this verse, which involved compiling what was virtually a thesaurus of the finest hymn-tunes in the world compatible with the metres of the words. The work took him two years, and cost him £250 out of his own pocket. (Dearmer had said it would involve an expenditure of some £5.) In it he incorporated a number of the folk-tunes he had recently collected—such as, for example, the fine tune which in the book is called *Monk's Gate*, after the place where he had first heard it, near Horsham. 'Why should we not', he remarked in the year of the book's golden jubilee, 'enter into our inheritance in the church as well as the concert room?' [1] In addition, he persuaded Holst and other friends to provide tunes for it, and his own contributions, which number four,[2] stand comparison with any of the fine melodies he had collected from divers sources, both ancient and modern. The quality of both words and music ensured for the *English Hymnal*, as it was named, a great success. Between the date of publication and the golden jubilee in 1956 over five million copies were sold. This was due to several factors. First of all, the music was forceful, strong and simple. Secondly, the theology was radical and clear-cut. Percy Dearmer, like Sharp and Holst, was deeply interested in the place of the arts in religious worship, and in the relevance of Christianity to social problems. He was an admirer of Charles Gore, and at the time when he walked into Vaughan Williams's office was secretary of the London branch of the Christian Social Union. The earnest radicalism and directness of outlook of the editorial collaborators on the book, together with their vigorous and fervent ideas on the place of the arts in Christian worship, ensured that, by the standards of its time, the *English Hymnal* was a really revolutionary work. It was revolutionary in its acceptance of the liturgical importance of hymns as well as their doctrinal necessity, in the freshness and

[1] *Heirs and Rebels*, p. 38.
[2] Increased to seven in the 1933 edition.

grandeur of most of its music and in the thoughtful arrangement and systematic layout of its component sections.

In its own way the *English Hymnal* thus played a part in the renaissance of English music. The event usually accepted as the beginning of that renaissance was the production of Parry's *Prometheus Unbound* at Gloucester in 1880, though Sullivan, in his work with Gilbert, had produced something distinctly English as early as *Trial by Jury* in 1875. Elgar's work is usually regarded as the culmination of the first phase, which in the main looked to Germany for its technical models; it is indeed no coincidence that the German conductor Hans Richter was one of the foremost protagonists of Elgar's music. The composers of the second phase—of whom the greatest was Vaughan Williams—were to make an even more decisive break with the German tradition. Whereas Parry's music, and Stanford's, spoke German with an English and Irish accent, as it were, and Elgar's spoke English with a German accent, Vaughan Williams and Holst quite consciously aimed at doing for English music what Smetana and Mussorgsky had done for the music of Bohemia and Russia respectively—developing it on its own lines independently of the Teutonic tradition. Basing one's idiom on English folksong, of which Parry and Stanford, for all their erudition, were virtually ignorant, was the most natural way of doing this, yet it was patently not enough simply to force 'English' themes into formal moulds derived ultimately from the structure of folk music of a quite different nature. Even at the age of thirty-six, when he had already published a number of works in a recognizably English idiom, Vaughan Williams felt that his technical equipment was not complete. It needed, he felt, a touch of lightness and colour.

So in 1908 he set off for Paris, to acquire 'a little French polish' at the hands of Maurice Ravel, taking a room in the Hôtel de l'Univers et du Portugal, and staying for three months. There can have been few people offering a greater contrast in external appearance: Ravel small, neat and dandified; Vaughan Williams tall, ungainly and never very careful about his personal appearance. It is typical of the new pupil's humility that he should choose to take lessons with a man three years his junior, and it is perhaps possible that Ravel mistook his humility for lack of experience at their first meeting. He told him to write 'un petit menuet dans le style de Mozart'. Vaughan Williams, who had had his song for chorus and orchestra *Toward the Unknown Region* performed at Leeds the previous autumn under Stanford, was not grateful for such advice, and proceeded to say so in his best French. (This was, incidentally, quite good; there are records of him speaking fluently in that language in French Society debates at Charterhouse.) Ravel set him exercises principally in orchestration, choosing mainly piano works by Russian composers, which were new to his pupil, and gave him lessons four or five times a week. He told Holst that the work was doing him just the good he hoped it would, and although Ravel was shocked that he had no piano in his hotel room with which to invent new harmonies, he was already quite capable of using old ones in a completely original context, as his work was soon to show. What he did learn from Ravel was a new, lighter, more colourful kind of instrumentation, and above all that he had not, after all, reached a dead end in composition, as he had feared. Ravel's own motto, 'complexe, mais pas compliqué', was carefully remembered, even if not invariably put into practice.

Before going to Paris he had visited Norfolk on another folksong collecting expedition, this time on the Broads not far from Lowestoft; some time after his return, he broke new ground by collecting songs in various parts of Hampshire early in 1909. The newfangled phonograph was used both on certain of these expeditions and later on that year, in July, when he went collecting with Mrs Leather in Herefordshire. The year 1909 also brought the first performance of a work which had lain unperformed since its composition in 1903, the cantata *Willow Wood*, which was produced at the first and only festival of the short-lived Musical League, in Liverpool, on 25th September. All the great names in English music of the day, including Elgar, Delius, Bantock and Arnold Bax, were associated with this organization, but it failed to attract either notice or support, and collapsed in obscurity. The renaissance of English music had involved a renaissance of English orchestral playing, and the rise to fame of conductors who frequently played new English works, such as Thomas Beecham and Henry Wood, the latter of whom Vaughan Williams and Holst

23

particularly admired. What it had not involved was any sensible and rational policy for opera production, and so although Vaughan Williams shared in Holst's disappointment when the latter's opera *Sita* was rejected for the Ricordi prize in 1908, it is not surprising that he himself, interested though he was in the stage, did not at this period of his life complete any operatic work. He did write some incidental music for various plays, including the music of Aristophanes' *The Wasps*, which has since become well known, and he had, as early as 1902, published an article on 'The Words of Wagner's Music Dramas' in the *Vocalist*.[1] In this he upheld Wagner's claim that the composer himself should write the libretto—an opinion he modified when he came to write operas himself. When choosing a text for music he therefore aimed at using the text as a peg on which to hang his musical thoughts rather than as a programme to be illustrated in music. This is an indication that he regarded the formal structure of the music and the general effect of a setting as more important than the impressionistic painting in of details. Yet he did not entirely neglect the latter at any time of his life. On returning from Paris, for example, he set to work on a song-cycle for tenor, piano and string quartet, choosing as his text the simple yet evocative verses from Housman's *A Shropshire Lad*, and giving it the title *On Wenlock Edge*, and critics were eager to catch glimpses of Ravel in it. The sentiments of the poems which Vaughan Williams chose for this work would not have suited Ravel's idiom, though there is a somewhat terse irony about some of them, but their plainness is not compatible with the sophisticated elegance of the French composer's style. The other compositions of about this time—mostly songs (including two to old French texts and one to a translation by Mabel Dearmer of a poem by Verlaine)—are small in scale, and include a string quartet and the fantasy quintet written for Walter Willson Cobbett, which won a prize in the series which he inaugurated. Two orchestral impressions, first performed about this time, were later scrapped.

In 1910, however, two major works had their first festival performances, one of which has gone into the repertoires of all the great

[1] An extract is printed in *Heirs and Rebels*, pp. 33–5.

orchestras. When editing the *English Hymnal*, Vaughan Williams had incorporated into it a magnificent Phrygian tune by the Tudor composer Thomas Tallis (No. 92); now appreciation developed into inspiration and he wrote a fantasy for double string orchestra on this melody. It was performed at the Three Choirs Festival. As Herbert Howells wrote, nearly half a century later, in his *Sunday Times* obituary notice of the composer:

Two thousand people were in Gloucester Cathedral that night,[1] primarily to hear *Gerontius*. But there at the rostrum towered the unfamiliar magnificent figure. He and a strangely new work for strings were between them and their devotion to Elgar.

In the same notice, he describes the conductor-composer as

thirty-nine, magisterial, dark-haired, clear-cut of feature; a physically magnified version of the then Sir Edward Grey.

There is nothing sensationally original about the *Fantasia on a Theme by Thomas Tallis* of the kind that might have been invented by Ravel on a keyboard; yet it is unquestionably the first work by Vaughan Williams that is recognizably and unmistakably his and no one else's. The same cannot quite be said for the *Sea Symphony*, which Stanford, again helping out his pupil, produced (with the composer conducting) at Leeds on 12th October of the same year. Yet when Parry heard the work for the first time he noted in his diary that it was 'big stuff—with some impertinences'. Needless to say, the 'impertinences' are what modern audiences find the most characteristic parts of the work.

But it was not only at Leeds and the Three Choirs Festival that Vaughan Williams was active at this time. In 1905 his sister Margaret and Lady Farrer had founded the Leith Hill Music Festival. Like many others founded at that time to encourage local choirs, it was

---

[1] Tuesday, 6th September; the *Musical Times* described it as 'a grave work, exhibiting power and much charm of the contemplative kind, but it appeared over-long for the subject-matter'. The work was later revised and abridged.

competitive, and as the years went on one particular composer became more and more the mainspring of the whole affair—as was the case, for example, with Elgar at Morecambe, and is with Britten at Alde-burgh. At Leith Hill, of course, it was Vaughan Williams, who was active as conductor, composer and organizer. In the earlier days the orchestra was composed mainly of competent amateurs with a leaven-ing of professionals, and rehearsals for the former were held, usually at private houses, in London. The administrative foundations of the festival were none too secure at first, and Vaughan Williams insisted on the words 'subject to alteration' being printed on all the pro-grammes for many years—but thanks to the energy of the organizers and the enthusiasm of the participants, the festival was built up into a national event to which even the main London newspapers sent their chief critics.

Holst too, despite tardy recognition from the critics, was maturing steadily, and dedicated his two *Songs without Words* to his friend. The music arrived while Vaughan Williams was staying at Meldreth, Cambs., at work on the *Sea Symphony*, and he wrote back, acknow-ledging the dedication:

It was nice to open y^r parcel and find my initials over your pieces—I don't know what you owe me—but I know all I owe to you—if I ever do anything worth doing it will be greatly owing to having such a friend as you 'at my command' as the folksongs say, always ready to help and advise—and someone whose yea is always yea & nay, nay—which is a quality one really wants in a friend and so seldom gets.[1]

Perhaps one of the things he owed to a Holst 'field-day' was the unqualified effectiveness of the scoring of the *Tallis Fantasia*—but perhaps not, for it should never be forgotten that for all his desire to find the most suitable means of expressing his musical thoughts, Vaughan Williams was from the first quite adamant if anyone tried to alter a piece of scoring which sounded exactly as he intended it to. Neither Ravel, Elgar nor Holst nor anyone else from whose work he picked up technical tips would have been able to persuade him to change his mind once it was made up. Another friend with whom he

---

[1] *Heirs and Rebels*, p. 40.

used to discuss his works in those days was George Butterworth, a gifted young man some thirteen years younger than Vaughan Wil-liams, who had been a scholar of Eton. Butterworth had led a varied and somewhat unsettled career in music; after finishing his studies at Oxford he had been a journalist, a public-school master and a student at the Royal College of Music, where he abandoned his course and went off to collect folksongs in Sussex. It was Butterworth who suggested that his friend might write a symphony. After rejecting the idea, Vaughan Williams reconsidered it. At that time he was working on a large orchestral tone-poem with London as its subject; he recast his ideas in the form of a four-movement work, and the *London Symphony* came into being. Butterworth helped him with the copying, and prepared the programme notes for the first performance, which took place on 17th March 1914 under Geoffrey Toye at a festival designed primarily to make the young conductor known to the public.

Vaughan Williams's ideas on the place of the composer in the society in which he lived were, in a sense, put into practice in this and other works written at the time; as those ideas themselves crystallized, so his choice of musical forms grew more venturesome and more ambitious. He at last turned his attention to opera, selecting as his librettist the journalist, and art and drama critic, Harold Child, who wrote the book of *Hugh the Drover*, the composition of which was spread over the years 1911 to 1914. He was elected on to the committee of the newly formed English Folk Dance Society in 1911. His friend Cecil Sharp's name stands at the head of the score of the *Fantasia on Christmas Carols* of 1912, and a less everyday side of Vaughan Williams's character shows itself in other works of this time—notably the *Four Hymns for Tenor* and the *Five Mystical Songs*. A more formal and explicit indication of the matters that were occupying his mind at the time is, however, given in a remarkable and outspoken article entitled 'Who wants the English Composer?', which appeared in the first number of Volume IX of the *R.C.M. Magazine*.

His growing reputation as a composer—aided perhaps by the fact that he had studied with Ravel—resulted in his being hailed by the French critic X. Boulestin as the leading representative of the post-Elgar generation in English music. Boulestin's article (in *La Revue musicale*, Jan. 1913) caused the following comment from a usually discerning English critic, at that time on the staff of the *Birmingham Daily Post* (16th February 1914):

As for Dr Vaughan Williams, he 'deserves more respect and consideration than some other English composers who are more perfect and more notorious'; he is, in fact, 'considered by some people the most interesting of the modern English composers'. Strange that it should be left to a Frenchman to discover a fact of which no one in England has hitherto been conscious! I have heard most of Vaughan Williams's works: I have been through the length and the breadth of musical England, and discussed English music with hundreds of musicians; strange that no one I have ever met had any intuition that Dr Vaughan Williams was our Messiah! We live and learn.

The truth simply is that M. Boulestin is insensitive to the greater English music because it is not French, and he prefers some of the minor English music because it coquets with the modern French idiom.

How directly Ernest Newman here misunderstood Vaughan Williams's aims and principles (to say nothing of his stature as a composer) can be discovered by reading the latter's article.

Its main point was that music, alone of the arts, was judged by standards which severed its connection with everyday life, and that as long as British composers continued to base their work on these artificial standards, they would remain unwanted and unready:

We English composers are always saying, 'Here are Wagner, Brahms, Grieg, Tchaikovsky, what fine fellows they are, let us try and do something like this at home', quite forgetting that the result will not sound at all like 'this' when transplanted from its natural soil. It is all very well to catch at the prophet's robe, but the mantle of Elijah is apt, like all secondhand clothing, to prove the worst of misfits.

He recommended 'cultivating a sense of musical citizenship', urging composers to live with their fellows and make their art an expression of the whole life of the community. Clearly, certain aspects of the *London Symphony* and of works such as *Hugh the Drover* represented his own attempt to do this, for he held that in order to do it it was necessary for the composer to share the community's experiences.

RALPH AND ADELINE VAUGHAN WILLIAMS AT CHEYNE
WALK, 1918
(By kind permission of Mrs Ursula Vaughan Williams)

Enlisting in the Army

Vaughan Williams himself was soon to be given an opportunity to do this very thing, an opportunity which pushed ballad opera, mystical poems, nature-lyricism (as is evident in *The Lark Ascending*, written in 1914) and folk music completely into the background. On 4th August 1914 war was declared on Germany, and Vaughan Williams, like the heroes in many of the folksongs he loved so much, felt it his duty to enlist as a soldier.

CHAPTER IV

SOLDIER AND TEACHER (1914-22)

ALTHOUGH he was nearly forty-two years of age when the First World War. broke out, Vaughan Williams did not take long to decide to volunteer for military service. The war was for him, as for many others, a turning-point in his experience, and there is a noticeable difference between the music he wrote before it and after it. Until then he had lived a comfortable life, with enough money to enable him to keep hard at work composing; suffering he had experienced at close quarters, for his wife had been gradually developing into a a cripple over the years as the arthritis that finally rendered her body helpless slowly spread over it. But active physical discomfort had not so far been his lot; as a student and a struggling young composer he had never suffered the penury that had fallen to Holst, for example. Now, by his own choice, he was to experience and to share grim and squalid suffering with millions of his fellows of all classes, and to discover other aspects of twentieth-century warfare—its waste, its futility and its brutal impersonal boredom punctuated by sudden violent death. Some of his closest musical friends were to be killed on active service, and one young composer whose work he greatly admired driven insane as a result of his war experiences. What he had formerly been able to envisage only by his sensitive and sympathetic imagination he was now to feel as a direct impact in its most intensive form.

He enlisted as an orderly in the Royal Army Medical Corps, joining a Territorial Army Unit, the 2/4 Field Ambulance, and it cannot honestly be said that he was a smart soldier. Though tall enough to have been a guardsman, his broad shoulders and his large flat feet ensured that he neither looked nor moved like one. He was always in trouble with his puttees, and invariably required assistance when expected to dress in a smart and soldierly manner. To some of the wags of the unit he was an object of considerable mirth when under

30

training, yet, as was invariably the case in all human contacts with him, his frankness and simplicity, and his sincere humility, made him respected at the same time. Few if any of his comrades knew his identity.

His first billet was near his home—the Duke of York's H.Q. at Chelsea—after which, in December 1914, the unit moved to Dorking, and his first occupation as a trained soldier was that of wagon orderly, once the unit had been issued with ambulances. He performed his military job conscientiously, and naturally accepted such musical opportunities as army life offered with zest and good humour. On one occasion, acting as organist in a garrison church, he improvised an organ voluntary on the popular song *Make your mind up, Maggie MacKenzie* while the troops were solemnly filing into church. No doubt, if challenged by the authorities, he would simply have replied that he was putting his principles into practice, and basing his inspiration on what he heard about him. He also organized sing-songs, and took quite a fancy to the mouth-organ, since it was so easily portable and therefore practical for supplying music on the march. Broad though his musical sympathies were, however, they did not extend as far as the R.A.M.C. march-past, *Her sweet smile haunts me still*; he dismissed it as 'sentimental humbug', left over to the corps after the 'real army' had stolen all the good tunes.

Thanks to his adaptability, his robust health and his complete lack of self-esteem, he bore army life well. Certain duties which army routine required of him he found boring, but few left him feeling that they were utterly useless. He always took his turn with fatigue duties, such as scrubbing floors, without complaining, although, like everyone else in the unit, he could see no sense in the form of stretcher drill in force at that time. Had he chosen to complain, there is no doubt that he would have done so effectively, and it is entertaining to imagine the dilemma in which his superior officers would have been placed had they been faced with the problem of sentencing a well-known composer to a spell of C.B. for insubordination. However, believing as he did that service to others was the basis of human life, he was prepared to accept any task, however menial, as part of the duty he had incurred by volunteering.

From Dorking the 2/4 Field Ambulance was posted to a camp hospital at Audley End Park. Vaughan Williams had the good fortune to be billeted on a musical family, which boasted a violist, a pianist and a clarinet-player amongst its members. Military service, like folksong collecting, brought him into contact with people with quite different backgrounds from his own. With his usual disregard of any prim conventions and his complete lack of snobbery, he won their respect, and in some cases their lifelong friendship. Such, for example, was the case with Henry Steggles,[1] who shared a billet with him from early days at Dorking until the middle of 1917 in Salonika. Steggles, whose background was as different as could be from Vaughan Williams's, became a firm friend and remained so all his life. At divisional concerts he would sing comic songs, such as *When Father papered the parlour*, aided by his illustrious room-mate, who accompanied on the piano. Their turn was in considerable demand after the war at reunions, which they regularly attended throughout the nineteen-twenties. Vaughan Williams's musical activities on active service were not confined to comic entertainment, however, and he encouraged his companions to take part in choral and instru-mental performances under his direction, forming choirs, and even, on one occasion, a drum-and-fife band, which he rehearsed and con-ducted—totally oblivious, as usual, of distinctions of rank or office when bestowing praise or reprimands.

Yet all the time he was uneasy because he felt that he was not as fully engaged as he ought to be, and he was relieved for more than one reason when, after further training on Salisbury Plain, the 2/4 Field Ambulance was posted to France on 21st June 1916. There he was engaged in work with motor ambulances, transporting the wounded between the trenches and the field dressing station. Once again he formed a choir, teaching them carols and Christmas hymns, many of which were quite new to his singers. He was utterly without fear, finding the danger of life in the trenches stimulating rather than frightening, and feeling somewhat pleasurably relieved to find that the dress regulations were rather less stringent at the front than in England.

[1] His detailed account of life in the army with Vaughan Williams is printed in the *R.C.M. Magazine*, Vol. LV (1959), No. 1, pp. 21-4.

Yet though his personal feelings at being usefully employed and at 'fitting in' were satisfied, he was aware of the great losses that others were suffering. The death of George Butterworth on the Somme in August 1916 caused him to write to Holst in these terms:

I sometimes dread coming back to normal life with so many gaps—especially of course George Butterworth. . . . I sometimes think now that it is wrong to have made friends with people much younger than oneself—because soon there will be only the middle-aged left—& I have got out of touch with most of my contemporary friends—but then there is always you & thank Heaven we have never got out of touch & I don't see why we ever should.[1]

In December 1916 the unit was transferred, as part of the 60th London Division, to the Salonika front, and stationed near Mount Olympus, where the Allies were expecting an attack. The medical units were among those who lived in bivouacs somewhat smaller than a double bed. These makeshift abodes had no doors or windows; the entrances were hung with old sacks or groundsheets, which afforded the occupants little comfort, even if ample ventilation. They were usually heated by means of improvised stoves, concocted from old oil-drums, mud, stones or bricks, fed with tree-roots or charcoal. Into such a 'bivvy' Steggles and Vaughan Williams packed all their worldly goods, among which were the indispensable Isaiah and Jeremiah, two empty pineapple tins filled with charcoal, which they used for warming it. The procedure was simplicity itself. They would rush into the 'bivvy', seal as many of the air outlets as they could, light Isaiah and Jeremiah, and swing them vigorously round outside until they were sufficiently alight to sit by in moderate discomfort.

Vaughan Williams's interest in folk music was not confined to English tunes alone, for in Salonika he would watch the Greeks dancing and listen to them singing in village shops, sampling the local wine and noting down the tune as he did so. Though this aspect of service in Salonika must have appealed to him (he was a connoisseur of wine) he still felt that he was not doing as much as he could in the war, and even when the division was moved to the

[1] Ibid., pp. 45–6.

Doiran sector—the scene of heavy fighting, where the British trenches were completely overlooked by a strongly entrenched enemy—he was not satisfied. He even managed to break security regulations in a rather novel way, sending home a postcard to his family with a Dorian scale on it in order to tell them his whereabouts! He was now engaged in anti-mosquito precautions, filling in puddles; this he did not object to, for although monotonous it was at least useful. Other activities, however, such as washing red bricks to be laid out in the form of a cross in order to ward off German aircraft, he regarded not merely as boring, but also as futile, and so he volunteered for a commission in a combatant regiment—the Royal Garrison Artillery.

During his last three weeks in Salonika, in June 1917, he was engaged on latrine fatigues at Summerhill Camp, a very unpopular transit camp some six miles from the town of Salonika itself. This unpleasant duty was the lot of all potential officers awaiting posting back to England, and it was better not to complain about it, since anyone rash enough to do so was instantly returned to his unit. Even though this particular duty was more or less inevitable, he could, had he so desired, have avoided others. Members of concert parties (there were two of these, the 'Roosters' and the 'Barnstormers', to one of which he could certainly have belonged) were excused fatigues. So were those in the divisional theatre group. His reason for not joining them was simply that he felt they were managing very well, and that his participation could not possibly have improved their standard of performance.

He detested the phrase 'Officers and Men'; so much so, indeed, that on being accepted as an officer candidate, he informed the officers of his regiment, standing stiffly to attention before them, that his greatest regret on leaving the unit was that he would cease to be a man on becoming an officer. A somewhat similar caustic comment on the class distinctions of army life occurred in the ship on the way home, where he saw no reason for the officers and nurses being railed off from the 'common herd' and occupying the fore part of the ship. In January 1918 he was commissioned, at the age of forty-five, in the Royal Garrison Artillery, and was posted to the First Army in France. In addition to performing the usual tasks of a regimental officer, such as looking after transport, etc., he was given the special task of organizing the musical side of educational activities within the division. This he continued to do until his demobilization.

While he was still serving in France, in October 1918, his old teacher, Hubert Parry, director of the Royal College of Music, died at the age of seventy. He was succeeded by Vaughan Williams's friend and Cambridge contemporary, Hugh Allen. The college expanded rapidly with an influx of ex-servicemen, and one of Allen's first tasks was to provide teachers for the new pupils. Between 1918 and 1920 he appointed no fewer than twenty-six new teachers, among them Gustav Holst and Vaughan Williams, who finally joined the staff in September 1920. He soon became a well-known character at the college, usually coming in on Wednesdays and bringing with him a collapsible bag which quickly became as much a legend among the students as its owner did. Holst, Stanford and Vaughan Williams were in charge of the principal composition students, and it is clear that the methods and aims of the younger teachers were somewhat at variance with those of the older. There had, of course, been a reaction against German culture during the war—a reaction which had in some cases been expressed in somewhat extravagant and ridiculous terms—but the new English musical art of which Holst and Vaughan Williams were two of the foremost representatives was too much for Stanford. Arthur Benjamin has related how Stanford almost pathetically begged him not to 'go mad', as all his 'lovely pupils: Holst, Goossens, Vaughan Williams, Bliss', had done. Vaughan Williams was probably not so gifted a teacher as his master, but there is no doubt that many of the post-war generation of students regarded him as more sympathetic to some, at any rate, of the contemporary musical developments.

His teaching methods were not orthodox, and he taught what has been described as not a style but an attitude towards composition. If convinced that a student had talent, but that he himself was unable to develop that talent, he spared no pains to find him a teacher who could—as was the case for instance with Constant Lambert. His attitude was based on the precept 'to thine own self be true'. Years earlier he had been deeply impressed by Parry's demand that an artist's foremost loyalty was to his conscience as an artist; this was simply his own method of imparting Parry's precept to his pupils. He discouraged them from any conscious attempts to be strikingly original, telling them that if they really were original, it would show itself in their work, and that if they weren't, no amount of technical jugglery would make them so. Among his colleagues was R. O. Morris, who had married Adeline's sister, and who shared the house at Cheyne Walk with them (working, so Vaughan Williams asserted, by candlelight, even when there was broad daylight outside). According to Dr Gordon Jacob, one of the pupils who studied under Vaughan Williams in those days, he had

a horror of professional skill and technical ability. As he grew older, he came to realize that these qualities did not necessarily add up to superficial slickness and his later pupils were put through the mill or, as he put it, 'made to do their stodge' methodically.[1]

He had, wrote Elizabeth Maconchy, one of his favourite pupils,

no use for ready made solutions: he had worked out his own salvation as a composer and he encouraged his pupils to do the same. Technical brilliance for its own sake he despised, and this perhaps made him rather too distrustful of brilliance in any form—though he overcame this distrust to some extent later.[2]

He did not believe at that time in making pupils work through text-books, even though he himself had learnt much as a student in that way; when studying counterpoint, for example, he maintained that they should study contrapuntal music written by great composers rather than synthetic examples concocted by clever academic theorists. No better comment on the mental attitude that underlay this precept can be adduced than his own *Concerto Accademico*, as his violin Concerto was first called. In it many of the most cherished rules of the academic teacher are deliberately broken—but the scale and the spirit of the work bring it much nearer to Bach than many an impeccably written copy of that master, and the fact that it is in every respect

[1] *R.C.M. Magazine*, Vol. LV (1959). No. 1. p. 31.
[2] Ibid., p. 34.

highly characteristic of Vaughan Williams differentiates it from the dry-as-dust copy that a lesser mind would have made it.

Although his own criticisms of pupils' work were usually couched in diffident terms and framed as suggestions rather than observations (even with amateurs), he encouraged the pupils themselves to criticize one another with the frankness that he and Holst always showed one another. He persuaded them to form a kind of club, performing one another's music, and directly discussing the works afterwards. There is a story, too, of a college student who had brought him an exercise in scoring with which he was displeased.[1] The next day he told the young man, with some concern: 'I have been worrying for fear that I was too severe with you. Will you take your piece and this note to Mr Holst?' The student, overcome by curiosity, opened the note on the way; this is what he read:

Dear Gussie.[2] You know so much more about orchestration than I do, will you look at this and tell me if I was too hard on it.

When Allen had embarked on the work of expanding the college's activities, he had been doing a good deal of practical music-making as a conductor—particularly of the Bach Choir. His duties as director of the Royal College and as professor of music at Oxford compelled him to give some of this up, and he chose Vaughan Williams as his successor in April 1920. The first rehearsals under the rather shy new conductor were not easy; his approach was different from Allen's vivacious, easy-going, extroverted bonhomie, but the choir soon settled down under its new chief. (It appears that his outsize boots and flat feet endeared him to the choristers in some way. 'As soon as we saw his boots, we knew it would be all right,' was the comment of one of them.)

Vaughan Williams introduced the choir to a number of unusual works—not only by Bach, but by other composers, such as Byrd,

[1] Ibid., p. 27.
[2] Vaughan Williams disliked and never used the name 'Gussie' in conversation, but the substance of this anecdote seems so typical of his modesty and respect for the feelings of others that the story may well be based on fact.

Holst and even Charles Burke, a Morley College pupil of Holst's who had begun his musical studies at the age of fifty-nine. Some of the programmes, following a tradition established by Allen, were brought before a newer public at the People's Palace in the Mile End Road; Vaughan Williams, having learnt much from the music of the ordinary people, was now in some measure repaying the debt.

A number of musical organizations bearing quasi-patriotic titles sprang up in the years after the First World War, their intention in every case being to promote new British music and artists. Foremost among them were the British National Opera Company, the British Musical Society and the British Symphony Orchestra. The British Musical Society had been set up in August 1918, and incorporated as a society in November 1919, largely owing to the zeal of A. Eaglefield Hull, who was its first honorary director. It chose the *London Symphony* as the chief native work for performance at an important Queen's Hall concert on 4th May 1920. The conductor was Albert Coates, and Vaughan Williams revised the work specially for this occasion, making considerable cuts in the finale. The work had already been performed in February and March 1918 under a young man who was to have much to do with Vaughan Williams's works, receiving the dedication of one of the greatest of them. His name was Adrian Boult.

It was Boult who rehearsed and conducted the first public performances of the first important work written after the war—the *Pastoral Symphony*, some of the most original features of which had germinated in the composer's mind during his war service. It received its first performance at a Royal Philharmonic Society concert on 26th January 1922, and was a puzzle for many listeners and critics. The apparently uneventful serenity of this and other works of this period (such as the one-act opera *The Shepherds of the Delectable Mountains* and the pre-war *The Lark Ascending*, which had been revised in 1920 during a stay in Gloucestershire with a friend and music patron, Philip Napier Miles) were at variance alike with the glowing opulence of the Edwardians and the acidulated tinklings of some post-war composers. They did not 'fit' in a hectic age, but regardless of any recognition from others the composer calmly went his own way.

Recognition there was, nevertheless. The International Society for

Contemporary Music (of which the British Musical Society was the British centre) took up a few of his works. The University of Oxford conferred an honorary doctorate on him in 1919. America was beginning to hear of him, and the gifted conductor of the choir at Westminster Cathedral, R. R. Terry, who had rejuvenated the liturgical repertory there by 'digging up' unusual works from the present and the past alike, performed the Mass in G minor as part of the liturgy, thus bringing it before a public which did not merely savour the music as part of a social round.

While other composers in the twenties were busy experimenting with new dissonant combinations and the reaction against romanticism was at its peak, Vaughan Williams was thus pursuing new and original lines of development. His own revolution was not sensational, and was only incidentally to be associated with any 'ism'; but it was none the less thorough and fundamental. It involved a complete rethinking of his musical idiom, which from now on developed in many directions, but still remained utterly and recognizably characteristic. He was never one of the 'smart', fashionable composers of the twenties, but he was a pioneer all the same, carefully assimilating all that he found useful in contemporary novelties, and just as carefully ignoring all that he felt was merely showy and deliberately provocative. How far he had now travelled along his own road can be measured by comparing the symphony performed under the auspices of the British Musical Society at Queen's Hall on 4th May 1920 with the one given by the Royal Philharmonic Society in the same hall some nineteen months later.

CHAPTER V

A PROPHET NOT WITHOUT HONOUR (1922–34)

THE development of the arts in the nineteen-twenties followed patterns which in many cases bordered on the bizarre and the ridiculous, even though they were often merely further developments of pre-war tendencies. Tolerance of extreme forms of experimentation became the watchword of a whole generation. There were various reactions against the direct expression of emotion in music; some took place because emotion was in some way held to be a thing of the past, a product of the mental climate of the pre-war era. Some good souls held it to be bourgeois, and therefore indicative of lack of sensitivity; some felt it to be aesthetically out of place, and some followed the fashion of being 'anti-Romantic', 'Romanticism' becoming in fact a meaningless vogue-word implying 'something-of-which-I-don't approve'. Nationalism, too, both political and artistic, was suspect. It was regarded as one of the root causes of the war, and the eager interest —and apprehension—with which the enormous social experiment following the Russian revolution of October 1917 was followed rested partly in a hope that the establishment of an internationally minded, classless society would ban warfare and lead to a world in which artistic and social progress would march hand in hand. In western Europe nobody was quite sure whether the 'new' art was to be some kind of 'art for all' under the aegis of some form of socialism, or an art for the select and initiate few—as appeared to be the belief of those following the lead of a number of White Russian *émigrés* centred on Paris or of the Bloomsbury set in England. Sir Osbert Sitwell's phrase 'amiable debility', used of Lytton Strachey, seems in retrospect to sum up the whole of many now forgotten 'daring' works of the twenties which, at their best, were chic and amusing, and at their worst snobbish epicene pretentiousness masquerading as art.

Vaughan Williams still felt that English composers should write music expressing something peculiar to their country and its people, but he never confused nationalism with cynical chauvinism of the Horatio Bottomley kind, something to be exploited for personal gain. His mind was much too honest and acute for that. Similarly, he never felt that a thing should be approved simply because no one had ever done it before; his standards were more solid. He used technical innovations only if they were a real expansion of the medium in which the artist chose to express his ideas. But he was certainly neither reactionary in his attitude to the present nor nostalgic towards the past. Flirtations with jazz, for example, of the kind which led to interesting works such as Lambert's *Rio Grande*, did not attract his attention much, but—probably under Holst's influence—he developed a 'back-to-the-past' technique of his own, as did other composers of the time, notably, of course, Stravinsky. Yet the reaction was not a volte-face; it was a logical development of what he had done before, a further stage in his emancipation as a composer. Indeed, he held strongly to the view that Stravinsky's greatest and most lasting works of the post-war period were those which most deeply rooted themselves in his Slavonic ancestry—instancing the *Symphonie des Psaumes* as an important example.

Holst's post-war works began to break strange new ground, and even Vaughan Williams was sometimes rather unable to give them the whole-hearted admiration that he would have liked to. For example, in a letter after the first performance of Holst's *Choral Symphony*, he expressed the hope that they would not 'drift apart' musically, and in his reply Holst implied that he, too, had felt disappointed about *Flos Campi*. They did not, in fact, 'drift apart', but it is evidence of the depth and sincerity of their friendship, as well as the independence of outlook of their characters, that they felt impelled to write to one another in such terms. As conductor of the Bach Choir, Vaughan Williams had earlier been responsible for giving Holst's *Ode to Death* twice at one concert—for which he earned his friend's enthusiastic gratitude. Holst said that it was what he had been waiting for for forty-seven and a half years, and his pride at the dedication of the Mass in G minor knew no bounds.[1]

[1] *Heirs and Rebels*, pp. 59–62.

As for the more controversial doctrines of the age, Vaughan Williams was by nature more sympathetic to Hindemith's *Gebrauchs-musik* than to the 'toute réaction est vraie' ideas of some of Diaghilev's *entourage*. But his kind of *Gebrauchsmusik* was, ironically, even if under-standably, more practical and more down-to-earth than Hindemith's own. We have already noted that he was the musical editor of *The English Hymnal*; just twenty years after it appeared the team that had collaborated on it set to work on two other anthologies—the *Oxford Book of Carols* and *Songs of Praise*, both of which were *Gebrauchsmusik* of an eminently sane and practical order. One aimed at improving the quality of the musical offerings at religious festivals, the other at providing 'a collection of hymns that should be national in character'. The response to both was immediate and enthusiastic. *Songs of Praise*, of which its musical editor claimed that there was not a single tune contained in it of which he was ashamed, was published in 1925, and ran to a greatly enlarged new edition two years later; *The Oxford Book of Carols* appeared in 1928 and was reprinted twice in the two following years.

A large number of the tunes included in these two collections came from traditional sources, and Vaughan Williams continued his activities as a folksong arranger by making a number of arrangements, and using folk music as the basis for a number of fair-sized works. These included the *Six Studies in English Folk Song*, written in 1927 for, and dedicated to, the cellist May Mukle, another work for cello and orchestra—the *Suite on Sussex Folk Songs* (1930), for Casals, to whom it was dedicated, and two ballets—*Old King Cole* (1923) and *On Christmas Night* (1926). Another work which comes into this category is the *Folk Song Suite* for military band, which was written in 1923 at the instigation of the commandant of Kneller Hall.

The two folksong ballets were by no means his only works for the stage in this decade. He had always been an ardent theatre- and opera-goer, and it seemed that such groups as the British National Opera Company would go far towards building up a public in the country which would at last accept opera as something natural, something English and something worth spending an evening in the theatre for.

So it was encouraging for him when, after a first production under S. P. Waddington in the Parry Memorial Theatre at the Royal College on 4th July 1924, Malcolm Sargent conducted the first public performance in a commercial theatre of *Hugh the Drover*. This was at His Majesty's on 14th July of that year, and Sargent later took the opera on tour with the same company. Vaughan Williams wrote three further operas during the twenties—*Sir John in Love* (a Falstaff opera which forms a natural counterpart to Holst's *At the Boar's Head*), *Riders to the Sea* and *The Poisoned Kiss*. The latter two had to wait until well into the thirties for their first performance, and even then the performance was not given by a professional company.

The expense entailed in mounting an opera demands a public which is prepared to listen to a work not once, but repeatedly; whereas anyone can go to a first performance at a concert and then forget about the music afterwards. But one more, at any rate, of Vaughan Williams's stage works reached a public theatre, and it was one of his most complex and profound ones—the 'masque for dancing' *Job*. Originally intended for Diaghilev's company, it had been suggested as a theme by Geoffrey Keynes, the distinguished surgeon whose many outside interests included a deep interest in English literature. Keynes and his sister-in-law, Gwen Raverat, worked out a scenario based on Blake's engravings to the book of Job to which they suggested Vaughan Williams might provide a score. The project fired his imagination, and when Diaghilev lost interest in it, he still continued work at it, devoting many 'field days' with Holst to the polishing and revision of the score. Thus both friends and family (Mrs Raverat was a Darwin by birth, and a cousin of the composer) contributed to the work, which was first performed as a concert suite at Norwich, on 23rd October 1930. In the meantime the Camargo Society had become interested in the possibility of producing the ballet as Keynes and Vaughan Williams had originally envisaged it, and the gifted young conductor, Constant Lambert, reduced the score for the smaller orchestra which would be available for performance in the theatre. It was danced for the first time at the Cambridge Theatre on 7th May 1931, the choreography being by Ninette de Valois, and Lambert, whose great gifts as a musician had been noticed and developed partly as a result of Vaughan Williams's guidance and encouragement when he was a student at the Royal College of Music, conducted.

Most of his works written during this period received their first performances at provincial festivals of one kind or another, and one, the *Pastoral Symphony*, was the occasion of his being invited to the United States for the first time, when he conducted the New York Symphony Orchestra at the 1923 Summer Festival at Norfolk, Conn. He had been invited there by Carl Stoeckel (the son of a Bavarian *émigré* musician who had become professor of music at Yale), who had established the festival in 1907. Although Adeline's illness was steadily rendering her more and more incapable of normal movement, she was able to accompany him and see him conduct, but by 1927 it was necessary for them to leave Cheyne Walk and find a bungalow as she was almost unable to climb stairs. They bought a house called the White Gates, near Dorking, and not far from Vaughan Williams's childhood home at Leith Hill Place, which quickly became the focal point of the now flourishing Leith Hill Festival.

In 1930 the festival celebrated its silver jubilee, and he wrote three works for it—one for each grade of choir involved, elementary, moderate and advanced. The largest and most complex of the works, the *Benedicite*, was selected by the International Society for Contemporary Music for its London Festival in that year, and was well received, particularly by the French critics. He was becoming an international figure, as well as a national one. It was in 1930, too, that the University of Swansea conferred an honorary doctorate in music on him; at a ceremony there on 22nd June he was presented by Sir Walford Davies for the degree in terms which showed how considerably his reputation had grown. Uttering what he loved with musical intensity, Davies observed, Vaughan Williams had become the unconscious leader of national musical thought and idiom. The main characteristics of his work, he went on, were naturalness and wonderment. Certainly some of the works he produced during this era of his life bore evidence of the latter quality—particularly *Sancta Civitas*, which Hugh Allen produced at Oxford on 7th May 1926, and *Flos Campi*, which had received its first performance in London on 10th October of the previous year. Vaughan Williams was now, in fact, the national

VAUGHAN WILLIAMS CONDUCTING THE LONDON
SYMPHONY ORCHESTRA AT A HENRY WOOD PROMENADE
CONCERT, 1946
(*B.B.C. copyright*)

musical standard-bearer, having largely taken Elgar's place as the principal public figure in music. Elgar himself had written virtually nothing since the death of his wife in 1920, though he had since become Master of the King's Musick. But it was to Vaughan Williams that festival committees now turned when commissioning important new works. Among these were the *Magnificat*, which was performed at the Three Choirs Festival at Worcester in 1932, and the Prelude and Fugue in C minor (Hereford, 1930). In a letter, written to Holst when the latter was in America in 1932, he mentions his intention to try and lift the words of the *Magnificat* 'out of the smug atmosphere' associated with them.[1] As always, even in works written in response to a commission, he went back to fundamentals, thinking of the *Magnificat* within the context of its origin—the song of an excited and awe-filled young woman—rather than as a staid cantata text.

Increasing demands on his time as a creative musician did not mean that he gave up his work in other fields, though it did mean that he had eventually to abandon some of his activities. After the war he retained an interest in the doings of his wartime comrades, regularly attending regimental reunions and delighting those present by accompanying sing-songs and burlesques at the piano, fitting into the company for all his shyness, which he never completely overcame. His 'bivvy-mate', Henry Steggles, was somewhat surprised to receive an almost illegible (and therefore indisputably authentic) postcard some years after the end of the war inviting him to a dinner at Simpson's and a performance of *Carmen* afterwards. This was the result of a promise made in Salonika which Steggles himself had long since forgotten, but Vaughan Williams had remembered. Moreover, it was as a result of Vaughan Williams's advice that Steggles had taken up his successful post-war career as a commercial traveller. In other fields of musical life Vaughan Williams was no less active than before; for the golden jubilee of the Bach Choir in June 1926 he organized a four-day festival, at which the two Passions and the B minor Mass were performed. The festival constituted a fitting climax to Vaughan Williams's career as their conductor. Shortly afterwards he handed the position over to Adrian Boult.

[1] Ibid., p. 79.

As a conductor he was no polished technician, but his experience with the Bach Choir certainly gave him more confidence in his ability and experience with the stick. His technique remained somewhat heavy and rigid, but he was able to rely on a witty tongue and a great ability to explain in simple terms what he meant. The rather ponderous exterior concealed a sharp mind, which sometimes exploded in a sharp temper. Outbursts of anger were quite frequent, but always over quickly and always followed by a genuinely humble apology. Professional orchestral players are usually regarded as somewhat hard-bitten, and they are almost always able to detect the charlatan on the rostrum; they willingly and lovingly played under Vaughan Williams, and they never let him down because he never let them down. There are many stories of him muttering asides to his players; one of the best concerns a rehearsal of his fourth Symphony—of which he conducted a magnificent recording just before the Second World War. A player was not sure what a certain note ought to be, and asked him what it was. Screwing up his eyes at the score, and then blinking at the player, he finally said: 'Well, it's B flat. I know it *looks* wrong—and *sounds* wrong—but it's *right*.' [1] When conducting some choral work, he always made sure that the chorus knew the story if, as in the case of the great Bach Passions, it was a narrative work. This enabled them to see the work as a whole, and not as a collection of isolated movements. He even timed the pauses between movements so that every single second which elapsed from the moment the performance began contributed to the total impact of the work. His view of the *St Matthew Passion*, for example, was dramatic as well as contemplative; he expanded the continuo part where it accompanied emotive or expressive phrases in the text, leaving it as dry chords where the words implied action or dramatic tension, and took care to bring out expressive inner parts in the string orchestra accompaniment to Christ's words—as at 'The same shall betray me'. Similarly, in any vocal work, he always stressed the importance of the words, which perhaps explains why he was able to make a body of three hundred singers perform with the flexibility of a small madrigal group—indeed,

[1] Bernard Shore in the *R.C.M. Magazine*, Vol. LV (1959), No, 1, p. 36.

to get them to perform madrigals themselves. There were times at the Leith Hill Music Festival when he would put down his stick after a few bars, knowing that the choir was sure of itself, and only resume conducting for the closing passage. His aim was to instil implicit trust in his players and singers, and this he did by showing them clearly that he trusted them.

It was as a conductor that he had paid his first visit to the United States; it was as a teacher that he paid his second. In 1932 the University of Bryn Mawr, Pennsylvania, invited him to deliver six lectures under the auspices of the Mary Flexner Trust, and he gave them in October and November of that year. Adeline was by this time so seriously crippled that she was unable to accompany him. The lectures were published under the title *National Music* in 1934. They are really a positive development of the provocative article published in 1912, and incorporate a number of ideas contained in other occasional writings of earlier years. The two main arguments he adduced in favour of a 'national' school of composers can best be shown by two quotations from the book:

. . . the St Matthew Passion, much as it is loved and admired in other countries, must mean much more to the German, who recognizes in it the consummation of all that he learnt from childhood in the great traditional chorales which are his special inheritance. . . . Is it not reasonable to suppose that those who share our life, our history, our climate, even our food, should have some secret to impart to us which the foreign composer . . . is not able to give us?

which discusses his theme from the listener's point of view, and:

It is by synthesis that the student learns. Early Beethoven is 'synthetic' Haydn. Early Wagner is 'synthetic' Weber, and I believe that for a student to do a little 'synthetic' folk-song writing is a better way of arriving at self-knowledge than imitation of the latest importations from Russia and Spain which after all only cause him to write 'synthetic' Russian or Spanish folk-song, and that at second hand,

which does so plainly from the composer's own.

It was while in America on this visit that he first made the acquaintance of the virtuoso conductor Serge Koussevitzky, who had a very high regard for him as one of the great composers of all time. Holst, who had been in America some four years previously, had urged Vaughan Williams to go and hear the superlative Boston Symphony Orchestra, and when its conductor asked which work of his he would like to hear it play, he decided, after much thought, to ask for the *Tallis Fantasia*, on account of the orchestra's fine string section. A delightful anecdote concerning the first performance of the work under Koussevitzky at Symphony Hall, Boston (the first of many there, it is needless to add), tells of the composer incurring the displeasure of two Boston matrons who were seated at the opposite end of the row of seats from him. Unfortunately the seats were only attached to the floor at one end, and as the composer, completely lost in the superb performance of his music, rose and fell 'with a decided thump' every time one of the numerous *sforzandi* in the work occurred, the ladies were hard put to it to retain either their balance or their dignity, as they found themselves unwittingly on one end of a rather unconventional see-saw. Unfortunately their reactions were not observed when the composer was persuaded to join Koussevitzky on the platform after the performance to share the applause; but certainly during the performance they cast intermittent baleful glances at this bulky, ill-mannered Philistine who was ruining the music for them.[1]

At the time of this second visit to America he was sixty years of age; in fact, he celebrated his sixtieth birthday in America. It is tempting to think that America provided a stimulus to him as London had to Haydn; certainly, although he was not commissioned to write any works for his visit, those which appeared after he came back showed a further development in his style—a development which seemed to indicate a more comprehensive outlook and a changed attitude to his art, culminating in the almost brutal power of the fourth Symphony, written during the early thirties. Yet the development was logical; it was merely a versatile artist revealing new aspects of his personality. All the shyness and diffidence were now gone, and the forthrightness and originality that they had so long overlain were revealed. He was now not merely a seeker but a leader, and though, in his modesty, he was as ready as ever to solicit advice, he really had

---

[1] Archibald Davison in the *R.C.M. Magazine*, pp. 27–8.

very little need of it. In any case his teachers and mentors, and those who had exerted a strong influence on his development or had suggested ways he might profitably explore, were dying one by one. Parry had already gone in 1918, Stanford in 1924 and Charles Wood in 1926. Walthew, Allen and Waddington continued to enjoy his friendship for many years yet, and new friends—such as Gordon Jacob, a former pupil whose advice he quite frequently sought on matters of scoring, and Cecil Forsyth—came into his circle, but they were in many cases disciples rather than guides, and there was not the same intimacy of equals as existed between him and friends of other days, for whom he retained an intense personal affection and enter- tained an almost fierce loyalty. He chose, for example, the occasion of Elgar's death, early in 1934, to come to the defence of Parry. In an article in *Music and Letters* on what he had learnt from Elgar, he devoted a considerable passage to refuting the charge that Parry had led a clique whose aim had been principally to keep Elgar down.[1] The charge had been made by none other than Bernard Shaw some fifteen years previously. Shaw's admiration for Elgar had induced him to denigrate those English composers (not including Vaughan Williams) for whose music he had little time, and Vaughan Williams took Shaw severely and somewhat acidly to task for it, with a force of invective worthy of its target.

Elgar, though he had been a friend, was not the greatest personal loss to him in 1934; not long after the death of the Master of the King's Musick, there came one which, as man and musician, affected him far more. On 25th May Gustav Holst, who had been ill for some months and had had to abandon a course of lectures at Harvard University on account of his illness in order to return to England, died suddenly at the age of fifty-nine.

[1] It is true that Professor Dent, writing in Adler's *Handbuch der Musik- geschichte*, had made a series of sweeping and quite unjustified assertions about the 'repugnance' which Elgar's music was said to arouse in 'English ears', and it is equally true that there had been a marked coolness between Elgar and Stanford for some years before the latter's death, but the 'clique' to which Shaw had referred existed more in his—and possibly in Elgar's— imagination than in reality.

CHAPTER VI

WITH HOLST's death Vaughan Williams was left as the only one of his generation of English composers who recognizably counted as a genius. Elgar, who had died a few months before Holst, is sometimes regarded as the musical laureate of the Edwardian era, and his appointment as Master of the King's Musick seemed to some a kind of belated recognition of this fact. It is slightly ironic that Vaughan Williams, who so ardently advocated going back to the roots of English music, and who himself had always done so, was quite rightly never regarded as the laureate of any age, least of all of the Georgian. His works do not in any way seem to sum up the spirit of any particular generation; their sense is too universal and the age through which he lived was too diversified. But none the less, when Elgar died, Vaughan Williams's fellow musicians showed their appreciation of his standing by electing him to the Collard Life Fellowship of the Worshipful Company of Musicians, which Elgar's death left vacant, and in the Birthday Honours list of 3rd June 1935 he was awarded the Order of Merit, as was his old friend G. M. Trevelyan. Both the musical world and the Crown—for the O.M. is of course a personal honour from the sovereign—thus showed their appreciation of what his work meant in the musical life of the country.

Official recognition naturally had no effect on either his versatility or on his outspokenness. Neither *The Poisoned Kiss*, which was at last performed for the first time on 12th May 1936, nor the *Five Tudor Portraits*, which were first performed at Norwich that September, can be regarded as a mere repetition of old formulae, for they showed qualities—a trenchant humour and a gift for satiric character-portrayal —that had, as far as the general public was aware, lain hidden before. The *Five Tudor Portraits* resulted from a suggestion made by Elgar that Vaughan Williams might find Skelton a sympathetic poet to set —an interesting example of the older man's insight into the mind of

50

the younger—particularly when it is remembered that Elgar also remarked on one occasion that he had originally intended to complete his two oratorios *The Apostles* and *The Kingdom* with an apocalyptic oratorio, but that on hearing *Sancta Civitas* he had realized that the work he had had in mind had already been composed.

Vaughan Williams's outspokenness caused him to be misunder-stood at times. Thus *The Times*, reporting a speech he made at the Musicians' Company dinner on 24th March 1936, misinterpreted some observations to the effect that the average Englishman hated English music as a plea for greater regard for the contemporary English composer. This drew a letter from him stating that he had merely implied that the fact he had mentioned pointed to something wrong, either with the average Englishman or with the present situation. He had always maintained that a composer should be able to stand on his own feet without being coddled, and in this instance he was pointing out a fact rather than begging for sympathetic consideration (which he, at any rate, did not need). What he continued to stress was that music and life were closely related to one another, and he showed what he meant by this when the Huddersfield Choral Society commissioned a work from him to celebrate its centenary on 2nd October 1936. Instead of a triumphant setting of a eulogistic text, ending in a stately climax, he wrote *Dona nobis pacem*. Critics, wise after the event, have asserted that the F minor Symphony is a prophecy of the 1939–45 war. Whether or not this is true there is no mistaking the topical relevance of *Dona nobis pacem* and its bearing on issues far outside the immediate field of a musical celebration. The text includes a quotation from John Bright's famous 'Angel of Death' speech, and the com-poser used to observe with a chuckle that he must have been the only man who ever set John Bright to music.

Musical celebrations of a more conventional nature came in 1937, when two works were commissioned for the coronation of King George VI. A *Flourish for a Coronation*, somewhat inappropriately performed for the first time on 1st April, and a festival setting of the *Te Deum*, first heard at the service itself on 12th May, were his con-tributions. But if the year 1937 brought him opportunities for express-ing joy in music, it also brought him sorrows. Ivor Gurney, one of the most tragic victims of the 1914–18 war among English musicians, died after years of mental suffering, the result of shell-shock. Vaughan Williams, who had been visiting and comforting him over the years, wrote a simple and sincere tribute to him in *Music and Letters*. A still more intimate and still greater loss was the death of his mother, to whom his own character owed so much. It was thanks mainly to his upbringing at her hands that, as well as being revered as an artist, her son was loved and respected as a person.

During the year he showed that his interest in folk music of all nations had not abated by publishing a number of settings of British, French and German folksongs. His continued interest in contemporary music, and his opinion of some of it is shown by his characteristic retort to an article in *The Times* in which the paper's critic had caustically dismissed an I.S.C.M. Festival Concert at Queen's Hall in June 1938. The article took exception to works by Riccardo Nielsen, Roberto Gerhard, Aaron Copland, Hindemith and the Swiss composer Willy Burkhard, for whose *Vision of Isaiah* it reserved such phrases as 'eschewing all ameliorating harmonies', 'decorating his chant only with dissonant orchestration' and 'ungainly fugue'. Vaughan Williams's letter ran:

SIR:

Your unfavourable notice of a choral work by Willy Burkhard performed at a contemporary music concert at Queen's Hall last Friday prompts me to venture to express my opinion that we have here a remarkable, often beautiful and often deeply moving composition. It seemed to me that evening to stand out amid a waste of arid note-spinning as a genuine and deeply felt expression.

I ought perhaps to add that in case my opinion should cause the composer to lose face among his fellow 'contemporary' musicians that he is fully as capable of inventing lacerating discords as any of them. But the discords seemed to me to come from a genuine emotional impulse and not from a desire to outshine one's neighbours in hideosity.

I hope that one of our choral festivals will perform this work, having previously revised the present English translation.

Yours faithfully,
RALPH VAUGHAN WILLIAMS.

The reference to 'one of our choral festivals' in the last paragraph is a head-on tilt at the *Times* critic, who had pontifically declared the work to be unfit for consumption by a Three Choirs audience. The mention of a 'genuine emotional impulse' and the contrast drawn with 'arid note-spinning' are completely consistent with what Vaughan Williams said and practised all his life; he never regarded music as a matter for the sheer creation of sound-patterns, any more than he regarded it as something invariably meant to illustrate an extra-musical programme. For him it was the emotional, even the spiritual, aspect of music that was all-important; a musical work represented a moral, spiritual or emotional experience expressed in terms of a coherent musical pattern, not simply a musical pattern which might or might not involve the listener in an emotional or spiritual experience. In this sense he remained a 'romantic' all his life, and it is plain that he regarded Bach as a 'romantic' too.[1]

Foreign audiences were beginning to learn more of him. On 20th October 1937 the Rector of Hamburg University announced that he was to be the first recipient of a Shakespeare Prize established by a Hamburg merchant, part of a scheme aimed at strengthening cultural ties between Britain and Germany. The presentation took place on 15th June 1938, and the celebrations included performances, under Eugen Jochum, of the *Fantasia on a Theme by Thomas Tallis* and the *London Symphony* as well as a speech by Vaughan Williams which pointed out that *das Land ohne Musik* possessed a number of other talented composers besides himself, and expressed the hope that musical ties would strengthen friendly links between the British and German peoples. He gave the money to help victims of the Nazis. At Brussels that autumn a performance of the *Tallis Fantasia* caused many Belgian critics to compare it most favourably with a Brahms symphony in the same programme. Though, as the Hamburg authorities had said, he had established a link with his country's musical past, he was also part of the European tradition.

But, as the Munich crisis showed, nationalism in politics was quite another matter from establishing a national tradition in the arts, and as

[1] See, for example, 'Bach and Schumann' (*Heirs and Rebels*, pp. 29–33).

war drew inevitably nearer, he decided that he must do something to help the numerous refugees entering Britain from the Fascist countries. A committee was formed at Dorking to administer their needs; it met once a month, and he was able to contribute much to its success because of his understanding of the nature and needs of ordinary people. He never forgot that suffering sometimes brings out the worst in people as well as the best, and thus he never failed to grasp the refugees' point of view when others overlooked it. When an indignant welfare worker complained that a German refugee, protesting that the hostel where he was billeted in Dorking was far worse heated than houses in his own country, was being ungrateful, Vaughan Williams simply commented: 'How right he is! And how excellent that he should still remember the good things in his country!' This breadth of sympathy and sense of proportion was extended to all—if they were sincere—no matter who they were or what they were doing. It mattered not whether they were touchy chauffeurs, charmed into good humour by a simple request such as 'Do you mind if I smoke in your car?' or young cockney campers who strayed inadvertently into the garden at Leith Hill Place admiring the rhododendrons, and were promptly given a standing invitation to come in whenever they were in the neighbourhood; the charm and the courtesy were inevitable, fundamental and natural, as were the desire and the belief that the good things in life should be shared by all, and that politeness was due, not only to the great, but to the humble as well.

In 1938 Vaughan Williams retired from his post as composition teacher at the Royal College—part of a process of gradually withdrawing from the more formal kind of regular musical activities—but he still gave lessons to private pupils and worked hard for the Leith Hill Festival. During the summer months he would be busy compiling the schedule; in December and January he would attend the conductors' conference, when a few singers from each of the competing choirs and their conductors would work through the festival music under his guidance. Later on in the season he would take the combined choir rehearsals, and when the festival was due to take place, the orchestral ones as well. His kindness and consideration showed itself on these occasions in numerous ways, ranging from his practice of starting the full rehearsal with five minutes' playing 'to see if you have room to play' to his friendly reminder to individual members of the orchestra that there was a meal provided for them after the rehearsal.

It was in 1938 that Sir Henry Wood celebrated his golden jubilee as a conductor, and Vaughan Williams wrote a work containing parts for sixteen well-known British singers who had been associated with the conductor throughout his career. The *Serenade to Music*—one of his most lovely occasional works—was the result. Another occasional work of that year for an unusual combination of voices resulted from a visit to Christ's Hospital. As Clement Spurling had done at Oundle, the director of music there, C. S. Lang, had built up a considerable repertory of arrangements for massed unison voices in conjunction with the normal chorus. Thus that section of the school which was not in the choir was able to take part in the singing: indeed, Lang had developed the school's massed singing technique to such a remarkable degree that he had even arranged a simple and effective part for the five hundred or so 'school' singers in certain choruses in the *Messiah*. Vaughan Williams was much impressed by this sensible and useful method of interesting the 'average' boy in musical performance; it appealed to his own belief that the English were at heart a musical nation. So he wrote a complete set of Canticles—morning and evening service—for unison voices, choir and organ, 'for C. S. Lang and his singers at Christ's Hospital'. Yet another quite new type of occasional music came from his pen in the early years of the Second World War. When war had broken out in September 1939 even Vaughan Williams had naturally been unable to join the forces, so he busied himself with menial but useful tasks such as collecting salvage and addressing envelopes (in his unique and almost illegible hand), occupying his 'leisure' with the composition of a provocative and deeply interesting essay on Beethoven's ninth Symphony—the outcome of a projected performance of the work for the 1940 Leith Hill Festival which the war caused to be cancelled. Early in 1940 Muir Mathieson, the director of music for London Films, called upon him and asked if he would be prepared to write the music for a feature film. This was the first introduction for the sixty-seven-year-old composer to a new type of *Gebrauchsmusik* (he was allowed four days in which to write the first batch!). Ever since Arthur Bliss had been called upon to write the music for the film of H. G. Wells's *Things to Come*, British film studios had been enterprising in their choice of composers, taking their lead from our documentary film groups. Vaughan Williams was thus the latest and greatest of a longish line of distinguished names, but he saw the possibilities latent in the combination of film and music more clearly than most, and wrote in an article [1] somewhat later:

Perhaps one day a great film will be built up on the basis of music. The music will be written first and the film devised to accompany it, or the film will be written to music already composed. Walt Disney has pointed the way in his *Fantasia*. But must it always be a cartoon film? Could not the same idea be applied to the photographic film? Can music only suggest the fantastic and grotesque creations of an artist's pencil? May it not also shed its light on real people? [2]

He was called upon to provide music for a number of films after *Forty-ninth Parallel*, and this provided him with a useful means (which he greatly appreciated) of serving the national cause by providing a component in people's relaxation and also in Ministry of Information propaganda work. As seems always to have been the case with him, his attitude and output were here again intensely patriotic without being in the least chauvinistic.

But he was not only busy with film music during the war years. The summer of 1940 saw a visit to his old school for the ceremonial opening of the new music school there, memorable also for a performance of the *Toy Symphony*, directed by the headmaster, Mr Robert Birley, in which Vaughan Williams ('solemnly, and, moreover, artistically') played the cuckoo. He was appointed chairman of the Home Office Committee for the Release of Interned Alien Musicians, and his quiet work behind the scenes resulted in a number of useful releases—one of the most notable being the bringing back of the pianist Peter Stadlen from Australia. He organized music for the

[1] Reprinted in *Some Thoughts on Beethoven's Choral Symphony* (1953), pp. 107–15.
[2] Ibid., p. 114.

forces at the White Horse Assembly Rooms, Dorking, since the Leith Hill Music Festival was adjourned 'for the duration' and the concert halls were filled with bodily rather than mental sustenance. These concerts took place once a fortnight, and Vaughan Williams acted as compère. Concerts of a more popular nature were also arranged by him. They were held at the Toc H depot behind the Red Lion Hotel, and combined with a happy informality popular pieces chosen by the audience and more unusual music selected by the organizer. He wrote occasional articles—one of the most typical being that published in the *Manchester Guardian* in 1943 on William Shrubsole, the composer of the hymn-tune *Miles Lane*, and one of the most profound being that on 'Nationalism and Internationalism'. And he continued to compose.

His wartime works did not neglect the needs of what he called the 'modest amateur', and, practical as ever, he thought of those who would wish to combine and make music together, yet would not perhaps be able to produce an orthodox complement of instruments. So he wrote his *Household Music* for four instruments, thus putting into practice the thoughts expressed in his article 'The Composer in Wartime', written in 1940. But other works for distinguished professional musicians combined the kindness of the graceful gesture and the practical purpose of extending the repertory. Such for example was the second string Quartet 'For Jean on her Birthday', two movements of which were sent by a personal messenger (Ursula Wood) to the violist Jean Stewart as a surprise birthday greeting in February 1941.[1] Miss Stewart, a member of the Menges quartet, had been urging him for some years to write a work for them. The complete work (incorporating in its Scherzo some of the music from *Forty-ninth Parallel*) was given its first performance on 12th September 1944 at a National Gallery concert. Léon Goossens was the dedicatee of a concerto for oboe and strings, also written during the war years.

[1] There is a delightful pendant to this story. In 1957 Miss Stewart's daughter (then aged eight), wrote a small piano piece called *For Uncle Ralph on his Birthday*; he spent twenty minutes with her on the occasion of his eighty-fifth birthday listening to her playing it and gently correcting inaccuracies in her manuscript.

But the most important work was unquestionably the fifth Sym-phony, which was first given under the composer's direction at a Promenade Concert at the Royal Albert Hall on 26th June 1943. As with Verdi, so with Vaughan Williams; in his gathering old age he achieved new greatness, nowhere more apparent than in this work. It was no mere courtesy when the B.B.C. celebrated his seventieth birthday with a week of concerts, nor when the Folk Dance and Song Society presented him with its gold badge; both organizations were expressing a respect both profound and sincere. It is indicative of his generous nature that he was willing to testify in court on behalf of Michael Tippett in June 1943—though he strongly disagreed with the pacifist views which Tippett held. What mattered to Vaughan Williams was that Tippett sincerely meant what he said, and that he was, as a composer of 'very remarkable' works and as director of music at Morley College, performing work which increased the country's prestige in the world. He judged people by such criteria as complete personal integrity, sincerity and moral convictions. Tippett's views were based on these qualities, and that was enough to guarantee him Vaughan Williams's unstinted assistance.

Life at The White Gates continued much as before.[1] A niece had described it thus, and though the description refers to the period after the war, it is typical of the atmosphere of The White Gates at any time:

All its activity was contained in a single large room which, with galleries and inglenooks, seemed to be full of false old oak. The piano stood at one end, the dining table at the other; Robin Darwin's childhood sketch of R.V.W. conducting hung side by side with a bad reproduction of Van Gogh's chestnut tree on the walls; an exceptionally large cat slept in the warmest patch. Here Aunt Adeline would sit with her silver hair and long black dress, immobile in her high chair and infinitely welcoming; Uncle Ralph would come lumbering in from rolling the lawn or taking a practice for the Leith Hill Festival—or sitting to Epstein; as a treat there might be

---

[1] Ralph's elder brother Hervey had inherited Leith Hill Place on the death of their mother in 1937, and when he died in 1944, Ralph presented it to the National Trust. The tenancy was kept in the family, however, as the property was taken by Ralph Wedgwood.

played a worn record of Noel Coward singing 'The Stately Homes of England', which reduced both to helpless laughter; there would be a delicious tea to which, when she could no longer use her crutch, Uncle Ralph would move Aunt Adeline, chair and all, with the greatest skill and delicacy. They were never alone. There was a student, perhaps, who needed quiet to prepare for examinations, a refugee, someone who happened to be homeless or convalescent, the little great-niece who sent a jet of fresh life spurting through the house as one of its wartime residents.[1]

Thus it was for those who knew him and were of his family circle, but it was also the case during the war years that he became a kind of embodiment in music of the wartime spirit of Britain. His musical idiom had been regarded simply as one of a number of 'isms' in the thirties; the wave of national pride which welled up in the forties, following Dunkirk and the Battle of Britain, was much more conducive to the true appreciation of those of his qualities which represented all that was best in the national way of life. After the shifting improvisations in policy which had marked the thirties, the nation responded eagerly to clear and forthright leadership from Winston Churchill's government. The directness and simplicity of Vaughan Williams's art, the strength of will and quiet but firm patriotism which underlay it and which it seemed in some strange way to symbolize—these qualities reflected the national mood well. His adventurousness and radicalism were in tune with the spirit of enterprise that had replaced the aimless drift of the pre-war years. It was not thanks to the war that he became the leading and most respected figure in British music, but it almost certainly was because of the war that people in Britain realized for the first time his true stature as a composer.

His music seemed in fact to say, with deeper, and more immediate effect, what he himself had written in 1942:

I believe that the love of one's country, one's language, one's customs, one's religion, are essential to our national health. We may laugh at these things, but we love them none the less. Indeed, it is one of our national characteristics and one which I should be sorry to see disappear, that we laugh at what we love. This is something that a foreigner can never fathom,

---

[1] Mary Bennett in the *R.C.M. Magazine*, p. 20.

but it is out of such characteristics, these hard knots in our timber, that we can help to build up a united Europe and a world federation.

In his music were embodied those virtues which the British in their more idealistic moments are capable of exercising, and it was this aspect of it—more obvious in time of war when illusions can lead to fatal mistakes and the truth, however harsh, must be faced—which struck a sympathetic chord in wartime audiences and revealed to the British how great a composer their foremost musical patriot really was.

RALPH AND URSULA VAUGHAN WILLIAMS
(*Copyright: Douglas Glass*)

CHAPTER VII

THE LAST YEARS (1945–58)

IN ANTICIPATION of the allied victory over the Germans in 1945, the B.B.C. had commissioned a work from Vaughan Williams entitled *A Thanksgiving for Victory*, for speaker, chorus and orchestra, which was broadcast on the occasion of the German surrender. Once again he identified himself with the spirit of the nation at large and showed himself a national composer in a larger, more profound sense than simply that of a kind of composer laureate. As was usual with him, he disposed the work so that it could be used on other occasions, for which it was renamed *A Song of Thanksgiving*. It was an appropriate coincidence that the season of Henry Wood Promenade Concerts which took place when the war with Japan was in its closing stages should have been the first to include all five of his symphonies. Everybody assumed that his symphonic output was now more or less complete, and no one could possibly have realized that he had actually only just passed the half-way mark.

For some years now he had required a copyist to help him with the preparation of his scores, and in his usual whimsical manner he would often introduce some friend who happened to be on hand when a work was being composed as 'the man who writes my music'. At this time it was his former pupil Michael Mullinar, a brilliant pianist, whom he had known since the twenties. Many people appear to have been misled by Vaughan Williams's joking assertion that others wrote his music for him, and although his usual process of polishing up a composition in his last years was far from simple, only he himself was ever responsible for his music. His normal procedure was to prepare a short score and send an advance notice to his copyist, so that the latter might come and play it over—no easy task, as Vaughan Williams's handwriting was never very legible even in his younger days. Then a fair copy would be made, and the first official play-through would take place before the composer and a few close friends.

Afterwards it would be discussed, and played through again. After this he would revise it—usually according to Boileau's precept, 'Ajoutez quelquefois et souvent éffacez', and some weeks later his assistant would be called in to play it over again, this time before several musicians whose opinions the composer particularly valued. He would then ask what they thought of it; when he already had doubts about the suitability of a passage he would often amend it according to their advice. If, on the other hand, they suggested alterations to a passage which he was sure was correct, no amount of argument or persuasion would cause him to change what he had written. More weeks would pass, and the work, further revised, would be played through again. As Roy Douglas, Mullinar's successor, remarked: 'Here and there a page, or a line [would be] stuck (slightly askew) over the original copy, and an extra bar added in some corner of a page with an arrow pointing to it.' The score was then ready to 'have its face washed', and then the difficult work really started, when the discrepancies in the parts were eliminated. Douglas (who as an orchestator had been responsible for the best-known version of *Les Sylphides*) succeeded Mullinar in 1947, and tells a charming story of an occasion when one passage (in *Hodie*) simply did not seem to fit; it was tried as a clarinet line, as a cor anglais (transposed a fifth), as a bassoon part in both tenor and bass clefs, but seemed equally irrelevant in all possible clefs and keys. He sent it off with a query to Vaughan Williams, who simply wrote back: 'Can't make this out at all; let's leave it out'—which they did.[1] Finally, at last, came the first rehearsals and the work was finished—for the time being.

Many of his works in the immediate post-war years were written to order or arranged from earlier works. The dedication of the Battle of Britain Chapel in Westminster Abbey was the occasion of the anthem *The Souls of the Righteous*; for St Cecilia's Day the same year (1947) the splendid 'Pavane of the Sons of the Morning' from *Job* was fitted with words taken from the Book of Job; in 1948 a poem by Skelton (in his sonorous rhyme-royal court poet vein, not as the mordant rhymester of *Five Tudor Portraits*) was selected for a short anthem in

[1] *R.C.M. Magazine,* Vol. LV (1959). No. 1, p. 47.

celebration of the centenary of Hubert Parry's birth. He continued to write film music, which culminated in a magnificent score for the Ealing film *Scott of the Antarctic*, awarded the first prize at the 1949 Prague Film Festival. But he also wrote works such as the sixth Symphony, which was first performed by the B.B.C. Symphony Orchestra at the Royal Albert Hall on 21st April 1948; it had been germinating in his mind since about 1944. And he contributed a challenging short analysis of music in English society under the title 'A Minim's Rest' for a collection of *Essays Mainly on the Nineteenth Century presented to Sir Humphrey Milford* during that year. A tribute was paid by a master of another art when Sir Jacob Epstein sculptured a bronze head of Vaughan Williams. On one occasion Vaughan Williams invited Epstein to a performance of the *St Matthew Passion* after a sitting; in his own autobiography, Epstein wrote:

Here was the master with whom no one would venture to dispute. He reminded one in appearance of some eighteenth-century admiral whose word was law. Notwithstanding I found him the epitome of courtesy and consideration, and I was impressed by the logic and acuteness of everything he discoursed upon and was made aware of his devotion to an art as demanding as sculpture.

The artist's eye caught the blend of immense power and warm, gentle, friendly dignity in the man which the listener hears so often in his music.

His reputation and the veneration in which he was held were now such that he was asked to lend his name and presence to all sorts of gatherings and organizations for prestige' sake alone. Any bodies which wished to enlist his name to glorify their own soon found, however, that his support was never purely nominal, and that he invariably took his duties as chairman or president very seriously. He succeeded Sir Hugh Allen on the latter's death as president of the British Federation of Competitive Music Festivals. Interest in new music showed itself in his presidency of the Committee for the Promotion of New Music, which gave its hundredth recital on 5th October 1948. Under his presidency it grew from what he himself called 'thirty or so composers more or less taking in one another's washing' to an important element in the assessment and performance of contemporary music. Though not particularly sympathetic to some developments in modern music, he never failed to give encouragement to any 'wrong-note' composer, as he called them, whom he felt to possess a real musical gift. Among the younger British composers he particularly admired the work of Elizabeth Maconchy. Against other developments in contemporary musical life, however—such as 'authentic' performances of eighteenth-century music on an intimate scale with small forces on reconstructions of old instruments,[1] or the revival of early nineteenth-century Italian *bel canto* operas ('shaking the dead bones of *Norma*', as he once put it)—he set his face most firmly, and for the 'bubble-and-squeak' tone of the baroque organ he entertained a contempt worthy of the Great Cham himself.

When his old school celebrated its quatercentenary in 1949 he wrote a masque for the occasion, a compliment which the school returned three years later by arranging special celebrations for his eightieth birthday. Anyone, as an individual or as representative of a body of opinion, who called on him for advice or assistance could always count on his laying aside whatever he was engaged upon in order to see what he could do for them. Such called on his time, together with his advancing age, neither slowed down his output nor in any way impaired his energy. As he grew older he grew, if anything, even more self-critical, still destroying much of what he wrote as unsatisfactory. But he continued to cultivate new ground. The war had caused him to lay aside a masque prepared for the Folk Dance Society, to a text based by Ursula Wood on Spenser's *Epithalamion* and called *The Bridal Day*; he revived it for a television broadcast in 1953. In 1951 the Schools Music Association required a work for children's voices in connection with the Festival of Britain. Protesting that he knew nothing about such works, he consented to write it, Ursula Wood

He became involved in a vigorous correspondence in the *Daily Telegraph* early in 1958 over the question of using a piano continuo when performing Bach's Passions; his own practice was to use a piano in what he would whimsically refer to as his 'Concerto version', for he could not stand the harpsichord any more than he could the 'baroque' organ.

again providing the text. *The Sons of Light* was performed for the first time at the Albert Hall on 6th May 1951. The harmonica virtuoso, Larry Adler, wanted a short work for his instrument, and approached Vaughan Williams for one. The *Romance* for harmonica and strings was the result.

During these years he and Adeline had been quietly living at The White Gates, as they had done for over twenty years; on 10th May 1951, however, she died at the age of eighty. He stayed on in the house for two years longer; it was, after all, the country in which he had grown up and with which he had so many musical ties. A consider-able number of communications in support of good causes and in denunciation of bad ones continued to issue from that address. Among the former may certainly be included a letter to *The Times* on 4th January 1950 appealing for funds for Cecil Sharp House, and among the latter a vehement and amusing broadcast, intended as a counterblast to certain attempts to relate Bach to the class struggle, emanating mainly from Eastern Germany as part of the Bach bicentenary celebrations in 1950. Provocative—indeed, one might say aggressive —as the text itself was, the spirited energy with which the almost octogenarian musician delivered it makes the printed version seem but a pale reflection of the original for those who heard it. He might have been expected to leave such matters to others; but he remained always willing to express a forceful opinion, too, on behalf of the prestige of British culture, and his wrath was as easily kindled as ever against those who sought to undermine that prestige. Thus, on 7th February 1952, *The Times* published a letter over his signature protesting against the closing down of the Crown Film Unit, which had commissioned much fine incidental music from promising young British composers, describing the decision as 'a sentence damaging to our colleagues at home and our prestige abroad'. Likewise, he came vigorously to the defence of his old teacher, Stanford, when *The Times* criticized his *Stabat Mater* on stylistic grounds. He informed an International Folk Music Council Conference in London in July 1952 that there was too much of a tendency to admire foreign products at the expense of the home-grown, a tendency not confined to Britain. Later on, in 1953, when Britten's coronation opera *Gloriana* was attacked for various reasons (many of them quite amusingly irrelevant), he voiced his own opinion with tact and frankness at the same time:

I do not propose, after a single hearing, to appraise either the words or the music of *Gloriana*. The important thing to my mind, at the moment, is that, so far as I know, for the first time in history, the Sovereign has commanded an opera from these islands for a great occasion. Those who cavil at the public expense involved should realize what such a gesture means to the prestige of our music.

Such words, coming from one who had full knowledge of what public neglect of his own operas implied, went completely over the heads of most of the other participants in the correspondence. Other topics, such as the inadequacy of royalties paid to composers on sales of gramophone records, the curtailment of the Third Programme and the future of John Nash's beautiful terrace houses in Regent's Park, also called forth trenchant comment, and sometimes vigorous action, from him—not the cantankerous spleen of a spiteful old man, but the passionate reaction of an agile mind.

In *Cakes and Ale* Somerset Maugham drew the somewhat cynical conclusion that longevity was more or less an essential of genius in England. While it is true that the beloved figure of the veteran composer was admired on account of the 'character' which the public saw and heard of, his compositions belie any idea that it was merely on account of his age that he was revered. When the Royal Festival Hall was opened in June 1951, two inaugural concerts were given by the B.B.C. Symphony Orchestra. The original intention was that they should be conducted by Arturo Toscanini, but he was unable to accept, and the programmes were taken over *en bloc* by Sir Malcolm Sargent. The first programme was devoted to Beethoven's first and ninth Symphonies; the second included Vaughan Williams's sixth, which was in no way overshadowed by the inevitable comparison that the short lapse of time between the two concerts invited. At the more formal and musically less intrinsically interesting concert which had commemorated the ceremonial opening of the hall, the *Serenade to Music* had been performed (in a choral version), with a special orchestra under Sir Adrian Boult.

Honours, both great and small, conferred on him and by him, continued to accumulate, but he still steadfastly refused any notion of a knighthood. As the most distinguished recipient of the Royal Philharmonic Society's gold medal he was responsible for making the presentation when it was conferred in 1948 on William Walton, and in 1950 on Sir John Barbirolli. At a concert in September 1951 at the Festival Hall he made a presentation to a great choral conductor who was also well known as an arranger of folksongs—Sir Hugh Roberton. On 14th December of the same year he received the first honorary musical doctorate of Bristol University from its chancellor—Winston Churchill. A man so much involved in public activities and so vigorous in the practice of his own art was, not surprisingly, equally vigorous in his human and personal relationships. The great and the little, the old and the young, all received forthright and kindly advice and criticism from him when it was required and deserved. Only for the sham and the affected did he have no time. In one particular case a friendship developed into something deeper. Ursula Wood, the widow of an officer in the Royal Artillery, had first met him in 1938, when they had collaborated on a masque for the Folk Dance Society adapted from Spenser's *Epithalamion*. Herself a poet and writer, Ursula Wood prepared a number of texts for him, including *Silence and Music* for his contribution to the symposium tribute by British composers to the second Elizabeth (a parallel to the *Oriana* madrigals for the first), certain parts of *The Pilgrim's Progress* and *The Sons of Light*. On 7th February 1953 they were quietly married: the bridegroom was just over eighty. In August The White Gates was put up for sale and Vaughan Williams moved to 10 Hanover Terrace, N.W.1, in Regent's Park, where he lived for the rest of his life.

He was still remarkably prolific, though perhaps rather less inventive. Economy in the use of themes originally thought of for other purposes is seen at its best in the *Sinfonia antartica*, a good deal of which was adapted from music written for the film *Scott of the Antarctic*. The quality of his own film music, and the human theme of Scott's voyage, appealed to him so much that he distilled the best of what had already been written into a new and original work, which he dedicated to Ernest Irving, the musical director of Ealing Films. It was first performed at Manchester on 14th January 1953 under Sir John Barbirolli, who was one of the most sympathetic and enthusiastic of Vaughan Williams's interpreters. Barbirolli in his turn received the dedication of the eighth Symphony some three years later. The Christmas oratorio *Hodie*, a tuba concerto for the London Symphony Orchestra's golden jubilee in 1954, a set of variations for a brass band festival (which he attended and at which he presented the prize), a violin sonata—all these broke new ground for him, as they were written either in a form or for a medium he had not tried out before. Even the eighth Symphony was not the last; the ninth followed in 1958. His lifelong preoccupation with *The Pilgrim's Progress* finally resulted in what, despite any quibbles about titles, is an opera on the subject, first performed at Covent Garden on 26th April 1951. Like Goethe's *Faust*, the work contains more than is readily digestible at one hearing, and, like most English operas, it was lavishly produced once and then dropped quietly from the repertory. Perhaps if it were sung by a star cast, in German, to Robert Müller-Hartmann's and Genia Hornstein's excellent translation, it would attract the attention it deserves, even if for wrong reasons. The parallel with Goethe can perhaps be extended further. Not only did both he and Vaughan Williams keep works by them all their long lives until they were ready to give them to the world, but both were men whose classic calm and dignity concealed a vigorous—even volcanic—temperament which does not always show itself in their work. Both were extremely versatile and willing to tackle almost any form. Both continued to work energetically until the very last days of their lives, and both owed much to the advice and stimulus of a younger friend whose acquaintance they had made when quite young, and who died considerably earlier than they did themselves. Both lived a busy public life, but neither forgot his calling as an artist. And both raised the art with which they were associated to a pinnacle which it had never before attained in their respective countries. When he was eighty-one, Goethe wrote:

> Diese Richtung ist gewiss,
> Immer schreite! Schreite!
> Finsterniss und Hinderniss
> Drängt mich nicht sur Seite.

Last Visit to U.S.A.

These words apply to no one with more force than to Ralph Vaughan Williams.

Early in 1954 the baritone singer Keith Falkner, who had been living for some time in the United States, was lunching at Hanover Terrace, when Vaughan Williams remarked that there were two things he had never done—visited Rome or seen the Grand Canyon. What should they do about it? His wife suggested 'See them both', and Falkner said that a visiting professorship at Cornell University might be the means of achieving one ambition, at any rate. So late in September 1954 he and Ursula arrived at Ithaca, N.Y., for the beginning of his third and last visit to the States; it lasted four months. As usual, his energy seems to have left everyone else save himself physically tired; after a hectic day seeing the sights of New York, he insisted that the whole party should go up to the top of the Empire State Building to see the sunset. It is reasonably likely that he would have insisted on this even had the lifts been out of order.

The Cornell lectures developed a similar theme to the earlier American course published as *National Music*, and they were published in 1955 under the title *The Making of Music*. During this visit he conducted and attended performances as well as lecturing, and wherever he went his robust vitality, his kindness and his humour seem to have deeply impressed everyone he met. Everyone, that is, with the possible exception of the unfortunate young student at Cornell who played over to him a movement from a somewhat dissonant quartet on the piano, at the end of which he simply peered down his glasses and observed: 'If a tune *should* occur to you, my boy, don't hesitate to write it down.'

The National Arts Foundation of America had voted him the outstanding musician of 1953, describing him as a 'Miltonic figure', and his music as 'full of splendour without tinsel', and he was naturally fêted wherever he went. He celebrated his eighty-second birthday at the University of Michigan, where the students and the music faculty arranged a special concert of his vocal works in his honour; he also went to Indiana University, which had recently been responsible for a performance of *Five Tudor Portraits*, and to California (via the Grand Canyon!), where he was able to experience something quite unique—Synge's *Riders to the Sea*, first as a play, then as his opera. At Yale he attended the centenary celebrations of the music department, receiving the highest award that the university can bestow—the Howland Memorial Prize. In Buffalo he was able once again to conduct one of the great American professional orchestras. The chief conductor there, Josef Krips, who had played many of his works with the London Symphony Orchestra in London and elsewhere, had arranged to conduct a performance of *Sancta Civitas*, to be preceded by the *Tallis Fantasia*, which he asked the composer to conduct himself. Krips had been very impressed by Vaughan Williams's method of rehearsing—despite his advanced age and the necessity for a hearing aid!—and the enthusiasm which ran through the audience of 3,000 when the composer bowed from the rostrum was such as the conductor had never seen before or since. It is difficult to know how much of the performance was due to the composer's conducting and how much to the sheer love and respect in which he was held by the players, for he was by now more or less unable to hear some orchestral timbres, such as the oboe, at all well. He possessed a veritable battery of hearing aids, the largest of which he referred to as his 'coffee-pot'. His advancing deafness somewhat restricted his enjoyment of music for large forces, but to the end of his days he continued to attend performances of works by composers—such as Holst—of whose music he was particularly fond. He regularly went out of his way to listen to new works by promising young composers, whether or not he found their musical idiom sympathetic. But what he enjoyed most was listening to small groups of musicians in his own home singing madrigals (always conducting them himself) or performing chamber music, while he sat in an armchair, attended by his two enormous cats, perhaps sipping a glass of sherry.

From time to time he continued to appear as a conductor almost up till his death, but naturally restricted his public appearances as much as he could. When he did attend festivals—such as the Cheltenham Festival of Contemporary Music, which he did regularly—he had such an appetite for new music that he would turn up punctually both for rehearsals and concerts, listening with deep attention and offering encouragement or criticism afterwards. His massive form, his thatch of white hair, his spectacles perched on the end of his long, rugged and prominent nose, his twinkling and expressive grey eyes and his uniquely untidy sartorial appearance rendered him an unmistakable landmark, and outside the concert-room an inspiration for distinguished artists as well, such as David McFall, who completed a fine bronze head for the Royal Festival Hall; Sir Gerald Kelly, who painted two portraits (one unfinished at the sitter's death); and Karsh of Ottawa, who spent four hours photographing him in 1952. Sometimes, it must be confessed, the landmark drew attention to itself by dropping off to sleep during a particularly dull work, but in general his stamina and alertness enabled him to offer shrewd and valuable comments. He had, Sir John Barbirolli remarked, the youngest mind of anyone the conductor knew, and this was coupled with an unquenchable zest for life, even though he gradually played less of a part in active public music-making. He handed over the conductorship of the Leith Hill Festival in 1955, but kept in touch with it till his death.

He was now not only a public figure, but a beloved institution. In November 1955 he became the first musician ever to receive the Albert Medal of the Royal Society of Arts. Any committee connected with the arts was eager to enlist his aid, and whenever possible he gave it. He arranged for a trust in his name to assist music and musicians. He retained his good health throughout the evening of his days, apart from a minor operation in September 1957, which necessitated a short spell in hospital, and so it was quite a surprise, despite his great age, when he died suddenly and peacefully at his home on the morning of 26th August 1958. It had been arranged for that morning that he should attend a recording session with Sir Adrian Boult and the London Philharmonic Orchestra, who were to record his ninth Symphony—thus completing the canon; they had recorded the other eight already.

Perhaps the greatest tribute that was paid to him of all the many hundreds all over the world was simply the almost universal surprise that he should have died at all, even at the age of eighty-five. He had, by his simple, strong personality, his direct and profound vision, already gained some foretaste of immortality as a person and as an institution. He had touched the hearts of the people as his predecessor

Elgar had done, but in a totally different way, appealing less to their patriotic pride in the splendour of power and responsibility than to their sense of the abiding beauty and worthwhileness of the better side of English life. He may not have been born great, but he achieved greatness of a rare quality. The Chancellor of Liverpool Cathedral based a sermon on his life-work, and the Dean of Gloucester justly pointed out that he had lived 'not in the clouds but in musical England as he knew it, in the churches, in the musical festivals, and other gatherings of ordinary music folk, speaking so often for the common man with the authentic voice of the English musical tradition'. Yet though he had not lived in the clouds, his vision had penetrated through them, as his greatest works prove.

His funeral service in Westminster Abbey on 19th September included, in accordance with his wishes, Maurice Greene's (1695–1755) *Lord, let me know mine end*, and the organ voluntary was Bach's Fugue in E flat. His own work was represented by *Five Variants of 'Dives and Lazarus'*, by *Rhosymedre*, and by the anthem *O taste and see*, written for the 1953 coronation, by his setting of the *Old Hundredth*, combining rich glory with its massed trumpets and warm common-sense solidity in the splendid Genevan tune, by the 'Pavane of the Sons of the Morning' from *Job*, and by *Down Ampney*. Craftsman and artist, *Gebrauchsmusiker* and visionary, the diverse facets of his inquiring mind were well demonstrated by these works. Not long after the Second World War he had told Professor Howells that all he required was a little time to glean his mind. The gleanings had included four symphonies, an opera and an oratorio; he left only one uncompleted work—a masque called *The First Nowell* to a text arranged from medieval plays by Simona Pakenham, who had recently published an enthusiastic and very discerning study of his music. The time he required had been exactly allotted him, and he had not wasted it.

CHAPTER VIII

THE SIMPLE KLEPTOMANIAC

A FAVOURITE word in Williams's vocabulary was 'cribbing'; he liked to describe himself as a man of little originality who plundered his predecessors and contemporaries, helping himself to whatever was of use to him. In the obituary notice which has been quoted in a previous chapter (p. 25), Herbert Howells called him 'a great original [who] liked to be thought a simple kleptomaniac let loose harmlessly among his creative peers—or inferiors'. What goods he pilfered and how he blended them into his own characteristic merchandise are a measure of his own originality.

The obvious starting-point is of course English folksong, and it is sometimes thought that folksong was just a model on which he based his style. It is certainly true that he studied folksong, loved it and found inspiration in it, and that many of his themes show a similar melodic contour to those of a genuine folk-theme. The majestic melody which occurs at the end of the first movement of the sixth Symphony, for example, might be described as an enhanced folk melody. How it arises out of its context is not a matter for discussion here and will be considered later on; what at present interests us is the elements from which the theme itself is built up. It is a noticeable feature of quite a few English folksong melodies that they are built up, not on the square repetition of balanced phrases, but by the fitting together of various musical fragments; *I will give my love an apple*, which Vaughan Williams himself arranged, is a case of this. There are a number of key motifs which are blended together to form a tune, and one complete phrase which is repeated almost note for note to form the second and fourth lines of the tune. The key-motifs are:

73

the complete phrase is:

and the whole tune runs:

The same process can be seen at work in the theme from the sixth Symphony, which is likewise built up from a number of motifs welded together by balance and variation. The tune itself could not be a folksong; its mode is too sophisticated, and its flow just a little too irregular, but it is a development from the same root as *I will give my love an apple*, and that root is an English root.

In his earlier works Vaughan Williams made much use of material that was so like some of the folksongs he had collected that critics and listeners were hard put to it to tell the difference, but it appears that he took some heed of Constant Lambert's rather malicious (but regrettably accurate) observation to the effect that 'the only thing you can do with a folksong when you have played it once is to play it again, and play it rather louder'. Vaughan Williams deviated more than a little from the folksong norm, but his deviations were of such a kind as rendered his material amenable to symphonic development rather than simple repetition. It was probably for this reason that he worked out forms which were rather different from the bipartite sonata scheme, with its two balanced but contrasting groups of subjects. Certain English folksongs, such as *It's a rosebud in June,* show a tendency to expand from an initial phrase, by varying the length of it, the shape of its intervals and its rhythm. In *It's a rosebud in June* the little phrase:

becomes:

and:

so that the whole tune seems to flower from the bud of the first phrase. There are a number of examples of this in Vaughan Williams's own themes; the theme quoted above from the sixth Symphony is one of them; so is this from the *Sinfonia antartica*:

and this, from *Flos Campi*:

That he regarded this as a definite way of developing symphonic material is shown by a passage from his long essay on the Choral Symphony, where he points out that when Beethoven wishes to develop the thematic fragment:

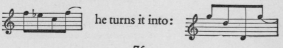

he turns it into:

This is exactly what Vaughan Williams does himself in the *Tallis Fantasia*, for example, where he takes the upward third at the beginning of the melody, and expands it (taking his cue from Tallis), first to a

fifth: (*a*) 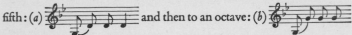 and then to an octave: (*b*)

before eventually submitting it to a further process of melodic expansion which is really only that of *It's a rosebud in June* on a much larger and more consciously applied scale.

In his Mary Flexner lectures he was careful to point out both the pros and the cons of using folksong as the basis for a style of composition, and threw an interesting light on its appeal to him:

In the days when Elgar formed his style, English folk-song was not 'in the air' but was consciously revived and made popular only about thirty years ago. Now what does this revival mean to the composer? It means that several of us found here in its simplest form the musical idiom which we unconsciously were cultivating ourselves, it gave a point to our imagination . . . the knowledge of our folk-songs did not so much discover for us something new, but uncovered for us something which had been hidden by foreign matter.[1]

Folksong was, in other words, a short cut to musical self-knowledge, not a model copied from the outside. This is why Vaughan Williams developed an idiom which based its inflections and methods on those of folksong but expanded the whole technique beyond the bounds of the folksong itself and into the realm of symphonic style. He neither cultivated the mosaic-like rhapsody nor fitted his themes into the Procrustean bed of sonata form, but developed his own new forms from his melodic idiom. There is thus a world of difference between his use of modal material, which is fundamental not only to his melodic idiom, but to his forms, and that of, say, Respighi in the second section of *The Pines of Rome*, where modality is a purely local colour effect. It is the difference between the swallow which incorporates material into the structure of its nest and the magpie which merely decorates it with garish objects.

[1] *National Music*, p. 75.

THE MANUSCRIPT OF 'BUSHES AND BRIARS'

(By kind permission of Mrs Ursula Vaughan Williams)

It was natural that these forms should bear some resemblance to the old sonata forms, simply because the sonata form, too, is a sophisticated extension of older and simpler purely melodic forms, but the difference between the two is caused by the difference between the tonal, melodic and rhythmic structure in English and German folksong.

It is not always realized just how original Vaughan Williams was in the matter of inventing new forms, simply because his respect for tradition made them appear as mere deviations from old ones (and therefore as shortcomings in technical ability). The process of grafting new sticks on to old stocks, as has already been pointed out, can be seen in the *Tallis Fantasia*; it is seen at work in the *Pastoral Symphony*, in the remarkable opening movement of the sixth—which, for all its pretence at being a sonata movement, is really a series of variations culminating in a theme instead of branching out from one—and the further development of this method in the first movement of the eighth, where the variations are 'in search of a theme', which is never stated, as the composer himself put it. (Even so, with his roguish sense of humour, he was careful to point out that the movement could be analysed on sonata lines.)

Realizing that folksong suffered from the great disadvantage that, being purely orally transmitted, its formal span was limited by what singer and listener alike were capable of remembering at one stretch,[1] he was simply bringing the processes of intellectual calculation and written transmission to bear on material which was ultimately of the same nature as the folksong itself. Elsewhere in the book, he quotes, with approval:

The best composers store up half-fledged ideas in the works of others and make use of them to build up perfect edifices which take on the character of their maker because they are ideas which appeal to that special mind.[2]

Of nobody was this statement more true than of Vaughan Williams himself. He often pointed out where he cribbed certain themes and ideas; Satan's dance, from *Job*, is a development of an idea first put on paper in Beethoven's F major Quartet, Op. 135—recognizably so, and the composer admitted as much. Similarly, the semitonal clash at

[1] Ibid., p. 75. [2] Ibid., p. 49.

the opening of the fourth Symphony was allegedly derived—or so the composer wrote—from the similar dissonance at the beginning of the finale of Beethoven's ninth. Much more interesting for us are those cases where—consciously or unconsciously—he adapts a scheme which another composer had used before and explores its meaning in a different, and sometimes more profound, way.

Two of the most striking cases of this are the fourth and sixth Symphonies. The former might well be described as a nightmare version of Beethoven's fifth. The superficial features of this can be seen in the groping lead into the finale from the explosive scherzo. There is the same build-up of a top-heavy harmony over a reiterated figure in the basses, the same powerful crescendo and the same three hammered minim major chords at the beginning of the new movement. But the differences show what Vaughan Williams learnt from Beethoven. Beethoven's three triumphant tonic C major chords and the great march that follows them represent a release from an almost unbearable tension; their effect is like that of a victory won after a tense and unremitting struggle. Vaughan Williams's three triads (F major, A major, D major) and his *marche macabre* are nothing of the sort. Thrown into the dissonant turmoil, they have the effect of a sarcastic perversion of a noble exhilarating message. In a certain sense this is exactly what they are. Various attempts have been made to read a programme into the fourth Symphony; it has been described as a prophecy, a diagnosis, a portrayal of a world dominated by vicious ideologies, and Heaven knows what else. It is not too far-fetched to say that it could equally well be said to stand as a demonstration of the terrible ultimate perversions of optimistic humanist liberal nationalism which were prevalent in the thirties, and that the likeness to Beethoven is extraordinarily apposite, even if completely unintentional. For Beethoven, of all composers, felt and expressed the liberating force of that liberal nationalism as a personal and social power, and his fifth Symphony is exactly the work in which the effect of its force on him might seem to be most clearly and tellingly demonstrated in musical form. The 'demonic' element seems to have come to the surface after the First World War, though it is foreshadowed in the first and fourth movements of the *London Symphony*. Power was always evident in his music, but the power in *Sancta Civitas*, for example, is of an entirely different order from that in the *Fantasia on a Theme by Thomas Tallis*. This elemental power dominates the fourth Symphony, is reconciled with and blended with the 'serene' element in the sixth, and 'tamed' into sardonic but harmless ribaldry in the ninth. The close formal structure of the fourth Symphony (which will be discussed later on) resembles that of Beethoven's fifth in some ways, too, particularly in the first and fourth movements. It is an exaggeration to say that Vaughan Williams explores the implications of Beethoven's fifth more profoundly than Beethoven did himself, but it is certainly true to say that he translated it into appropriate modern terms in more than one sense.

The sixth Symphony takes its point of departure in this matter from Holst's *Planets*, particularly in the second and fourth movements. The menacing, swirling string passages in octaves which occur in the Moderato movement, and the terrifying trumpet figure which appears from outer space as it were (though it is really derived from a phrase of the main theme, and merges into it when that theme reappears) and swells up to dominate the whole movement are—intentionally or not —a crib from 'Mars', but Vaughan Williams's use of them is both actually and deliberately different from Holst's. Similarly, the tenuous web of sound, *pianissimo* throughout and ending in an indeterminate cadence, which constitutes the finale, is very like 'Neptune'—but again, on account of its context, the impact of the music is totally different. The relationship between the two friends here bears fruit twelve years after Holst's death.

Vaughan Williams is not usually thought of as a composer who thought much of, or even about, jazz, though he did make the following point in *National Music*:

You will tell me you are tired of jazz and that it represents only a very small part of your psychology. I think you are wrong in despising jazz, but I do not go so far as to say as some thinkers do that it has in it the seeds of great further development. But it does show this: that there is musical vitality in America. . . . At all events jazz, whether you like it or not, is a purely indigenous art. No-one but an American can write it or play it.[1]

---

[1] Ibid., p. 126.

The raucous saxophone solo in the third movement of the sixth Symphony has many of the superficial characteristics of a jazz solo, the repeated changes in stress, the insistence on the repetition of one small phrase with minor variations, the quasi-improvisatory aspect of the whole tune, for example, which are thrown into relief when, later in the movement, the theme is 'straightened out' and blared out in augmentation by the whole orchestra with something of the brutal bravura of the last movement of the fourth Symphony. What had been a torrent of molten sound has now solidified into rugged shape, and the 'jazz' element has fulfilled its purpose of acting as the raw material of which the later version is the finished product. It is not a very prepossessing article—nor is it meant to be.

Another theory developed in *National Music* is that of music being a heightened form of excited and emotional speech; Vaughan Williams cited an example from his own experience in support of it. Listening one day to a Gaelic preacher on the Island of Skye, he was unable to understand a word, but was able to note the musical lilt of some of his phrases when he was obviously stressing a point. In *Riders to the Sea* he develops this side of his theory—and it is no coincidence that he chose a play with a Gaelic setting to make use of it. The vocal line is simply a recitative, rising to a kind of *arioso* when the situation demands it on account of emotional or dramatic stress. This is an experiment which had been tried out by other composers before, but it was the first time that the method had been applied to an English text. The cribbing here is from a verbal rather than a musical source.

Vaughan Williams's composing career lasted longer than that of any other major musician except Verdi. It is true that Sibelius was older when he died—ninety as opposed to eighty-five—but he had written nothing important since about his sixtieth birthday. Vaughan Williams, on the other hand, wrote his first published work when he was nineteen, and his last shortly before his death. His span as a composer therefore covers over sixty-five years—or something more than twice Schubert's entire lifetime, and nearly three times the length of his creative career. During that time serious music passed through the romantic twilight, impressionism, neo-classicism, dodecaphony, polytonality, socialist realism, socialist idealism and flirtations with jazz; in the years before the First World War alone, Strauss, Stravinsky, Schönberg, Debussy and Sibelius were all, in differing ways, writing music which was intensely individual, and at the same time a development from or reaction against nineteenth-century tradition. With the possible exception of Schönberg, Vaughan Williams's own development included elements which can be traced to each of them; yet in every case those elements are welded into a congruent style by the fertilizing influence of the melodic premises of English folksong. He is a master of the original use of the musical commonplace. We have already seen how, by its context, the formula of three major triads in succession is given a new significance by the use he makes of it. He once wrote that Sibelius made the chord of C major sound stranger than the maddest polytonalities of the maddest central Europeans. The same could certainly be said of him. On a first hearing of the *Pastoral Symphony*, for example, a progression at the beginning of the slow movement sounds strange and unreal; inspected more closely, it turns out to be a succession of major and minor triads cunningly juxtaposed so as to give an air of remoteness to the very simple melodic

line:

Or in the sixth Symphony a harsh and overbearing passage on the brass, which sounds more cruel and unsettling than any sequence of crude dissonances, proves to be simply the same device as the other, used in a different manner:

This mastery over the dramatic function of the common chord was a feature of Vaughan Williams's music from his very earliest days. It is already to be found in the *Songs of Travel*, for example, and plays an important part in his music from then onwards. Successions of triads grew to be a mannerism, yet it was a mannerism often used in an inspired way. This is a touchstone of greatness and originality which has nothing at all to do with his being English or basing his idiom in any way whatever on folk music, and it is one of the reasons why musicians like Cecil Gray and Arnold Bax, who abhorred folksong composers as such, were ready to admit Vaughan Williams's great-ness, as their autobiographies testify. His originality here is not the result of his having based his art on nationalist premises, but his 'nationalism' was the yeast which brought his genius to fermentation.

Cecil Gray, in his autobiography, also remarked that Vaughan Williams criticized a work of his by saying: 'You never attempt anything which you know you cannot do.' The corollary of this remark sums up Vaughan Williams's own attitude to composition admirably. He spent much of his life doing just that—attempting what people thought he could not do—and it is not surprising, therefore, that some of his works were gallant failures rather than outstanding successes. Once he had developed the tools of his craft—his idiom and his style—he set them to work to create things which even he himself could hardly have visualized as a young man. Remembering that the basis of all music is melody and rhythm, he set out to devise forms and harmonies that were congruent with his style of melody and his type of rhythm. He made technique his servant, not his master; he rebuilt his music from its foundations upwards, and always had a point of reference from which he could take his bearings.

Moreover, he was never satisfied that a work had fully expressed what he wanted to say. His musical integrity was of a peculiar kind. On the one hand we have anecdotes like that told of him as a student at Cambridge: when the local Musical Society intended to perform Beethoven's fifth Symphony at an orchestral concert, he found out that they could not afford a double-bassoon for the finale, and were intending to dispense with that instrument. Vaughan Williams set about collecting the money, on his own initiative, so that a player could be hired, rather than allow a performance which weakened the force of Beethoven's music through lack of funds. On the other, we remember that he was quite capable of giving a performance of the *St Matthew Passion* with different instrumentation from Bach's own, provided that all the parts were present—tone-colour being in this case a secondary consideration, and half a loaf better than no bread at all. Similarly, in nearly all his scores there is considerable provision for performance with smaller forces than those he originally envisaged. This is true, for example, of all the symphonies. In a certain sense it is a mistaken respect for his wishes which ensures that these works are not performed until the full—in some cases very large—orchestra is assembled which the composer calls for, simply because the aim of the 'cueing' was to allow the works in question to be performed by smaller and therefore less expensive combinations than the ideal forces. Even the formidable impact of the organ in the 'Landscape' movement of the *Sinfonia Antartica* can at need be replaced by a blast from the full orchestra.

The mixture of integrity and respect for what is practicable shows itself throughout his music, with few exceptions (the accompaniment of *The Roadside Fire* is one). He never thought of music apart from performance and frequently, as in *The Spirit and the Letter*, said so; he was, of all twentieth-century composers, the *Gebrauchsmusiker par excellence*. Amateurs, professionals, children and adults, the orthodox and the strange—all found him ready and willing to write for them. This in part explains his cavalier attitude to some of his own works, and his willingness to rearrange them and revise them. Unlike many modern composers, he was willing to go much more than half way to meet his audience and did so without sacrificing his artistic integrity. This attitude, which we find in other English contemporary musicians, too, notably Britten, derives in Vaughan Williams's case from his ideas on the place of music in society. Without attempting to interpret nationalism in Marxist terms, we can at any rate say that, as Constant Lambert points out in *Music Ho!* nineteenth-century artistic national-ism was a reflection of political liberalism and nationalism. Vaughan Williams's 'nationalism' was rooted, on the other hand, in a love of the underdog 'whose day was to come'. But his radicalism was of the William Morris kind (as was that of Dearmer, Sharp and Holst), which rebelled against contemporary conditions in the interests of a fuller, deeper and more beautiful life for the individual; it was not professed in the name of any particular political party or class of society. It may have been political at one remove; it was certainly (for want of a better term) 'anti-bourgeois' in its rejection of shabby, overdone ornament and second-hand values. Its aim was an enrichment and elevation of national musical standards and a re-establishment of national faith in the country's musical prestige. He believed that the English composer should have, and that he himself did have, something to say to the community that the foreign composer could not say.

The more obvious features of his style can be briefly and quickly mentioned. It is a matter of common knowledge that many of his themes are modal, and that some are pentatonic. Because the basis of his style is melodic, so too are most of his mannerisms, though his predilection for strings of consecutives (particularly of fifths and full common chords) is a harmonic mannerism obvious to all. Fingerprints of his melodic style are the drooping triplet

which returns again and again to its apogee:

Another is the formula best set out as: which

occurs in works as different as the canticle *Famous Men* and the fifth Symphony. Yet another is a relentless, striding crotchet bass—as in *Sine Nomine, The Vagabond,* the slow movement of the *Sea Symphony* or, again, *Famous Men*—which is a quirk inherited from Parry. Another is the habit of hammering or moulding a theme out of piled-up fourths, as in the scherzo movements of the fifth and sixth Symphonies. His themes often begin with an arching phrase which expands by extending its arch through the incorporation of new but similar material (see above). His use of chromaticism and of false relations in the melodic line often occurs in contexts where the music appears to portray violent and usually unpleasant emotion—a procedure surely developed from the art of Bach, whose music he loved. All these quirks bespeak a directness and a simplicity of outlook of a mind interested in great truths, which are usually simple, rather than in subtle technicalities, which are rarely profound. Yet he was capable of subtlety, too—in his use of new material (such as the common chord) in new and startling contexts, rather than in those of tone-colour.

His scoring and his sense of orchestral texture, though not obviously brilliant, are often intensely ingenious. The instrumentation of the fourth Symphony, for example, harsh to the point of rawness in places, is notable for unobtrusive ingenuity of colour and texture throughout. The spacing of the stringed instruments at the opening of the slow movement, after the wood-wind introduction—to quote a single example—has a sense of unspeakable remoteness, yet there is nothing very obviously striking about it. Virtuoso scoring he generally eschewed, and, despite his lessons with Ravel, he usually eschewed impressionistic effects too. Yet those who describe his scoring as clumsy would do well to listen to *Jane Scroop's Lament, Riders to the Sea*, or some of his scherzos—the trio section of the fourth Symphony, or the whole of the second movements of the fifth and eighth, for example. Here every effect is calculated to a nicety. Even when the orchestral texture is lighter than air, as in the coda of the scherzo from the *Pastoral Symphony*, there is no glitter to it. But this is deliberate—it is not the result of incompetence. Usually what is more remarkable is his sense of the colour-effect of acoustic spacing rather than that of orchestral timbre. The vast spread of the string chords in the *Tallis Fantasia*, the slow movement of the *London Symphony*, or in the sombre coda to the finale of the sixth contrasts most vividly with the close-textured richness of the slow movement of the violin Concerto, yet each has an atmosphere peculiar to Vaughan Williams alone. The eloquent use of wind instruments as soloists, winding expressive counterpoint in and out of one another's lines, is another feature—a linear rather than a textural or atmospheric one, yet the pitch at which the instruments intermingle is always neatly calculated. Sometimes his fondness for reinforcing the melodic line leads to thickness—but on far rarer occasions than his detractors would suppose, for the gain in colour and weight offsets the loss in clarity. One has only to compare the second movement of the eighth Symphony with the opening of the slow movement of the Brahms violin Concerto to see the difference between a texture that is rich and one that is simply thick.

This technical originality is further shown in his harmonic technique.

Rather than force his modal tunes into tonal harmonic frame-works, he gradually evolved a method which led him from purely modal harmony, via strings of consecutive common chords, to a striking yet effective amalgam of old conventions and modern 'discoveries'. It is not that chords are just treated as sensations; their occurrence in a given context depends less on the relationship of the bass notes to one another, than on that of the tensions between the notes and intervals of the melodic line. In other words, the harmony works from the top downwards, not from the bottom upwards. Where the intervals are wide, and not 'pure', the harmony is bitter and dissonant; where they are even and diatonic, it is placid and—by 'modern' standards—conventional. But in whatever case, it is always logical, and the logic depends on the shape of the melodic line. As Deryck Cooke has pointed out in a superb analysis of the Sixth Symphony in *The Language of Music* (pages 252–70), this method, at its most effective, results in an amazing monolithic unity of melody, form, texture and harmonic movement.

His originality, his willingness to try anything, the broad range of his musical sympathies, his Elephant's-child curiosity; all these contribute to give his music the unity, variety, symmetry, develop-ment and continuity which he asserted in *National Music* were the principles of great art. But allied to them was a vision which soared to greater heights than that of almost any other musician of his time. His art was rooted in the earthy, and its roots were solid. But from those roots it sent forth shoots which left the earthy far behind. And this was the result of his temperament, not of his technique.

CHAPTER IX

SMALL-SCALE WORKS

IT IS not given to many great composers who excel in large-scale works to achieve success as song-writers also, and Vaughan Williams was not a great song-writer. His melodic gift was fertile and original, and his ability to set words aptly and simply was undoubted, but his songs rarely rise above competence, and only very few of them are complete, rounded, successful works of art. Despite this many of them are attractive, and most of them serve the purpose for which they were written. More than any other works of his they cover the whole span of his long creative life, for the first extant song by him was written in 1891 and the last not long before his death. If in the general title 'songs' we include part-songs, folksong arrangements, hymn-tunes, unison songs, etc., the total of compositions in this *genre* exceeds 150, not counting *On Wenlock Edge* and the three roundels *Merciles Beauty*. which are chamber works on account of their instrumental accompaniment. This is a far cry from Schubert's total of over 600 original compositions in the field of accompanied songs, but it still forms a considerable corpus.

The most important of the early songs for solo voice which can be performed with accompaniment for one player are the *Five Mystical Songs* and the song-cycles *The House of Life* and *Songs of Travel* (the seven songs in the latter constitute perhaps a collection rather than two song-cycles proper). All these, to which can be added the *Four Hymns* for tenor, piano and obbligato viola, were written before the First World War. The earliest of them is the Dante Gabriel Rossetti sonnet sequence *The House of Life*, which was published in 1903 and contains six numbers: 'Lovesight', 'Silent Noon', 'Love's Minstrels', 'Heart's Haven', 'Death-in-love' and 'Love's Last Gift'. Only the second of these—'Silent Noon'—has achieved any popularity. Rossetti's imagery is of a kind that is not easy to set to music, for dealing as it does in images which appeal to other senses than the ear, it tempts the composer to display his technical finesse by catching each word-picture as it occurs. Vaughan Williams eschews impressionism throughout this cycle in favour of straight and rather rich lyricism confined within fairly strict forms. Piano and singer are treated with more imagination than is sometimes the case, and in 'Heart's Haven' there is dramatic music of a kind which makes it look like an early sketch for the operas which were to come.

Although intended as a single song-cycle embracing not only the seven songs as published, but also 'Whither must I wander?' and a concluding epilogue, 'I have Trod the Upward and the Downward Slope', which quotes from *The Vagabond* and *Bright is the Ring of Words*, and ends with the striding bass of the former *pp* in the major key, the *Songs of Travel*, to poems by Robert Louis Stevenson, divide naturally into the two sets in which they were published, both in atmosphere and in musical technique. In the original form, the songs were intended to be sung in the following order: 'The Vagabond', 'Let Beauty Awake', 'The Roadside Fire', 'Youth and Love', 'In Dreams', 'The Infinite Shining Heavens', 'Whither must I wander?', 'Bright is the Ring of Words' and 'I have Trod the Upward and the Downward Slope'. (The manuscript of the final song was found by the composer's widow among his papers after his death.) The first set displays the extrovert, vigorous Vaughan Williams, who sometimes relaxes his grip (as in the central section of 'The Roadside Fire') and on other occasions indulges his fancy for remotely related chords in juxtaposition (as in 'Bright is the Ring of Words'). The first of the set is defiantly cheerful, a song of the open air. The odd key change in the second—a cadence in D major leads without warning into a chord of E flat:

is really a preparation for the words: 'After the singer is dead.' What Vaughan Williams might have become as a song-writer is shown by 'The Roadside Fire', which displays an imagination not yet matched by the technical ability needed to express itself fully. Thus the accompaniment is merely awkward instead of delicate. The word-setting on the other hand is imaginative; a subtle point here is the lingering stress placed on the word 'I' by the shape of the opening vocal phrase, which gives the effect of a wheedling, coaxing lover revealing his most intimate romantic ambitions to his beloved, where a syllabic setting would have been duller. The second set is considerably more chromatic in idiom than the first, and the effect of the songs is more introverted and lyrical, less brisk and hearty. When the complete cycle is performed together, these elements set one another off very well, and the cross-quotations (from 'The Roadside Fire', 'The Vagabond' and 'Bright is the Ring of Words') which occur in 'Youth and Love' and 'I have Trod the Upward and the Downward Slope' assist in unifying a cycle whose musical style is sometimes rather derivative—even though a quasi-modal cadence in the vocal line here and there, as in 'Whither must I wander', enables the critic to be wise after the event. There is little originality but much tender beauty in these songs, particularly in 'Youth and Love', with its gently hovering accompaniment, like drifting leaves on an autumn breeze. 'The Infinite Shining Heavens' is interesting as a yardstick of what Vaughan Williams had so far been able to achieve before his technique had ripened in that field of remote visionary meditation which he was to make peculiarly his own.

It is in the accompaniments that the early songs fail: song accompaniments may either simply fill out the harmonies implicit in the vocal line with more or less elaboration, or else they may enhance the effect of that line by setting and illustrating an atmosphere—Gretchen at her spinning-wheel, the young nun with a storm around her but calm in her heart, and so on. Vaughan Williams's accompaniments are usually of the former kind, though he was capable of introducing illustrative details too. The greatest difficulty for a song-writer is to find a figure for the accompaniment which will both illustrate and underline the sense of the words and at the same time provide harmonic flexibility and support. In the Savoy operettas Sullivan, with his great love of Schubert, was an adept at this. Vaughan Williams, however, threw all the emphasis on to his vocal line, and the piano was left a very poor runner-up. Thus it is that the best of the early songs, like *Linden Lea*, win acceptance on account of their tunes but despite their accompaniments. Often there is too much unnecessary doubling of the melodic line in the top part of the piano harmony; one feels that the piano is there, *faute de mieux*, to fill out the texture. Even his arrangements of folksongs tend to this fault. Sharp's accompaniments may not be perfect but they are, surprisingly, more ingenious and imaginative—even though Sharp solicited advice from his friend on how to arrange the songs. The piano, in fact, was not Vaughan Williams's instrument.

A type of *Gebrauchsmusik* that is peculiarly English is the unison song, and Vaughan Williams composed a considerable number of these. With the encouragement of the folksong movement in state schools, the tradition of singing hefty, swinging melodies on occasions of patriotic display—coronations, Commonwealth Day and so on—and even the English habit of bursting into community song at cup finals (to say nothing of the Welsh at Rugby internationals), there is a fine opportunity open to any composer capable of writing a broad, simple melody with a diatonic outline and straightforward rhythm. The ancestry of the unison song goes back as far as Purcell; not that Purcell wrote such airs, but simply that a number of his finest melodies (*Fairest Isle, Come if You Dare* or the fine *I Come to Sing Great Zempoalla's Story*) have exactly these characteristics, which Handel and Parry and Elgar, in their turn, were able to turn to good account. Vaughan Williams was able to follow in the same tradition, and though none of his unison songs has quite captured the heart of the nation to the same extent as *Jerusalem* or the tune to which *Land of Hope and Glory* was set, such melodies as *Famous Men, The New Commonwealth* or *Land of our Birth* constitute a worthy contribution to what is after all a part of our national life. In keeping with the age the texts are much more subdued and less chauvinistic than Elgar's, but the characteristics of the melodies they inspire or to which they are fitted are the same—strength, simplicity and dignity. Moreover, in the best of these compositions—such as *Famous Men*—Vaughan Williams makes good use of some of his salient stylistic features without placing the music beyond the bounds either of what is suitable or of what is practicable for such songs. In *Famous Men* itself, for example, there is the dramatic effect of placing E major alongside E♭ major to illustrate the anonymity of those with no memorial:

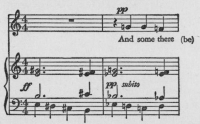

In these songs an elaborate accompaniment would be lost in the mass effect of hundreds of singers declaiming the same tune, and so there is no call for any other kind of background but strong supporting harmonies 'giving the singers their note' as and when required.

A more sophisticated kind of accompaniment is to be found in the four *Poems by Fredegond Shove*, published in 1925. 'Motion and Still-ness' sets the composer some stimulating problems of imagery, with its sea-shells 'cold as death', its clouds like a 'wasted wreath', its sleeping cows and its ships 'like evanescent hopes'. Vaughan Williams contrives to solve them by basing his setting on hollow fourths and fifths in the accompaniment; the chords drift slowly along, forming a more static, but thinner and less substantial, line than that of the *Pastoral Symphony*. Of the other songs, 'The Water Mill', which reminds one of a Dutch painting in its loving attention to the small details of a scene, simply cries out for a quasi-illustrative setting and duly receives one. It is a charming miniature, with the piano gently picking out little allusions from the poem—the rhythm of the mill-race, the clock ('very tall and very bright'), the twilit pool; even the cat. 'Four Nights' starts off by telescoping two lines of text to one phrase of music, and the accompaniment avoids the lower reaches of the piano for most of the first section. The vocal line is square but not facile; an instance of avoiding the obvious occurs when Vaughan Williams slows up the regular rhythm of the phrase for the last (and most important) words of the line, minims weighting a line predominantly of crotchets. Again, the way the poem divides into associations of the four seasons invites an illustrative setting. 'The New Ghost' is the best known of these songs; it is a kind of English *Doppelgänger*, where sweetness and love replace the grim and the macabre. The dramatic picture of a soul's flight to its Lord after death:

> He cast the garment of his flesh that was full of death
> And like a sword his spirit showed out of the cold sheath,

is enhanced and transcended by the rich lightness of the accompaniment—it lies entirely in the treble stave until the words 'late spring'. As befits the subject, the final cadence reaches out into remoteness.

The Whitman poems—again death is a central theme—of the set of three songs to this poet, also published in 1925, are more simply set. 'Nocturne' develops from a shadowy, wandering quasi-ostinato in octaves low down in the piano, out of which emerge a slow vocal line and sombre minim chords; the effect is simply achieved, and the setting is a noble one. 'A Clear Midnight', with the grave dignity of its descending minims in the bass, is a kind of *Sine nomine* in slow motion, rather like a sterner and maturer version of 'The Infinite Shining Heavens'. No attempt is made at illustrating images in the poem. 'Joy, Shipmate, Joy' is a sacred shanty on the theme of life as a sea voyage, ending *fff* on a chord of G with no third. All in all, these songs are nearer to the Robert Louis Stevenson sets than to the Shove settings. The Shakespeare songs, published in the same year, are again simple. The accompaniment is concerned with unobtrusively supporting the vocal line, and the interest in the songs is almost exclusively melodic. They are pleasing but not more. The *Two Poems by Seumas O'Sullivan* carry the tendency to stress the melody even further, for the accompaniment is optional, and therefore, as Frank Howes points out, tenuous. 'The Twilight People' points backward at *Hugh the Drover* in its 'folkiness', and forward to *Riders of the Sea* in its sombre strength and Celtic shadows. At about the same time Vaughan Williams experimented with settings for voice and violin, though these songs—to poems by Housman—were not published until 1954. Such songs are bound to be much more linear (and there/fore congenial to this composer) than any accompanied by a chord/playing instrument such as the piano. They set an interesting technical problem in that the compass of the violin cannot reach below G, and depth and weight of tone cannot readily be achieved. In most cases the violin plays a kind of descant to the voice part, but on occasion it supplies chords filling out an implied harmony, and in *Fancy's Knell* catches at the implications of the text by playing a spirited dance/tune in counterpoint to the voice. Fiddle and singer are thus much more equal partners than singer and piano, and the economy of means in these songs makes them interesting from every point of view—technically, structurally and melodically. The last *Songs for Voice and Oboe*, settings of ten poems by Blake, show similar artistic economy in limning the substance of the poems. In some (e.g. Nos. 4, 'London', 6, 'The Shepherd', and 9, 'The Divine Image') this is done purely by an expressive melodic line, the songs being entirely unaccompanied. In others (No. 5, 'The Lamb', for example) the oboe is skilfully interwoven as a pastoral background into the voice part. In yet another (No. 3, 'The Piper') there is a lilting dialogue between voice and instrument. No. 9 contains an effective *coup de théâtre* in the effective use of a tonal last verse in a song which has up till then been modal in implication.

Partnership in equality is a feature of the writing in most of Vaughan Williams's part/songs. These are mostly early works, and at least one set—the *Five English Folk Songs*—is well known. These 'arrangements' are very free and differ widely in their approach; the songs are virtually recomposed in some instances, as, for example, in 'Just as the Tide was Flowing', with its elaborate choral cadenza, or in the quasi/*canto fermo* treatment of 'The Lover's Ghost'. Indeed, the former song might almost be described as a *concertino* for four/part chorus; the proliferation of runs in the middle section has to be pulled up with a jerk before the chorus somewhat breathlessly rattles off the last verse. On a more grandiose and less intimate scale than most of his un/accompanied choral settings are works such as *O vos omnes* and *Prayer to the Father of Heaven*. Percy Young has said of the former that it possesses the anguish of Vittoria. The latter shows both Skelton and Vaughan Williams in a radically different light from that of the *Five Tudor Portraits*; sonorous and dignified, it was admirably suited to commemorate Hubert Parry. These two works are half way towards being major works in their own right; certainly they are more important in his output than some of his longer works. Of the other works of this kind, the slight but deeply moving O *Taste and See* deserves special mention.

The *Five Mystical Songs* are written for solo voice, chorus and keyboard accompaniment, but the chorus is optional (though 'Antiphon' can be performed as a choral song and exists in two versions on that account). It is worth remembering that it was not Herbert, the poet, but the composer who grouped the songs under this title. The songs were first performed with orchestra at the Three Choirs Festival; nowadays they are more frequently heard as solo songs. They are admirable examples of early Vaughan Williams, particularly 'I got me Flowers' and 'The Call', though they tend to mannerism and the last of the set, 'Antiphon', is noisy rather than energetic. A feature of the second—as Frank Howes and Percy Young have pointed out—is the flexibility of the voice-part, a kind of enhanced recitative. These settings are interesting for what they foreshadow rather than for what they actually achieve; they are serious, thoughtful, well-wrought works by a composer whose personal idiom was not yet capable of expressing the inspiration that the poems sparked off in him. The direct vision of God to which they aspire, and which Herbert so tenderly expressed, was later to find full expression in *Sancta Civitas*. The *Four Hymns*, which were written slightly later (Howes gives the date 1912–14 for these, and 1911 for the *Five Mystical Songs*), are a different matter altogether. Here the idiom is fully developed. The viola threads a reflective descant through the texture; indeed, the intimate nature of these songs entitles them to the description 'mystical' far better than the earlier set. There is none of the mannered, rather contrived ecstasy of *Love Bade me Welcome*. A comparison of that song and 'Evening Hymn', the last of the four, will show what a remarkable development had taken place in a mere two years or so.

On the smallest scale of all are the hymn-tunes, which number fifteen. As in every *genre* that Vaughan Williams tackled they display a very considerable range, from the rather recondite harmonic experiments of *Mantegna* to the simple serenity of *Down Ampney*. Yet even the latter, with its surreptitious false relation:

is a token of things to come. The settings in the *Oxford Book of Carols* are a mixed bag; they range from the mere dullness of 'Snow in the Street' to the unsentimental grace and charm of 'Wither's Rocking Hymn'.

All in all, Vaughan Williams's small-scale works for voice show a mind which is prepared to experiment, one given more to a combination of reflection and heartiness than to great subtlety or delicacy, and more interested in the strength and flexibility of a vocal line than any striking harmonies underlying it. For the most part, however, there is not sufficient integration of voice and accompaniment in the solo songs, nor sufficient scope for the composer in the part-songs, to warrant counting any of the works in these categories as masterpieces, attractive—and sometimes moving—though some of them are. The sureness of touch shown in the handling of words and the shaping of the melodies, however, are evident almost from the very start, and the best of his works in these fields show an epigrammatic concision which is at its best in a tune like *Down Ampney* or the melody of *Linden Lea*. Such compositions show that he, like the anonymous composers of folk melodies, was capable of producing a tune that would bear infinite repetition and not suffer from it, simply because its strength was its simplicity, and its simplicity its strength.

His other small works are, at their best, captivating; at their worst, dull. Vaughan Williams was never a pianist of the calibre of Britten, and his experience as a church organist depressed rather than inspired him. Yet he managed to produce at least one work involving each instrument which reflects his genius, if not at its greatest, at any rate at its most charming. The *Preludes on Welsh Hymn Tunes* for organ must be well known even to those who cannot put a name to them; 'Rhosymedre' is a particular favourite with parish organists all over the country. It is deservedly so, for it combines sympathetic and imaginative treatment of an attractive melody with grateful, though not too difficult, technique. The Prelude and Fugue in C minor sounds somewhat like an offshoot of *Job*, and received its first performance not long before that work. The Introduction and Fugue for two pianos is the most worthwhile of his other keyboard works. It combines closeness of structure with rhythmic vitality and a remoteness of atmosphere which is in some places—notably in the Prelude —oddly reminiscent of a late Beethoven slow movement without being in the least derivative from that source. It is noteworthy that a composer who wrote so little and so reluctantly for the piano should all the same have added at least one significant work to the limited repertory of two-piano works available without in the least descending into the archness that sometimes seems to be associated with music for that combination.

CHAPTER X

LARGE-SCALE WORKS FOR VOICES

IF A British composer wished to announce himself as ambitious in the days when Vaughan Williams was young, he had to do so by writing cantatas and oratorios for one of the great choral festivals for which even *das Land ohne Musik* has been renowned, at any rate since the days of Haydn. Vaughan Williams's first important works on a large scale conformed to this. Yet despite the fact that he developed in an age when a critic could say that a leading composer was 'sickening for another oratorio', Vaughan Williams himself only wrote two works that can be classified as oratorios; all his other works are called by such titles as 'Song for Orchestra', 'Cantata', etc.

The earliest of them is the Rossetti cantata *Willow Wood*, written in 1903 and first performed in 1909; there is little that it contains which could not have been written by any other competent musician of the period. *Toward the Unknown Region*, the next of them, forsakes Rossetti for Whitman—an interesting and important change. The eagle was spreading his wings, and the composer's challenge to himself is unmistakably there in the text and title of the work. It is called, not a cantata, but a song for chorus and orchestra, and its central feature is a great flowing melody which was later detached and arranged as a unison song. The work is not quite free from the trappings of late romanticism, with chromatic inner parts in the orchestra; they are used, however, to impart a surge and flow to the music, not to enrich the texture or render it voluptuously luxurious, and they are essentially developed as parts of the melodic rather than the harmonic structure. Frank Howes and Percy Young have pointed out the modal feature of the opening bars—further evidence of a new mind at work on old devices. The Parry-Elgar spaciousness of the work and its aspiring ending are full of strength and confidence.

The *Fantasia on Christmas Carols*, first performed at Hereford in 1912, has remained a favourite with choral societies, with good reason.

97

It is neither great nor profound, but it is (naturally enough) tuneful and singable. The harmony is straightforward, the structure simple and unsubtle. The text is so arranged that the story of the fall and of Christ's redemption of the world is succeeded by an invocation to rejoicing. An indication of the shape of things to come is shown by the way in which the solo cello introduction unwinds itself,

a fragment of the first phrase:

evolving, by means of a small rhythmic change, into:

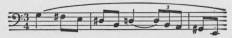

and finally, by a kind of musical pun, into the carol 'The Truth Sent from Above'. After an exultant climax the music finally dies away into a *pianissimo* ending—no mystery here but simply attentive devotion.

'The oddest thing', says Hubert Foss of the Mass in G minor, 'about this splendid reincarnation of the other world of sound is that it is not austere.'[1] But why should it be austere? We are used to thinking of cathedrals in their post-Reformation whitewash, not in the colourful and probably garish decoration of the late Middle Ages. All the same, the observation is correct; it is not an austere work. The soft richness of the *Pastoral Symphony* and the solidity and power of the *Tallis Fantasia* are here pressed into the service of the liturgy, and from the stylistic point of view an excursion is made into the remote past in order to create something quite new. One device which pervades this work is the use of consecutive triads; another, that of false relations. This latter was adopted for three reasons; firstly, because it was regarded as a peculiarly English procedure; secondly, because it is essentially a contrapuntal device, brought about by the free movement of independent parts (though it is here used on occasion to impart piquancy to the sound-effect of a chord); and thirdly, because it is a method of freeing the modes from limitations—enabling them, as Frank Howes points out, to modulate. As with modern tricks, so with old ones; Vaughan Williams always uses them to expand his

[1] *Ralph Vaughan Williams* (1950), p. 190.

technical range of expression, not simply to be 'in the swim', which is essentially a limitation of technique.

The main formal problem in any setting of the Mass lies in unifying the diversity of the Credo, and this Vaughan Williams achieves first of all by using the same music for 'Patrem omnipotentem' as for 'Et resurrexit'—thereby perhaps symbolizing that it was the same force which created the world as raised Christ from the dead, and possibly also symbolizing that the resurrection was as significant a demonstration of divine power as the creation itself. Overall unity is further strengthened by using the same phrase for the opening of 'Miserere nobis' in the *Agnus Dei* for the *Kyrie*. Another means of strengthening the unity of the work is Vaughan Williams's procedure of developing an initial motif set to different words as it expands from a similar opening phrase—the method of the baroque fantasia, in fact. Thus, in the 'Et in spiritum sanctum' section of the Credo, the phrase:

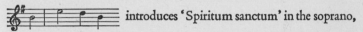 introduces 'Spiritum sanctum' in the soprano,

'et vivificantem' in the tenor, 'qui cum patre et [filio]' in the bass, 'simul ador[atur]' in the soprano (with a slightly altered rhythm), 'qui locutus est' in the soprano again, 'et unam sanctam ca[tholicam ecclesiam]' in the second chorus, and so on, each time leading to something slightly different.

There are so many lovely touches in this fine work that they cannot all be mentioned, but one of the most effective is in the 'Et incarnatus' section, where the introduction of the chord of A♭ major alters a trite tonal progression into one of veiled radiance exactly suitable to the mystery of the incarnation. Incidentally, the theme of the *Benedictus* bears an odd resemblance to the 'Alleluia' from *Sine Nomine*! The Mass is not a work for the festival platform; it belongs unreservedly in the church or chapel, preferably as part of the liturgy. Designed as it was for Holst's Whitsuntide Singers, it requires a good choir with a really musical conductor. It is *Gebrauchsmusik* which is not merely an adornment to the service but a revelation of its meaning, and it should be in the repertory of every cathedral choir in the country.

Sancta Civitas, Vaughan Williams's first oratorio, is anything but

Gebrauchsmusik. Anyone who thinks of oratorio as a stately and not too thrilling exposition of one of the gorier prophetic stories of the Old Testament would certainly find it difficult to accept this mighty vision of the new Heaven and the new Earth which are to come. It is white-hot in its intensity, fierce in its energy. Even the remoteness of the opening reminds one of a distant vista of stars which one knows to be infinitely hot. It is possibly his most thrilling work, and certainly one of his most compact. Every time an imaginative illustration of the words is called for, Vaughan Williams is able to provide it—even, despite Frank Howes's criticisms (which are after all the reservations of one who clearly admires the work profoundly) the curious chords describing the precious stones of the Holy City. These dissonances are—to one pair of ears, anyway—not opaque, but glittering and incandescent:

The hot shiver caused by the merging of the two dissonant flute chords at the beginning when the semi-chorus enters, the rapt bitonal effect when the distant chorus comes in, the manner in which the accompaniment swells to a gigantic chord of G minor on the word 'fierceness', and then vanishes abruptly leaving the ecstatic chorus supported only by the timpani—all these are strokes which make one wish, like Thackeray, to bang the table and yell: 'Genius, by God!' It is huge, yet it is concentrated (it lasts three-quarters of an hour); it is an oratorio, yet it is not churchy. If it has any antecedents, they are Holst's *Hymn of Jesus* and possibly Parry's *Vision of Life*. Yet no three works could be more totally different. Paradoxically, Vaughan Williams's work with its ostensibly more objective point of departure is the most fervent. The lament for the fall of Babylon is weird and unnerving (and, in passing, note that in outline it foreshadows one of the themes in the Moderato of the sixth Symphony), the description of the Holy City itself awesome and serene at the same time. In its scope this work reminds one far more of the Beethoven whom the composer did not like rather than the Bach he loved. Vaughan Williams had overthrown his Babylon (the left-overs of German romanticism and the square, obvious folkiness of some of his earlier works, which was a necessary reaction against it) and caught the flame of St John's apocalyptic vision. The rapture of that vision had already been shown in works like *The Shepherds of the Delectable Mountains*; here, however, we have a vision in terms of almost frightening power. In its 'beyondness' and its fierce, athletic energy it reminds one of the *Grosse Fuge*—yet the energy is less wilful than Beethoven's. Here the unknown region had been reached, and the composer was showing us what it looked like. Its nature is such that one has only to compare the lament for Babylon here with the equally effective one (to the same text) in *Belshazzar's Feast* to see that Walton was aiming at an effect which appears almost sentimental in comparison to Vaughan Williams's.

After *Sancta Civitas* no big choral work appeared for nearly ten years, but in the meantime there were a number of smaller ones. The three short works for the silver jubilee of the Leith Hill Festival are admirably suited for their purpose, combining robust rejoicing with gentleness and intimacy (in the *Three Choral Hymns* and the *Benedicite*, at any rate). The *Magnificat* (written for the Three Choirs Festival, 1932) is something more again, a vision, not a formal setting of a well-worn lyric text. Hence the use, not only of the *Magnificat* text itself, but of its context, which emphasizes the mystery—Mary's astonishment, her joy and rapture and, finally, her apprehension in case she prove unworthy of the great charge laid upon her. It is typical of Vaughan Williams that he set out to illustrate, not merely the semantic meaning of the text, but also its significance as a piece of history. The work is thus not liturgical but expository, dramatic and mystic in that it seeks to express a direct contact with the unknown Godhead. The atmosphere is conveyed from the outset by swaying chords and a melismatic flute solo. Mary's astonished joy is evident in her florid vocal line. At the end of the work the favourite device of a quiet epilogue after a big climax is used to bring us back to earth—to Mary's meek humanity after her heavenly vision. There is, then, plenty of illustration in this setting; it is the ecstatic song of a humble young woman to whom is revealed the greatest mystery of time and eternity—the 'Incarnatus' of the Mass, in fact, seen from the inside.

That the same composer could turn to write the *Five Tudor Portraits* for another musical festival (Norwich, 1936) is proof of his protean versatility. The salient qualities of Skelton's text are his directness, his vigour and his speed of movement. The verse is irregular and short-winded, but long-limbed; that is to say, it proceeds in short, jerky macaronic lines cast in lengthy paragraphs, and it is metrically stimulating. It has none of Gilbert's smooth regularity and verbal cleverness, and is completely lacking in any form of polish or gentility, offering plenty of scope to the composer's racy humour. This work is the reverse side of the medal of which the Scherzo of the F minor Symphony is the obverse, and its nearest counterpart in the rest of his output is perhaps to be found in the cocksure Scherzo of the eighth. The pulse of the music is for the most part heavy but rapid—particularly in 'The Tunning of Eleanor Rumming'; as in the fourth Symphony, the music goes crashing on its way, but here the irresistibility of its onrush is not the result of brutal and explosive violence, but of impetuous *joie de vivre*, and—in the case of 'John Jayberd', at any rate, of malice as well. The whole suite is aflame with passion and feeling, whether tender (as in 'Jane Scroop'), or sarcastic (as in 'Rutterkin'), or splenetic ('Jayberd'). This is a portrait gallery as vital and as colourful as Miss Power's *Medieval People*; here are gargoyles, carved out with glee and impatience rather than carefully worked miniatures (except of course for 'Jane'). The religious visionary of *Sancta Civitas* descends from the heights and sets his chisel to work hewing out human grotesques rather than soaring vaults.

'Eleanor Rumming' is a huge patter-song for full chorus and orchestra, but far rougher mannered than most patter-songs are. The ale-house commotion of the opening—coarse or *cantabile* by turns—carries the music along in one vast sweep until the procession breaks into a rampaging scherzo at the change to 9-8. All the rudest instruments in the orchestra have a field-day, particularly at the advent of

Drunken Alice. What is all this doing in a festival cantata, declaimed by a respectable contralto? Belching and hiccuping, the bassoons, the double-bassoon and the double-basses punctuate her ribald narrative, and once she has fallen into a stupor the party comes to life again, with pipe, bowl and high spirits, suddenly breaking off into an abrupt close after a riotous *fugato* which appears to cock a snook at the one in Weber's *Euryanthe* overture.

'My Pretty Bess' is an intermezzo, a charming love-song for the baritone solo, with the chorus supporting his plea. 'John Jayberd', for male chorus only, is sarcastic and uncouth, completely disregarding, both in words and music, the old saw 'De mortuis nil nisi bonum'. There is a raucous trill, an augmented fourth apart, for the whole chorus, which Howes fittingly describes as a 'parody of the sacred office which ends this pre-Reformation skit on the clergy and their ways'.[1] The lament for Jane Scroop's sparrow, Philip, is the only number in the suite devoid of any hint of parody, and its pathos is all the more marked after the bitter impoliteness of John Jayberd's epitaph, since it underlines the fact that the little girl feels the death of her pet sparrow far more acutely than anybody does John Jayberd's. Delicacy is not a predominant trait in Vaughan Williams's music, but it is most marked here. In 'Jayberd' all went at a rasping allegro; here it is lento doloroso. His tunes and harmonies were jagged; hers flow. His obituary was bawled out by the men; hers is half-crooned by the ladies. The orchestration is picturesque—one can perhaps instance the miniature tone-painting at the Poco più mosso for 'Sometimes he would gasp When he saw a wasp', with its piccolo, muted horns and muted trumpet, or the delightful procession of the birds, called in by Jane to mourn her pet. With the brilliant Waltonesque finale, 'Rutterkin', we are back with Jayberd and Eleanor again, but this time mincing elegance rather than blowsy coarseness is the target of the satire. It is a crisp scherzo with a little chromaticism and a lot of cross-rhythm, and brings the suite to a lively close.

Dona nobis pacem received its first performance one week after the *Tudor Portraits*, and is *Gebrauchsmusik* of a very serious order; a

---

[1] *The Music of Ralph Vaughan Williams* (1954), p. 177.

propaganda pamphlet, as has been pointed out. This does not prevent it from being a work of art any more than flattering references to the Stuarts prevent *Macbeth* from being one. It may be that the lack of unity to which sympathetic critics like Percy Young and Frank Howes have drawn attention is a stylistic one, but certainly the text is simply but skilfully put together. The six sections begin with a prayer for peace. This is followed by a vivid objective portrayal—from Whitman's *Drum Taps*—of the brutality of war and its effect on the community. There follows a description of the impact of war and death on the individual, again from Whitman; although the dead man is an enemy he is still a man 'divine as myself', which increases the pathos of the situation. Then follows the 'Dirge for Two Veterans' (already written some twentyfive years before the rest of the cantata), which is related to present circumstances by a quotation from John Bright's famous 'Angel of Death' speech, increasing the urgency and the relevance of the petition of the opening, which is supported by an invocation to God who alone can protect men from the horrors of war. This leads to a confident call to trust in God and a vision of a world at peace from the Old Testament. Whether or not the music is unified, the text is certainly logically laid out.

The finest sections of the work are the elegiac 'Dirge for Two Veterans' and the last section of all, which calls to mind the finale of *Flos Campi*, though the mood is less sensuous and the vision less exotic. Here, as there, a theme rises from below to be met by another descending theme which is a modified inversion of it—the second theme appears at the words 'Truth shall spring out of the earth'. The dirge emphasizes the pathos and eeriness of death rather than its glory or nobility, although the theme itself is powerful and dignified, and there is a solemn climax in C major at the words 'And the strong deadmarch enwraps me'. As with the 'Dona nobis pacem' of Beethoven's Mass in D, the reference to war is aimed at strengthening the prayer for peace, but Vaughan Williams's picture of warfare and its effects is more detailed than Beethoven's and less a prayer for inner than for communal peace. The core of this work is that it is a prayer—witness the short, quiet epilogue, Poco più lento, for unaccompanied chorus, which brings us back to earth with a prayer after the vision of a world at peace has dazzled us—and the more lurid parts of the work are there simply to say 'This is why'. It may be, therefore, that the 'Dirge for Two Veterans', splendid though it is, draws too much attention to one particular facet of war, and the memory of it is not quite effaced by the bustle of the next important choral section, when, as in the 'Dies irae' of Verdi's *Requiem* (from which there is a 'crib' in the soprano's opening 'Dona nobis pacem'), it starts forth in passionate terror. Vaughan Williams's treatment, however, is on a smaller scale than Verdi's, which is perhaps why it does not entirely offset the moving effect of the funeral march.

The *Serenade to Music* is one of Vaughan Williams's most sensuous works, and although (like *Dona nobis pacem*) it was composed for a special occasion, its appeal is universal, as long as men are prepared to allow music gently to steal over them and glory in the sheer beauty of silken sound. Written for sixteen singers and a large orchestra, it is, as a vocal *tour de force*, a graceful and serene counterpart to the magnificent fugue from Verdi's *Falstaff*, as English as the other is Italian, yet as rewarding and attractive as music for voices. The *Song of Thanksgiving*—like *Dona nobis pacem*, a commissioned work with text drawn from diverse sources—is a prayer, too, redolent of patriotism and praise, with a quietly breathed close for the solo soprano. The cantata *Folksongs of the Four Seasons* offers an interesting example of how Vaughan Williams lived up to the precept 'Limitation provides inspiration'. Asked to provide a work for the Federation of Women's Institutes festival at the Albert Hall, and knowing that the choir would be roughly divisible into three sections—a large body for unison singing, a smaller one for part singing and a small number for an unaccompanied passage—and that they would all be women, he laid out his work accordingly. The next thing was to provide a unifying theme, and he found it in the calendar. Each movement, accordingly, refers to one of the seasons of the year, and the musical material is based on seasonal folksongs. This work is, in many ways, a larger, more mature and more comprehensive *Fantasia on Christmas Carols*; four movements instead of one, and less elaborate movements at that. A cantata written under similarly restricting but inspiring circumstances was *The Sons of Light* for the Schools Music Association. It is direct and uncomplicated, lively and cheerful—as a piece written for children should be, and as music written by a man of seventy-eight might well not be. The *Oxford Elegy* is a stage further in the direction pointed by *A Song of Thanksgiving*—a recitation with orchestral accompaniment. The choir is used sparingly, and the orchestra is a small one. In its use of the wordless chorus as a background to the speaker's meditations, just as in *Flos Campi*, it provides a background to the solo viola's.

Hodie, the last of Vaughan Williams's large-scale choral works, was performed when he was nearly eighty-two. It is scored for a large orchestra and is a kind of symposium of all his choral writing. It is appropriate that the cover of the vocal score of the work should contain a reproduction of a Piero della Francesca painting, for *Hodie* has exactly that somewhat naïve vitality and delight in praising God that appears to have been such a feature of early Renaissance Italy. The solid rejoicing of the Prologue is the kind of music expected from a man of twenty-two rather than eighty-two. Even the cheerfulness of the opening movement of Bach's *Christmas Oratorio* seems tame by comparison. Perhaps the text has something to do with it, for instead of Picander's skilful adaptation of words already written for a secular celebration, Vaughan Williams has simply a joyful statement of fact, with an 'Alleluia' tacked on to the end. The 'Alleluia' itself, with its accompaniment of off-beat chords, owes its tang and mystery to its use of the tritone:

The somewhat sweet artificiality of the narrations enhances the effect of the work's being like an Italian painting. The melismatic incantatory recitative, over a chord formula, is gentle and matter-of-fact, the dramatic strokes being reserved for the fanfare of consecutive triads on the brass at the mention of the word 'Jesus'. Throughout the work, recitative is more a kind of varied chant-formula than a flexible dramatic device such as Bach was wont to make of it. Time and eternity, history and the present are linked by such devices as introducing the rest of the *Gloria* from the Mass into the narration representing the Angels' song to the shepherds, who meanwhile continue 'Let us now go even unto Bethlehem', and by following this by creating a present-day atmosphere with Hardy's *The Oxen*. This is set with extreme simplicity, with wood-wind solos gently hovering with a motif which varies in shape with each entry. The orchestration throughout is masterly, outstandingly clear and imaginative. *Hodie* is a child's view of the Christmas story, told with all the wit and sureness of a wise man of much experience who has a clear understanding of what lies behind the story. And for once in a way, despite the mystery of the last movement, an Epilogue setting of verses from the first chapter of St John's Gospel and Milton's *Ode on the Morning of Christ's Nativity*, the work ends in a jubilant peal of sound.

Many of Vaughan Williams's choral works were written for performance on a particular occasion—as were nearly all of Bach's, for example. Yet most of them contain passages which transcend their immediate purpose, and all of them are rewarding to sing. Some—like *Five Tudor Portraits*, an uncomfortably unique work, not at all the thing for a best-bib-and-tucker occasion like a choral festival—will in all probability never be frequently performed; that does not mean that they are not worthy of frequent performance. Others—such as *In Windsor Forest* and *A Cotswold Romance*—have not been discussed here because they are adaptations from works best considered under another heading. They constitute one of the most important facets of the work of this versatile musician, and their range of expression is very wide. There is no place in them for religiosity or staidness; every one of them is alive and shows that the composer's mind was fully employed in their composition, whether he was writing a tract for the times, enjoying a mystic vision of the Apocalypse, or simply describing a rather disreputable harridan of Henry VII's day. It is clear that he enjoyed writing them; whether he wrote them as a duty or as a pleasure, both elements invariably merged into one.

CHAPTER XI

OPERAS

THE PROOF of a pudding, as the saying is, lies in the eating, not in the recipe. We may regard the vocal or orchestral score of an opera as a recipe, but we cannot fairly judge the work until we have seen it on the stage. Anyone who wishes to assess the qualities of Vaughan Williams's operas is therefore immediately placed at a disadvantage, since one of them—*The Poisoned Kiss*—has never been professionally performed, and the others have been mounted only infrequently. Moreover, even in these days of long-playing records, no British gramophone company has seen fit to issue a recording of even the shortest of them—*Riders to the Sea*. Indeed, not until thirteen years after its original production was Britten's *Peter Grimes*—certainly the most internationally famous opera by a contemporary British composer —available on gramophone records. This suggests either timidity or ignorance on the part of the great men of the gramophone world—or both, since thirty years ago excerpts at least from *Hugh the Drover* were available on acoustic disks.

There is little need to stress the shortcomings of operatic life in the United Kingdom. There are, in fact, only two regular opera houses in the whole of the British Commonwealth, and except at Sadler's Wells (and since 1946 at Covent Garden), repertory opera, such as it is known in Italy, Germany, France, Switzerland, Austria or Russia, is virtually unknown, simply because the musical activities of the stage and the concert platform have never been anything like as closely integrated here as they have been in those countries. Instead of the tradition of regularly performing well-known operas with a professional cast at the local theatre and recruiting an orchestra from the theatre pit for concerts, as has been done in continental countries for over a century, we have allowed London to become the sole centre of opera, save for the gallant attempts of the Carl Rosa company, the English Opera Group, enthusiastic patrons such as Mr Christie and the universities and music colleges. No wonder there has never really been an English school of opera composers. But Vaughan Williams's operas suffered from the age in which they were composed as well as from the country in which they ought to have been cherished. What opera of the era since 1918, with the possible exception of *Turandot* and Berg's *Wozzeck*, has gone into the permanent international repertory? The conventions of operatic writing, even those of the post-Wagner era, have not exactly encouraged popular appreciation, which demands sentiment, lyricism and 'good old Italian bawling' (even if it happens to be in German or French).

Since the days of Monteverdi there has been unceasing argument as to what constitutes a good opera libretto, and as to what constitutes suitable dramatic music. There has also grown up a certain intellectual snobbishness which regards what is called theatrical effect as cheap, and an even more deplorable inversion of it which over-values what a previous generation has deplored simply because the previous generation did deplore it. Thus Vaughan Williams's *Pilgrim's Progress* was damned with faint praise, the music being described as lofty and uplifting, but the scenario and libretto deemed unsuitable for operatic treatment. Fault was found with the static nature of the action of the opera and the music's appositeness to the text was therefore adjudged a shortcoming—even Vaughan Williams himself shrank from calling it an opera. Yet if the effect of the spectacle, the music and the performers' conception of the work is thoroughly integrated, as was the case in a series of notable amateur performances under Boris Ord at Cambridge in 1954 (Dennis Arundell being in charge of the production), the hearer goes away from a performance of this great work enthralled and convinced of its vital message—just as he will after hearing and seeing *Fidelio* or *Die Zauberflöte* or *Aida*. Moreover, the absurdity of a libretto or its dramatic unsuitability does not mean that a great opera cannot be built upon it. The plot of *La Bohème* is trivial, sickly and absurd, yet Puccini takes his sugar-doll heroine and her irresponsible lover, writes astonishingly powerful and emotive music for them to sing, and in so doing turns them into real people by the sheer vitality of his lyric outpouring—just as the tom-fooleries and absurd coincidences of the libretto and the completely unconvincing character of the protagonists in *La forza del destino* are swept aside by the excitement and the magnitude of Verdi's score. We have grown so used to great operatic music being written round trivial, sentimental or preposterously far-fetched situations that we have forgotten that even music which is spiritually uplifting can also be dramatically—even theatrically—apt to a vision of the great, trans-human elements in our life and being. Thus we fail to recognize the *St Matthew Passion* for what it is—a superb music-drama setting forth the greatest drama of all time—and regard it as a solemnly pious exercise.

Vaughan Williams's first opera, *Hugh the Drover*, was written during the years 1911 to 1914, to a libretto by the Gloucestershire journalist and dramatic critic Harold Child. The west country aspect of Vaughan Williams should not be exaggerated; he lived in Glou-cestershire, where Child set the scene of his opera, for the first three years of his life only. All the same, the Cotswolds and the Surrey downs are not so very different—or at any rate were not in those days. Thus scene, atmosphere and theme—the wanderer motif, so evident in many of Vaughan Williams's early works—should have combined to attract and inspire the composer.

Hugh the Drover is precisely what it sets out to be—a ballad opera. It is not (as has rather unjustly been implied) an English attempt to write a *Bartered Bride* or a *Boris Godunov*. The plot has neither the human appeal of the one nor the patriotic surge of the other. Such pride of folk and ancestry (despite references to Bonaparte) as occur in the work are local rather than national; such romance and comedy more conventional and less conceived in terms of live character and situation than in Smetana's masterpiece. If we want a parallel to it, we must search our own musical history, not those of Bohemia or Russia. On the one hand, the works of Gay and Dibdin and perhaps *The Yeomen of the Guard* are its forerunners, and on the other, Benjamin Britten's Suffolk village in *Peter Grimes* its nearest contemporary—in setting rather than theme or style, however. The situation is a stage cliché: Mary, the heroine, is unwillingly to marry John the Butcher, as her father, the town constable, has arranged. She falls in love with Hugh, and the plot revolves around the struggles of true love to assert itself against convention. Hugh stands for the carefree life of the open air, which the more conventional of the townspeople regard as irresponsible if not dangerous; John, presumably, if he stands for anything at all, stands for a settled prosperous middle-class life. But need such a person be so trivially unpleasant? He arouses neither our sympathy nor our antipathy, and the result is that we cannot really understand what made the Constable choose him as a husband for Mary. Neither Child nor Vaughan Williams makes him a convincing villain; he has neither the *élan* of a melodramatic figure like Pizarro, nor the sinister power of a real one, like Iago. He is not even as funny, boorish lout that he is, as Gilbert's Wilfred Shadbolt in *The Yeomen of the Guard*, who is somewhat similar to him in outlook and behaviour.

Hugh and Mary, on the other hand, do come to life; the former's ballad 'Horse hoofs' has both confidence and vitality; his song 'Sweet little linnet' is both tender and strong—a strength and tenderness which are well balanced by Mary's 'Here, queen uncrown'd in this most royal place', and merged finally with his in the duet which begins 'Lord of my life, unworthy I to bear you company'. Even when her love for Hugh is being tested, as in the first scene of Act II (written twenty years after the original composition of most of the work), the orchestra does not lie:

The music is both romantic and unsentimental, without being either grand or insubstantial. One of the features of the opera is the manner

III

in which Vaughan Williams deploys his tunes according to the characters who have to sing them, and not simply according to the basic emotions they are required to illustrate. Hugh's, for example, are mostly warm and impulsive, Mary's expansive and—rare adjective for an English opera—passionate; John's are rough and uncouth. The *ensembles* are mostly vigorous and bustling; there is certainly both warmth and life in this music. Yet the opera is undoubtedly a failure. Hubert Foss has, I think, put his finger on the real failings:

> Hugh . . . is so picturesque, with his boxing match, his stocks, his escape, and his love triumphant, as to be unconvincing.[1]

This is, I feel, a little unfair; it is not Hugh himself who is unconvincing as a person but the situation into which he is placed; as Foss continues:

> Harold Child, we feel, had read the archives of, the poems about, that Cotswold village, with its stocks and its fair. And for once . . . Vaughan Williams accepted this charming compromise between literature and life as the real thing. . . . Here he was forced, partly by the words and partly by his own ideas, to produce *pastiche*.[1]

All the same, it is a robust pastiche, and a most enjoyable one, more substantial than operetta, with a touch of the flamboyant heroism of the folk ballads of which it unpretentiously attempts to be an extension. In any other country but England it would have achieved the popularity of Lortzing's *Zar und Zimmermann* in Germany or Charpentier's *Louise* in France.

Sir John in Love has all the robustness of *Hugh*, with much more convincing characters, more or less credible situations, and the world's greatest poet as principal librettist. It was the second product of that short period from just after the 1914–18 war till about 1927 during which Vaughan Williams wrote no fewer than four operas—two short and two full length. Like *Hugh the Drover*, it received its first performance at the Parry Memorial Theatre of the Royal College of

---

[1] Op. cit., p. 177.

Music, in this case under Malcolm Sargent, on 21st March 1929. It is not Vaughan Williams's greatest opera, but it ought to be his most popular one, for it has all the necessary qualities—broad tunes, spectacle, wit, attractive characterization and invention which almost invariably matches music to dramatic requirements. The character of Falstaff inspired two other great English musicians to some of their very best work—just as it did the greatest opera composer of all. Is *Sir John* overshadowed by Verdi's superb work? If it is, the composer knew what he was taking on, and said so in the published preface to the score.

The main thing needed in any comic opera is speed of movement, which is not a characteristic for which Vaughan Williams's music is notable. Without swift movement even the most amusing situation cannot be exploited; both composer and librettist must see to it that nothing congeals in the dramatic action. That *Sir John in Love* is going to move apace is indicated by the seventeen-bar prelude with its interplay of 3-4 and 6-8. When the curtain rises we are immediately presented with the main threads of the action: Shallow and Evans are busy bemoaning Falstaff's behaviour—which serves as a useful 'build-up' of the main character, Slender is hard at work in the corner writing a sonnet to Anne Page. Comedy and romance respectively, then, are to be the warp and woof of this opera. This is at once a step forward from *Hugh the Drover*; whatever merits that libretto possessed, comedy was not one of them. But in an opera comedy must be underlined by music that suits it, and in this opera the comedy is one of situations. The problem to be solved is whether a composer noted—as Vaughan Williams was at that time—for the seriousness of much of his output was able to distil humour and wit out of his normally full-blooded and robust idiom. *Hugh the Drover* provided evidence of his gift for writing appropriate lyric music for romantic situations; *Sir John in Love* shows that he could do the other too. Vaughan Williams always claimed that over-scoring was one of his vices; if this was so he was singularly virtuous when he worked on *Sir John*. It is one of his airiest scores, and the nature of the melodic invention is also light. Light, that is, without any hint of triviality. When required to he writes music which deftly hits off the farcical nature of, for example, the Caius-Quickly intrigue to marry off the delectable Anne to the preposterous Frenchman:

Or he depicts Falstaff's cocksure boastfulness thus:

By a skilful blending of Shakespeare's text with other lyrics taken from the works of his contemporaries, such as Jonson, Fletcher and Campion, Vaughan Williams fills out the romantic part of his libretto and at the same time develops his main character beyond what is to be found merely in *The Merry Wives*. Boito had added weight and depth to his Falstaff by borrowing from Henry IV; Holst and Elgar had based their musical studies of him almost entirely on the Falstaff of the histories; Vaughan Williams presents us with a more lyrical Falstaff, no 'knight, gentleman, and soldier', perhaps, but still a creature of sack rather than thin potations. He is hero and villain at the same time, and his villainy is essentially the harmless gallimaufry of a yeoman squire. He is no Almaviva, no scheming aristocrat out-witted by his astute servant; he is much more a bourgeois—a Schumannesque Falstaff. He is just as much a part of the middle-class country-town scene as Mrs Ford and Mrs Page; indeed, he is un-commonly like an irresponsible Hans Sachs. Not so wise, not so tolerant, not so resourceful, but as likable, as genial and as warm-hearted. The change in the title of the play may be significant; the central feature of the story is not so much the discomfiture of the fat amorous buffoon but the lively and lyrically romantic atmosphere of the play as a whole: it is a Midsummer Night's Dream, as the some-what sententious finale of Act IV—warning us not to take it all too seriously—seems to indicate.

Romance and knockabout comedy are cleverly interwoven, both in the dramatic situations and in the music which underlines and ex-ploits them. Thus, in Act I, the noisy abuse of the sextet with Falstaff,

Nym, Pistol and the others gives place to Anne Page's appearance with Mrs Page and Mrs Ford. The music pays most of its attention to Anne, who is yearning for a true love; romance merges into comedy again when Slender tries to fill the bill for her, and deepens into melancholy when she considers what her parents have in store for her —Dr Caius. The first appearance of Fenton both cheers and disturbs her; cheers her, because she knows that she has found her true love, and disturbs her because she knows that her parents will not agree to the match. This leads naturally to a depiction of the match they are prepared to countenance, and Caius is presented to us in a different light; he is not merely a mannered fop, but also capable of lyric sentiment (with his *Vrai dieu d'amours, comfortez moy*) even if not true passion. We have already heard what that entails in Fenton's music. Falstaff, who has been off the stage a considerable time, now brings us back to the central theme of the opera—his plot, divulged before Bardolph, Nym and Pistol, to cuckold Ford. They of course imme/diately decide to inform the intended victim, whose jealousy and rage at the mockery of the others grow to dominate the closing pages of the act.

The complex plot demands a similar helter-skelter development of emotional situation in the other three acts of the opera. Certainly there is none of the dramatic marking time that mars the plots of some other fine operas, and the music is sufficiently varied to retain the listener's interest all the time. A most remarkable feature of the work—as of its Shakespeare model—is that so much trickery and deception do not lead to more serious consequences. The nearest, in fact, that the plot gets to a tragic issue is when Evans and Dr Caius come near to fight/ing a duel over Anne Page—of which Vaughan Williams takes advantage by cleverly illustrating the confusion in Evans's mind. The poor man tries to calm his fear by reading a book of poems, but confuses Psalm 137 with Marlowe's *Passionate Shepherd*, with dis/astrous results. In the main the plot of the opera follows Shakespeare very closely, omitting only the episode of the fat woman of Brainford, the most difficult to accept, and the most unnecessary. As in Shake/peare, the last act is a final discomfiture of Falstaff interwoven with a satisfactory resolution of Anne's emotional problems—to the glorious melody which Vaughan Williams writes to the words 'See the chariot at hand here of love, wherein my lady rideth'. Falstaff reconciles parents and daughter and all ends happily—save for the finale on the theme 'All the world's a stage' and 'Nothing under the sun is done in true earnest', which includes the dance 'Half Hannikin'.

Sir John in Love represents a great advance on *Hugh the Drover*; not only is the plot more interesting and the lyrics of a far higher quality, but the music is infinitely more supple, varied and apposite. There is far less self-conscious open-air heartiness, and far more wit and rich-ness of emotion. The characters are much more skilfully portrayed, they have more substance and more depth—they are, in fact, English in a way that those in the ballad opera could not be. They are colourful, whereas those in *Hugh the Drover* were merely picturesque. Fenton and Anne give the impression that they have at least some idea of the practical side of life, whereas Hugh and Mary, for all their vitality, sometimes seem to thrill to the glorious unknown simply because they have no idea of the implications of the known. Moreover, the 'folky' element in the music of *Sir John in Love* is handled much more skil-fully; there is more true development of the themes. Frank Howes points out how 'See the chariot' is carefully prepared in the first act, and how the allusions of both words and music of such folksongs as are quoted or hinted at suffice to make a dramatic point, rather in the same way as Bach might quote the melody of a chorale in a cantata, without its words, so that the listeners might be affected on two levels, as it were. And the opera is suffused with sheer happy delight in the foibles and weaknesses of all men.

Hugh the Drover is a ballad romance; *Sir John in Love* a romantic comedy. *The Poisoned Kiss* is entitled 'a romantic extravaganza'; a better title would be 'a romantic farce'. For that is what it is, and as such it is almost unique in the field of opera, which may be one reason why it is so seldom performed. The plot is taken from a short story by Richard Garnett, whose rather sly, slightly donnish wit is not readily translatable into terms of effective theatrical dialogue. Nearly all his stories—at any rate those in the collection *The Twilight of the Gods*—turn on irony of situation and reveal a gentle sceptic's fun poked usually at dons, church dignitaries, the supernatural and philosophers.

'RIDERS TO THE SEA' AT SADLER'S WELLS

(By kind permission of Sadler's Wells Theatre)

(Satan himself appears in a number of the tales, and usually finds himself the butt of a farcical plot.) The name immediately called to mind by a study of the plot of *The Poisoned Kiss* is that of W. S. Gilbert; but Gilbert, unlike Garnett, would have worked out his idea of a young woman fed from birth on poisons in order to kill off any prospective lovers in general and one in particular in terms of remorse-less and absurd logic, including topical satire. So Evelyn Sharp's trans-lation of the mock-mythological legend, on which the opera is based, into modern terms, with fake mediums, satire on advertising and so on, is natural. The trouble is that Miss Sharp, talented writer and strong personality though she was, lacked Gilbert's spicy verve and genuine lyric vein, though her libretto is considerably better con-structed than some of Gilbert's. And even though a good opera can be written round a silly libretto, an opera with spoken dialogue depends not only on its music and lyrics, but also on the spoken words, which cannot afford to be merely facile or fatuous.

Mention of Gilbert prompts the inevitable question: Was Vaughan Williams capable of playing the part of Sullivan? In a number of his occasional writings, such as *A Minim's Rest* and *Nationalism and Internationalism*, he showed a distinct admiration for Sullivan, lament-ing only the fact that light music was obliged to be trivial in the Victorian age and asserting that Sullivan was born out of his time. Yet Gilbert gave Sullivan enough opportunities to show how national characteristics could be expressed or burlesqued in a conventional enough musical idiom. Such things as 'Prithee, pretty maiden', from *Patience*, or 'When Britain really ruled the Waves', from *Iolanthe*, or Giuseppe's 'Rising early in the morning' from *The Gondoliers* are recognizably English (and not in the least trivial, either.) In *The Poisoned Kiss* Vaughan Williams was challenging Sullivan on his own ground—the fanciful musical romance, spiced with satire. It is not entirely his fault that his challenge failed, but it is not entirely Miss Sharp's either. Yet we should remember that *The Poisoned Kiss* is Vaughan Williams's only attempt at writing what is in effect, even if not in intention, a less trivial counterpart to the Savoy operettas, whereas Gilbert and Sullivan wrote no less than thirteen pieces together. And even the most devoted Savoyard is unlikely to know much of *Thespis*, *The Sorcerer*, *The Grand Duke* or *Utopia Limited*, because they have been deservedly dropped from the repertory, to say nothing of such a work as *Princess Ida*, which contains some of Sullivan's most delightful music and some of Gilbert's best situations. The trouble with the libretto of *The Poisoned Kiss* is that the humour and wit in it smack of the smart revue rather than the romantic operetta, and the satirical elements, while entertaining in themselves, are not nearly so carefully integrated into plot and character as Gilbert would have made them. The music is at its best in the patter *ensembles* and the lyrical songs, and when Vaughan Williams is called upon to produce a really good tune he does so. But even when he tries his best, summoning up all the resources of his sense of irony, as in the Tango in Act III, for example, to drop into burlesque or musical comedy, he cannot really manage anything better than archness. *The Poisoned Kiss* is an embarrassing work, not because it is a complete failure, but because it is a half-success. It is too substantial for an operetta, not sentimental enough to be a musical comedy and too sophisticated to be a lighter and more playful version even of *Hugh the Drover*.

The main characters, Tormentilla and Amaryllus, are a kind of small-scale Pamina and Tamino, to whom Angelica and Gallanthus stand in the relationship of Papagena and Papageno. What Vaughan Williams was capable of providing in the way of dramatic *ensemble-writing* is shown by the following quotation:

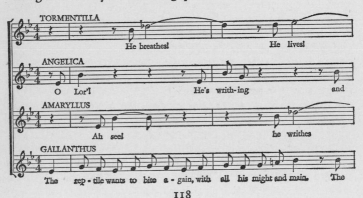

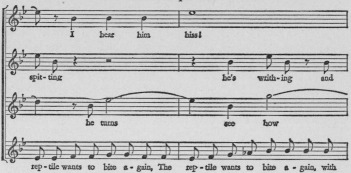

from the episode in the first act when Tormentilla's pet cobra has been
brought back to life after Amaryllus, thinking to save her from its
deadly poison, attempts to kill it. The whole of this longish *ensemble*
is beautifully contrived; it has pace and vigour, a clear texture and a
cleverly placed climax (at which Tormentilla sings: 'Oh joy',
Angelica 'A kiss', Gallanthus '[might] and main', and Amaryllus
'he spits') on a modulation into G major. Moreover, the change from
major to minor at the moment when the reptile actually comes to life
again is a delightfully ironic touch, and the madrigalian counterpoint
works gently into a combination of Tormentilla's lullaby, Angelica's
and Gallanthus's patter and Amaryllus's love-song. It is a pity that
not all the opera rises to this level. The minor characters suffer particularly in comparison with Gilbert and Sullivan. Alongside the
latter's absurdly dim-witted aristocratic primitives Arac, Gurion and
Scynthius in *Princess Ida*, so ably brought to life by Sullivan's ponderous mock-Handelian music, Lob, Hob and Gob are merely silly;
moreover, a comparison between No. 5 of Act I in *The Poisoned Kiss*
and the trio 'We are warriors three' in *Princess Ida* show the difference
between succinct musical characterization and mere setting of words.
Or, to take another example, both words and music contribute far
more satisfactorily to the illumination of what is basically the same
situation—the confession of a fickle young man who ought not to be
taken too seriously—in Edwin's first solo song from *Trial by Jury* than
they do in Amaryllus's 'It's true I'm inclined to be fickle'.

Frank Howes points out that the main characters dominate each act in turn, and also says that the opera has a 'theme'—that love triumphs over hate. This is surely carrying things a bit too far. Granted that the work tries to avoid triviality (and even this is not certain, as we shall see), can we really recognize the farcical emotion displayed by the sorcerer Dipsacus as hatred? And is the sentiment which exists between Amaryllus and Tormentilla really carefully enough delineated to be called love? The great appeal of the greatest comedies, from Aristophanes to the present, has depended on the satisfactory comic treatment of universal human types and situations known to every generation: Falstaff, the genial boaster who is continually getting into scrapes on account of his mendacity and out of them by means of it; Figaro, the resourceful schemer paying off his social superiors who try to delude him; Don Quixote, the bungling yet appealing lunatic with misplaced ideals. Even Gilbert's characters and plots are generally recognizably abstracts of certain universal human foibles, but this cannot be said of *The Poisoned Kiss*.

Howes also draws attention to the note of deliberate bathos, sounded time and again through the opera. Perhaps the bathos is deliberate, but much of it finds its way into the dialogue and lyrics of the servant couple, Gallanthus and Angelica. This reverses the convention of opera and operetta, where the servants are usually clever and their social superiors romantic. There seems little point in turning a soubrette —which Angelica certainly is, both in her actions and in the music with which Vaughan Williams provides her—into a purveyor of platitudes. Surely, if bathos is required, it is required in order to deflate the romantic and the mighty, not the patter-men. No amount of cutting and trimming will make *The Poisoned Kiss* into a really satisfactory work, which is a great pity. There is much that is good in it, but there is no doubt that it is a failure. The fact, however, that Vaughan Williams took on the task of writing it, and put so much music of a high quality into parts of it, is further evidence of the extraordinarily wide range of his mind and sympathies. The attempt was worth making at any rate.

If *The Poisoned Kiss* is Vaughan Williams's one undoubted failure in the field of opera, *Riders to the Sea* is surely his greatest success. It is a masterpiece which succeeds in being dramatic, colourful and deeply moving simply by relying almost entirely on reticence and under-statement. This chamber opera in plainsong, as it almost is, is an operatic treatment of the theme of the *Sinfonia antartica*. It deals with the same situation—man (or, in this case, woman) versus Nature. *Hugh the Drover* lacked a convincing antagonist; here the villain remains offstage all the time, and is the most terrible that man can face, because its whole activity is unguided by any conscious purpose. The sea—Nature the destroyer—is here not the majestic arena for epic human endeavour, as in the *Sea Symphony*, but an antagonist in that arena against whom man must unceasingly fight. In Synge's tragedy it is ostensibly the sea which wins, but in actual fact the triumph is with the old woman Maurya who has lost her six sons victims to it, for it has deprived her, not of her capacity to love and her inner serenity, but merely of the concrete objects of that love. So we have the interest-ing contast that whereas in the *Sea Symphony* the sea is itself a symbol—of the innermost self that man can and must discover and explore just as he explores the sea—here it is the human beings whom Maurya loves, her six sons, who are tokens of her spiritual power in the struggle between her spirit and the sea. She prevails in that struggle by suffering all that it can possibly inflict, and when it has stripped her of all her possessions she realizes the dignity and power of her own spirit, which it cannot destroy. Thus in both cases the sea is an instrument of self-realization.

The real drama, then, in Synge, as in Vaughan Williams, takes place within the soul of Maurya herself. Hence the intimate scale of the work—hence also its enormous power, locked up inside as with an atom. Synge was an appropriate choice in more ways than one; like Vaughan Williams, he collected folk poetry, only his medium was words rather than music, and he collected colourful expressions, not songs. Many of these expressions he included, by his own ad-mission, in the texts of his plays. The drama, which Vaughan Williams set virtually word for word, is short, concise and simple. The opera lasts little more than half an hour. It is scored for single wood-wind with a second flute (the only clarinet being a bass one), two horns, a trumpet, strings and percussion, which includes a sea-machine. The female chorus is wordless and forms an eerie back-ground as the climax of the drama approaches, leading to Maurya's great solo Adagio lament beginning 'They are all gone now', which in its austere grandeur ranks alongside 'When I am laid in earth' as one of the supreme tragic utterances of English opera:

As Dr Percy Young points out, the supernatural elements in the opera merge pre-Christian Celtic beliefs with Catholic Christianity. The combination enhances the tension of the drama, for it is the former which warns Maurya of the tragedy which is to come, and the latter which strengthens her and enables her to overcome its assault. It is perhaps this element which aids the astonishingly effective reticence of the vocal line, which conveys both the atmosphere of plainsong and the lilt of Celtic speech simultaneously. This is not local colour, painted in for the sake of decorating an otherwise un-impressive canvas; it is an integral and necessary component of the work, arising from the nature of Synge's plot and dialogue.

When a composer deliberately adopts such a restrained method of setting a text, the differentiation of character and the marking off of dramatic events within the action of the drama have to be done by other means than those accepted by convention—sudden modulations, strange harmonies, agitated rhythms and striking orchestration. Vaughan Williams manages it here by keeping his vocal line within so restricted a pitch that the moments of urgency and tension can be simply indicated by rising from the usual chant. But delineation of character within such restrained limits must be achieved by tiny details of vocal phrasing and rhythm. Fortunately all the important characters in Synge's play are members of the same family, and their characters can be expected to be similar, at least in part. The danger is, of course, that melody confined within such a range can become not merely monodic but also monotonous. What ought to have the effect of a hypnotic incantation might degenerate into a soporific chanting. This is skilfully avoided throughout; the vocal lines are a triumph of subtle melodic organization. The Vaughan Williams technique of generating a complete long-phrased melody out of a single thematic germ is used here with infinite subtlety of gradation and concentration of purpose. When the two sisters open the bundle of clothes which happen to belong to their missing brother Michael, for example:

the manner in which the chord at the apex of the phrase is resolved, first of all back on to the germ from which it grows, and then, through the continuation downwards of the phrase to the words 'God spare his soul', leads naturally on to the next phrase, grows organically out of the previous context, and marks off a moment of tragic realization at the same time. This is merely one phrase typical of the whole opera. Though certain of the themes can be designated as *leit-motive*—constantly recurring when a certain emotion or element in the action is mentioned—the music is so arranged that they grow organically out of their context without for one moment surrendering their dramatic effect. The texture of the opera is decidedly symphonic—in the sense in which Vaughan Williams understood the term.

Dramatically and musically, this is one of the most effective and moving operas ever written. It deals with a heroic situation without bombast, it illuminates an urgent and noble human tragedy in a powerful manner with great economy of means, it is utterly unique in its use of original dramatic effects and it is so concise that not a single bar of the music could be cut. Had Vaughan Williams been anything else but an Englishman, it would now be in the repertory of every good operatic theatre in the world.

The last and longest of Vaughan William's operas incorporates his other one-act piece, *The Shepherds of the Delectable Mountains*, which was actually the first of his operas to be publicly staged. It is true that Vaughan Williams himself refrained from calling *The Pilgrim's Progress* an opera, but it is surely just as much an opera as those seventeenth-century works with their allegorical characters and personified virtues which enjoy that title. Perhaps he called it a 'morality' because the lyrical love-interest which is almost a *sine qua non* in conventional opera is entirely missing. Or perhaps he did so because, as the critics were quick to point out, dramatic tension and character development in the normal sense are also entirely missing. Yet it is surely straining at a gnat to swallow a camel to say that *The Pilgrim's Progress* is less suitable for stage production than *Parsifal* or *The Thrie Estates*.

The text and the music divide into tableaux rather than acts, each one depicting a different stage of Pilgrim's journey; it is as if the composer picked up and surveyed different aspects of his theme rather than developing it. This means that each scene is dominated by an overall atmosphere rather than by any expansion of the plot. Characters in the normal sense disappear; their place is taken by allegorized virtues and vices, or symbolic personalities such as Mr By-Ends, and the music does not fill out their human qualities by developing phrases associated with individual people. Such characterization as there is is reduced to rudimentary motto-phrases which recur but are not, as a rule, submitted to a process of symphonic growth. The Evangelist, for example, has his utterances prefaced by two chords— just as in *Hodie* he is introduced by what Simona Pakenham aptly calls 'a little twist of theme'. Such a musical procedure, nearer to the mosaic-like build-up of *Hodie* rather than the 'symphonic' style of *Riders to the Sea*, is suited to the black-and-white, 'either-or' setting of Bunyan's allegory, and it constitutes a *dramma per musica* of a kind that Bach's librettists provided for him in his secular cantatas, rather like the sententious choruses in German seventeenth-century drama from which the baroque secular cantata of Bach's day developed. The minor characters represent 'might-have-beens' in Pilgrim's life rather than definite influences on it, and there is therefore much narration and some dialogue, but very little *ensemble* combination between solo singers.

The range of this music is greater than that of any of the other operas. Whereas the concentration of *Riders to the Sea* left no room for anything other than grim tragedy, and *Sir John in Love* was light and romantic, this music is serene, powerful, minatory, grim, ironic and downright evil by turns. The scenes are arranged so that each particular element is followed by something which contrasts with it in nature and in tempo; thus the noise and flashy activity of the Vanity Fair scene are immediately contrasted with the Florestan's dungeon atmosphere of its successor. The 'action' runs through despair, spiritual enlightenment, resolve, solemn statuesque conflict, gaudy spectacle and light comedy to the ineffable serenity of the Delectable Mountains and the closing *Verklärung*.

The emotional layout of the opera follows a kind of parabola, from the radiant opening of Pilgrim's journey (when, having cast off his burden of sin, he is sent forth on his way by the Shining Ones), through the struggle with Apollyon, the confusion of Vanity Fair and the despair of the dungeon, until he passes the trivial and amusing By-Ends and reaches the Shepherds of the Delectable Mountains, leaving them for his final destination, the Heavenly City. The impetus of the music, then, arches upward, as Pilgrim's fortunes arch downward; it gathers momentum through the fight with Apollyon, reaches its zenith of frenzied movement in Vanity Fair, touches sublimity and broadens out to the noble close. Strands of repose and tension are thus woven into an enormous design which sums up the whole of Vaughan Williams's musical career. Not for nothing does he quote from his own fifth Symphony and there are thematic motifs reminiscent of—and sometimes identical with—themes from the fourth and the sixth, as Deryck Cooke pointed out in an article in the *Listener*; and every aspect of his genius appears in some guise or other. Even the mordant irony which is a feature of such works as the fourth Symphony and *Five Tudor Portraits* finds a place when Lord Hategood pronounces sentence in a kind of gabbled plainchant which is just as much a distortion of the 'real thing' as is Satan's 'Gloria in excelsis Deo' *fff* on the muted brass at the end of his dance of triumph in *Job*. This is Vaughan Williams's comprehensive vision of life in all its aspects— a huge, integrated and colourful pageant, leading inexorably towards the unknown region of whose existence the composer had always been aware, and of which he had experienced a vision. His last opera, like his first, contains a scene set in a fair—but this time the fair is not an excuse for local colour; it is a metaphysical fair, portrayed and realized by a genius who has rightly—even if somewhat vaguely— always been regarded as a mystic. When this great work is criticized for being 'undramatic', what is really meant is that it is not theatrical in the conventional sense—which is an entirely different matter, and even in the conventional sense, the chilling effect of the music when the inhabitants of Vanity Fair pronounce Pilgrim guilty and sentence him to death is intensely skilfully contrived in dramatic terms. If the listener lays Bunyan's allegory, Vaughan Williams's music and his own head together, as the text enjoins him to, he will find that *The Pilgrim's Progress* is drama: it shows in vivid and comprehensible form those elements and attitudes which go to make up human life here on earth—and, unlike nearly all other dramas, transcends this life to offer a vision of what, in the composer's opinion, awaits those who are faithful to the light within them.

CHAPTER XII

OTHER STAGE WORKS, FILM MUSIC AND SHORT ORCHESTRAL WORKS

THE FIRST incidental music known to have been written by Vaughan
Williams was for *Pan's Anniversary* in 1905; the last was in a film on
Blake, to which parts of *Job* were fitted as incidental music, and which
was released not long before his death. There is incidental music to
Aristophanes' *The Wasps*, three ballets, a good deal of film music
and a masque written as a kind of folk-dance ballet, but first produced
on television. In addition to this, the B.B.C.'s West of England studio
asked him to provide music for a radio adaptation of Hardy's *The
Mayor of Casterbridge* in 1951. Relatively little of this music is of great
importance, but some of it is well known and some of it was adapted
for other purposes by the composer himself. One of the works is a
masterpiece; indeed, Dr Percy Young devotes a whole chapter to it
in his study of the composer's music. Vaughan Williams has been
better served by the recording companies in this field, for not only is
Job available, but also *Old King Cole*, and a suite from the music to
The Wasps (all recorded by Decca, who have shown much more
interest in Vaughan Williams than all the other companies put
together), as well as some of the film music.

Since the music to *Pan's Anniversary* has been scrapped, the first
extant work we have to consider here is the music to *The Wasps*,
written for an undergraduate production at Cambridge in 1909. The
overture—the only one by Vaughan Williams which is ever heard in
the concert hall—is a bright and tuneful piece, conceding only the
opening flourishes in the strings to the title of the play, but based for
the most part on 'folky' material, with themes which hop about
in what Professor Tovey aptly described as 'rowdy counterpoint',
worked out in simple sonata form and scored for a modest orchestra.
The other movements are for the most part light-hearted; the 'March
Past of the Kitchen Utensils' displays a saturnine wit in its glum

theme, the two entr'actes are charming, and the finale tableau a scurrying romp—a forerunner of *The Tunning of Eleanor Rumming*.

Old King Cole, commissioned by the Cambridge branch of the English Folk Dance Society, was first performed at Trinity College on 5th June 1923. The scenario fills out the pipe, bowl and fiddlers three of the nursery rhyme with some historical speculation on their origin. The King's daughter, who really existed (she married the Roman Emperor Constantine, becoming the mother of Constantine the Great), brings a pipe home from her travels abroad. She also arranges for a competition between the three fiddlers which is the central episode of the ballet. Nearly all the music used is of folk origin, and the third fiddler, who wins the competition, does so by dint of catchy tunes such as 'The Oyster Girl'. A feature of the score is the use of a wordless chorus, which sings a brisk tune in unison.

On Christmas Night is based on Dickens's *A Christmas Carol* and appropriately enough weaves a number of traditional carol tunes into the musical texture. As with all Vaughan Williams's ballet scores, the music is intended for a rather different style of dancing from conventional ballet. This particular ballet was devised by Adolf Bolm, who was with the original Diaghilev company, and it was to his choreography that it was produced at Chicago in 1926. But it was re-choreographed for the English Folk Dance Society, and first performed in the new form at Cecil Sharp House on 29th December 1935. In its present form it interweaves various Christmas motifs into a kind of dream-sequence of Scrooge's youth. Musically it is a folk-song rhapsody on an extended scale, with the tunes woven in according to the demands of the story.

By far the greatest of Vaughan Williams's music for the ballet theatre is the masque for dancing, *Job*, which many commentators would rank as his finest work altogether. In a performance of this work no fewer than four major artists combine—the composer, the choreographer, William Blake, on whose engravings the choreography is based, and the anonymous genius who wrote the Old Testament poem which inspired Blake. Moreover, unlike the merely sentimental or pathetic legends which inspire some ballets, we have here in choreographic terms a quest into the nature of man's place in the universe and his eternal spiritual destiny. It will probably never be a popular ballet, for the only virtuoso part in it is that of Satan, and it offers no display dances for a *prima ballerina*, but the concentrated impact of superb spectacle, magnificent music and a profound theme make *Job* one of the most irresistible aesthetic experiences imaginable.

Blake's interpretation of the Book of Job was that God was Job's spiritual self and Satan his material self. In addition he portrayed Job's three comforters not merely as self-righteous but also as hypo-critical, and this is caught up by Vaughan Williams in their music, as is Blake's suggestion that they were 'Satan's Trinity of Accusers'. Most of the dances are cast in the mould of old-fashioned courtly dances of the Elizabethan period—pavane, galliard, minuet—or of English country dances. This adds a certain statuesque formality of a rather heavier nature than is usual to the miming which must be part of them in the airiness and fantasy of conventional ballet. Again, as with the operas, it is the overall effect that matters—music, dancing and story; but since the music is not a setting of a verbal text, a concert performance or a gramophone recording is more rewarding than is the case for the operas. Moreover, a magnificent record of the score has been made by Sir Adrian Boult (to whom the work is dedicated) and the London Philharmonic Orchestra for the Decca Company.

The main characteristic of the figure of God in this score is immense power and majesty—his music is firm and tonal. Satan is represented by a demoniac energy and a majesty which is a perverted vision of the majesty of God. His music is notable for odd melodic leaps, the sudden juxtaposition of unrelated chords and violent scoring. No-where is Satan's awful majesty more apparent than at the terrible moment when, after being ministered to by the three comforters, Job is visited by a vision of heaven with Satan enthroned in God's place. Here, in the concert version, the sombre sound of the full organ contrasts grimly and dramatically with that of the orchestra, and with immensely powerful effect. The whole work is full of *coups de théâtre* of this kind—whether they be points of scoring, such as the ghostly hollowness of the restatement section of 'Satan's Dance of Triumph', or of dramatic anticipation, such as in the long first movement, when a few wood-wind instruments foreshadow in mysterious chords what is to become the opening motif of one of the grandest tunes ever written:

or of structure, as when the accompaniment to the main theme in the 'Minuet of the Sons and Daughters of Job' appears right at the end without its theme, or when the evanescent wispy pattern of the 'Job's Dream' theme reappears, not as a single line in canon with itself, but as a fully harmonized block of chords, still in canon with itself.

The work is set, like a medieval morality—or like Stravinsky's *Petrouschka*, for that matter—on a double stage; in this case the two planes represent Heaven and Earth. The opening movement sets the scene; Job, surrounded by his family, good, prosperous and happy, is observed by Satan. At Satan's request God puts Job within his power. The contrast between Satan's snarls and the ineffable majesty of the 'Sarabande of the Sons of God' is very striking, but not so striking as to obliterate the fact that the whole of this movement is built up on a familiar pattern of developing embryo-elements: a phrase: ♪♪♪ and its reversal: ♪♪♪ two sharply juxtaposed chords (B♭ minor and A major) to represent Satan, and a rising scale passage, which assumes various forms throughout the movement.

'Satan's Dance of Triumph', cribbed—angular theme, whirling ostinato and all—from the scherzo of Beethoven's Op. 135,[1] is a *tour de force* of destructive energy. Has real evil ever been more convincingly

[1] Might not the association of this ostinato with the Devil derive, however, from a much less exalted source than a late Beethoven quartet—i.e. Gounod's *Faust*, where the same whirling figure occurs in the orchestral introduction to Mephistopheles's 'Ballad of the Golden Calf'?

portrayed in music in all its fascinating illusory dignity than in the powerful 'Trio' section, with its augmented fourth in the trumpet theme and its ponderous trombone and tuba accompaniment? The sinuous tranquillity of the following dance is interrupted by thunderbolts from Satan, anticipated by scoring which can rightly be described as uncanny, and as the dance proceeds it is accompanied by a meandering counterpoint on the viola—a favourite trick of Vaughan Williams's, and one which recurs in the 'Dance of the Three Comforters'. The main theme of 'Job's Dream' grows, like a folksong melody, from an initial germ:

and is interrupted by hideous visions before it leads into the desolation of the 'Dance of the Messengers', and the cortège of Job's sons and daughters, with its curious reminiscence of a theme in the finale of Brahms's *German Requiem* over a throbbing bass. The three comforters present themselves—or rather Satan presents them—each by means of a characteristic phrase, which all develop into a rich and ironic pattern as the friends work up their self-righteous indignation against Job, and the icy smoothness of a high note on the saxophone leads back into a mocking reprise, complete with crocodile tears on a solo viola. No wonder Job turns and curses God. 'Elihu's Dance of Youth and Beauty' leads us upward (as it were on the wings of *The Lark Ascending*) to a further celestial vision, and the action moves back to heaven, where Satan is banished and the Sons of God expel him from the Almighty's presence with a galliard which might well be a sea-shanty, so square and hearty is its melody. Earth too joins in (to a theme whose opening phrase exactly follows the outline of a theme in *Flos Campi*, but in a different rhythm) and Job is restored to his former state, and sits musing peacefully upon his story, surrounded by his family, in the epilogue, which has the serene inevitability of a summer sunset.

The Bridal Day was written for the Folk Dance and Song Society shortly before the Second World War, and was the first work in which Ursula Wood (as she then was) collaborated with Vaughan Williams. Its first production in 1953, on television, drew down criticism on the B.B.C. for cramming so rich a spectacle within the confines of the television screen. Like *Job*, it bears the title 'A Masque for Dancing', and has something of the pageantry of the earlier work, but naturally little of its sublimity and power.

Vaughan Williams approached the composition of film music with zest. It is the fate of most film music to be an unobtrusive partner in the heightening of emotional tension in the action of the film, and since Vaughan Williams threw himself into the composition of this kind of music with the whole-heartedness with which he attacked everything he did, it is not surprising that he felt that much of his film music was worth publishing or redeveloping. Thus the title music for *Forty-ninth Parallel*, with its processional, Parryish theme, became the unison song *The New Commonwealth*, with words by Harold Child, the librettist of *Hugh the Drover*. Another theme from the same film was incorporated into the scherzo of the second string Quartet. The epilogue of the same quartet is based on a theme originally intended for a film on Joan of Arc—hence the superscription in the score of the quartet 'Greetings from Joan to Jean'. Much of Vaughan Williams's film music is good, workaday music, designed to enhance the effect of an individual scene, but hardly more remarkable than that. The score to *Scott of the Antarctic* was used as the basis for a complete symphonic work, and though it has been criticized by an expert [1] for technical reasons, its value as the basis of a symphonic work is notable, and it was awarded the first prize at the Prague Film Festival in 1949. The normal process in composing film music was reversed when music taken from *Job* was dubbed into a film about William Blake which included shots of the *Job* engravings; in this case the music was simply fitted into the film sequences, and hardly counts as a separate composition. Yet it does represent a tentative step in the direction suggested by Vaughan Williams himself, where a great film might be built up round a great piece of music. And if ever a composition deserved such homage from other arts it is surely *Job*.

[1] Hans Keller, 'Film Music', in Grove's *Dictionary*, 5th ed., vol. ii.

'Fantasia on a Theme by Thomas Tallis'

Since the greatest of Vaughan Williams's ballet scores is heard fairly frequently in the concert hall, it is but a small step to his other orchestral works, some of which, like all his film music, were written for an immediate purpose. (Into this category, for example, falls the *Concerto Grosso*.) A number of these works, again, like some of his ballet scores, are firmly based on folksong material. Indeed, the first of his extant works for orchestra is the first of the three *Norfolk Rhapsodies*, developed from his discoveries at King's Lynn. (A *Bucolic Suite* and a *Serenade*, written earlier, which had pleased Stanford, were rejected.) The scoring and structure of the first *Norfolk Rhapsody* (the other two were destroyed later) are not strikingly original; the work is neither better nor worse constructed than Dvořák's *Slavonic Rhapsodies*. What was original in the work, which received its first performance in London in 1906, was that here was a composer working up tunes which he had collected himself among the people— a thing virtually unheard of in early twentieth-century England. Some idea of Vaughan Williams's future line of development is betrayed by *In the Fen Country*, originally written in 1904 and revised in 1905, 1907 and 1935. Here the themes themselves are original, though modelled on folk-tunes. Again there is little that foreshadows the great composer who was to come; the craftsmanship is competent, the orchestration rather heavy, the form conventional, the harmonic treatment unambitious.

The first of the truly characteristic orchestral works remains one ot the greatest of all his works, yet there is hardly a chord in it that could not be found in a classical work. The *Fantasia on a Theme by Thomas Tallis* for double string orchestra and string quartet is massive, spacious, powerful and ruminative. Yet for all its mass and power it is intimate and possesses a gentle richness which sometimes blossoms into a lyric ardour. The huge climax of the movement, before it settles down into the serene recapitulation, is not emotional or erotic but weighty and reflective; there are no sudden hammer-strokes but a steady growth of relentless pressure. The texture throughout is rich but never thick, the lyricism warm but never sticky. The work's originality consists neither in its melodic structure nor in its freedom of rhythm, and certainly not in its use of unconventional harmony, but in the mentality which gave rise to it, that of a quietly confident mind which combined the ardent devoutness of Bruckner with the stern sense of purpose and controlled will-power of Beethoven. There is no sense of struggle or conflict (and hence no dramatic sonata-form layout, as the structure is entirely monothematic) but rather a concentrated discussion of various aspects of one thought which, like the tributary streams of a river, flow together into a giant flood of sound whose course is inevitable and irresistible. It is typical of the work that its supreme climax is partly based on a phrase which has developed out of the theme without being a part of the original theme itself. The interplay of third and fifth is part of both the melodic and the harmonic scheme of development. Thus the theme itself starts with a jump of a minor third, which becomes a fifth in the second phrase. Vaughan Williams takes the fifth, and expands it later to an octave. Similarly in the introductory passage fragments of the theme are heard which resolve on to an open fifth; when the passage is restated at the end of the work they resolve on to a major triad—a harmonic device as simple, and as subtle, as that used by Beethoven at the opening of the ninth Symphony, when the bassoon sideslips into D from the violins' open fifth. Here the strings have been holding a chord of F minor and resolve quietly into G major; the effect is like a shaft of golden sunlight in the aisles of a great cathedral:

This great work makes an immediate appeal, largely because of the nobility of Tallis's own theme; yet the more closely one listens to it, the more one becomes captivated by the ingenuity and inevitability of the manner in which Vaughan Williams develops it, and the variety and subtlety of the scoring. Here is something as old as the soil of England itself, yet for ever fresh and original. Why is it that the time-worn device of an exceedingly loud chord followed by a very soft echo seems so utterly new in this work? Or that the use of *pizzicato* cellos and double-basses under a high held note in the violins sounds so dramatic a trick—as if it had never been thought of before? In the words of the schoolboy quoted by Vaughan Williams in his essay on Beethoven's ninth Symphony: 'I could have written all that Shake-speare stuff myself if only I'd thought of it.' [1]

The other extended work for string orchestra the *Partita* (originally a double trio)—also laid out for two contrasting and unequal bodies—is much more of a lightweight. Neither orchestra has second violins, and the two orchestras are used much more as backgrounds to one another than as contrasting bodies, which is the case in the *Tallis Fantasia*. Moreover, where the one is dignified, serious and sublime, the other is genial, for the most part light, and earthy. It contains a whirring scherzo and a syncopated intermezzo entitled 'Homage to Henry Hall', both cast in moods that would have been quite out of place in the earlier work, and a finale rhythmically built up from a scrap of theme recalling the 'Hoy-da!' expostulations from the finale of *Five Tudor Portraits*, though perhaps in a less sardonic and more lyrical vein.

A problem not merely textural but also technical was set by the commission of the Rural Music School to write a *concerto grosso*. Some of the instrumentalists were defined by the composer as those 'who prefer to use only open strings'; another group was capable of more advanced playing, and a third of more difficult work still. The *Concerto Grosso* gives the lie to those who believe that Vaughan Williams was technically a clumsy amateur; like Benjamin Britten, he knew how to introduce material playable by the most elementary

[1] *Some Thoughts on Beethoven's Choral Symphony* (1953), p. 34.

members of a group of musicians which was both grateful to play and served a useful thematic purpose in the work in which it occurs. It is a jolly work, full of broad, simple humour (in the *Burlesca ostinata* and the scherzo), of vigour (in the opening movement and finale) and fresh warmth (in the *Sarabande*).

The *English Folk Song Suite* and *The Running Set* are ingenious and successful arrangements of folksong material; *Five Variants of Dives and Lazarus* is a cross between a folksong arrangement and an original composition—a meditation on folk-material which is more shapely and more 'learned' than a rhapsody, reaching up, like the *Tallis Fantasia*, to a big, firm climax, dying away again to a remote hushed ending, serene but not sublime. Each variant gives a different section of the orchestra (strings and harp) a chance to enjoy itself, and in all of them the composer enjoys his haunting theme.

CHAPTER XIII

THE SYMPHONIES WITH NAMES

JUST AS Vaughan Williams's first orchestral works are of the 'fantasia' kind, so his symphonies are not formally conventional. This does not mean, however, either that they are entirely formless or that their composer misunderstood the meaning of symphonic form. By a combination of conscious thought and unconscious instinct he felt his way towards a kind of symphonic form which is quite different from that of the eighteenth- or nineteenth-century symphony yet in many respects as satisfying a design. The sonata plan is gradually and carefully modified until, by the first movement of the eighth Symphony, it has all but developed into something entirely different, yet the form is still organic. The themes do branch off, develop and recombine.

When Vaughan Williams had settled on his own particular personal idiom—which did not happen until he was nearly forty years of age—he realized that the type of theme which inspired him could not be pressed into the conventional symphonic mould, which depended on the balance of keys between, and the contrast of, groups of material, each of which displayed some individual melodic or rhythmic turn. This in turn hinged upon the use of the major-minor key system and the acceptance of certain rhythmic and harmonic devices within it. Modal themes do not readily fit into a pattern dependent on tonic and dominant in contrast and in collaboration— and the rhythmic vagaries of the English folksong are difficult to strait-jacket; after the *London Symphony* he never made the mistake of trying to make them fit into the conventional form. Instead, he built up his large-scale movements, as has already been said in a previous chapter, in a manner analagous to the way in which some English folksong melodies blossom from an initial motif. The forms he created, in fact, were determined by the structure of his melodies and not based on any tonal centres leading to harmonic experiments and key-contrasts. This is only what might be expected from a composer whose strength lay in his melodic gift, and whose attitude to form was always that form and style were something alive, not a mass of rules and formulae to be culled from textbooks.

The variety of mood in the nine symphonies is impressive; no one could possibly accuse him of having written the same symphony nine times over. Perhaps a glance at the scherzos shows this better than anything. In the *Sea Symphony* the scherzo is robust and hearty; in the *London Symphony* it is impressionistic and colourful; in the *Pastoral* it is heavily mysterious and boisterous, but it finally vanishes like a will-o'-the-wisp. In the scherzo of the fourth Symphony sardonic humour and high-pressure emotional steam burst forth abruptly and almost maliciously when they can; in the fifth the will-o'-the-wisp coda of the *Pastoral* is raised to the *n*th power of subtlety and developed into a complete movement. In the sixth the atmosphere is strained, flushed and hectic; in the *Antartica* elusive and pictorial by turns; in the eighth there is wit and gaiety—somewhat braggartly and vulgarly whimsical in its manner of expression. The scherzo of the ninth has something of the sneering insolence of the fourth but is rather less forceful in its manner.

It is not necessary for a composer to write for a large orchestra or for a work to last an hour in order to create big music; Beethoven's Quartet, Op. 95, is unquestionably a big work, yet it lasts little more than a quarter of an hour and employs just four players. But it is unquestionably Vaughan Williams's intention in most of his symphonies to write big music, and he realizes his intentions. The *Sea Symphony* takes up where *Toward the Unknown Region* left off; whereas the former work resolved a mysterious beginning into a bold and confident ending, the latter proclaims its scale and comprehensiveness with its very opening bars. The sudden leap from a chord of B♭ minor to D major has the effect of an enormous curtain being swept majestically aside: 'Behold the sea itself!' After this magnificent rhetorical gesture the waves immediately roll back, as it were. In the text of the poems chosen the world is Whitman's oyster; he seeks the secret of the Universe in the deep waters. The choice of poet and poems was deliberate. Vaughan Williams knew where he was going; if he was unsure of anything, it was how to get there. One can say without offence that this work is largely rhetoric—magnificent, powerful and determined rhetoric evolved by a man whose confidence in his message was sure, not the rodomontade of the boaster thumping his tub. As Parry wrote, it is 'big stuff' indeed. The texture is kept firm and clear and strong by a good deal of doubling at the octave in the voice parts; the melodies are powerful and diatonic, the scoring full and glowingly opulent. On occasion there is a dash of the shanty—as Dr Percy Young points out, one theme in the first movement resembles *Tarry Trowsers*, and *The Golden Vanity* and *The Bold Princess Royal* are quoted in the scherzo. (The text of the latter can hardly have been included in the allusion; it refers to the gallant crew of a ship who, attacked by pirates, made off and congratulated themselves on their escape afterwards.) The influence of Parry is perhaps evident in the slowly and majestically descending scale-figures in the bass which occur on a number of occasions, and in the outline of some of the themes: this, for example:

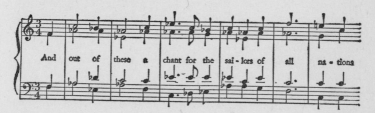

in the second main theme of the slow movement, which swells up into a gripping climax for the voices alone to the words:

> This vast similitude spans them
> And always has spanned
> And shall forever span them
> And shall compactly hold and enclose them.

to which the orchestra adds a kind of comment in octaves, based
on this phrase:

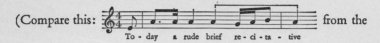

(Compare this: ... from the

To - day   a rude brief   re - ci - ta - tive

first movement.) But the real size of the work, and the nature of its
composer, is actually revealed only in the last pages. After a huge
climax on the words 'Steer for the deep waters only', somewhat like
the valedictory paean at the end of Part I of *The Dream of Gerontius*, it
is not the grandeur of the impression that is left with us; the towering
structure vanishes, and opens out a new, mysterious vista beyond—
Molto adagio e molto tranquillo. This is the first of Vaughan
Williams's symphonic epilogues; here is no nostalgic looking back
with regret, but a glance forward towards, even if not into, a new
unknown region.

The *London Symphony* was one of the composer's favourite works; it
is indeed lovable. It is packed with attractive melodic ideas—so many
are there, in fact, that one is reminded of Sullivan's good-natured
grumble on seeing an exercise by Ethel Smyth: 'An artist is supposed
to make a penny do the work of a shilling, and here you go chucking
sovereigns away for nothing.' The formal problem in the *Sea Symphony*
lay in reconciling the sprawling lyric rhapsodizing of Whitman with
at any rate something resembling orthodox sonata form, and the
introduction of two soloists in addition to a chorus did not greatly
complicate matters, for it seems that Vaughan Williams (like Sullivan,
prompted by Gilbert) felt that if a thing was worth saying it was worth
saying twice. Thus some important themes in the *Sea Symphony* are
given out by the soloist and taken up by the chorus immediately
afterwards. In the *London Symphony*, however, the problem is quite
different. It was the problem faced by Dvořák and Tchaikovsky,
and, like them, Vaughan Williams did not entirely succeed in
solving it. It was how to adapt 'folk-like' material to symphonic
form.

A lot of nonsense has been written about the fact that the country-man Vaughan Williams was perhaps not in his element in London. Quite apart from the fact that he lived there for much of his life, and that he died there, it should not be forgotten that his grandfather, his father and a number of his uncles were Londoners by birth. Neither the fact that he was born in a west-country vicarage, nor the fact that his father was born in London, has the remotest bearing on the success or failure of the *London Symphony* as a piece of music. Any failings it may possess are due to the composer's imagination, not to his pedigree. And those failings are structural, not programmatic or illustrative. Perhaps one of the troubles with the symphony—its diffuseness—derives from the fact that it was originally intended as a kind of tone-poem, and that material which started by being program-matic did not quite fit together well when the programme was suppressed. Yet the mosaic of themes which constitutes the main part of the first movement has the air of sketchy views of fascinating streets and people seen perhaps from a fleeting train.

The work begins with a phrase based on a rising fourth, starting deep down in the lower strings, which works its way upwards into a shadowy tune, swelling up into a crescendo which is usually cut short by a comma. After an allusion to the chimes of Big Ben the Allegro risoluto begins. Every listener can decide for himself which aspect of London inspires each of the numerous thematic fragments which the composer fits together in the long exposition; the main impression left is that, whether like an impatient cabby:

or a group of sailors singing a shanty:

or a cockney street-urchin whistling:

they are all busy and all in a very great hurry. This profusion of tunes is by no means complete with the end of the exposition; as in Elgar's E flat Symphony there is an episode containing new and more reflective material in the working-out. The 'shanty' becomes a new, lyrical

theme on the flute:

and a theme previously hinted at in the exposition expands into a self-contained episode. Scored for harp and string quartet, it is another example of Vaughan Williams's ability to make a quiet passage the culmination of a movement. The restatement begins quietly and is more compressed than the exposition, finally bursting out in a grand climax in which one of the themes combines with itself in augmentation (a procedure which Brahms used sometimes—notably in the *German Requiem*). Throughout the movement the emphasis is mainly melodic; harmony and harmonic subtleties are secondary. There is indeed one passage in the introduction where a chord of the dominant seventh arises out of the movement of the parts. It is not resolved in the conventional manner; the parts simply continue on their way, thus foreshadowing a practice used much more consistently in the next symphony. The chord is an incident in a progression of themes, not a pivot for the harmony and key-relationships arising out of them.

The slow movement (Lento) begins with a series of chords in the strings, spread out over a huge span, into which is projected a cor anglais solo, vaguely similar in outline to *I will give my love an apple*. The contrast after the glittering end of the first movement is striking—but no more striking than the effect of some of London's quiet spaces, often only a few minutes from her busiest streets. The tune is played over again by the strings in unison. A feature of the way the secondary themes develop in this movement is the manner in which solo instruments are allowed to meditate on them in imitation, each soloist breaking off in turn and leaving the field to the newcomer. This kind of texture derives ultimately from the old fantasy type of composition and became an important constituent of Vaughan Williams's orchestral style later on. This is a gentle intimate movement, for all its massive size, and a reflective one, for all its quotation of the lavender-seller's street-cry on the clarinet, and its odd, episodic foreshadowing of the march movement from *Flos Campi*, and it ends mysteriously.

In the scherzo, fragments of theme loom out of a mist: this 'Nocturne', as the composer entitles it, is like one of Whistler's rather than one of Chopin's. As in the first movement, there is a profusion of themes. Some of them consist of a head and a tail which are interchanged with the heads and tails of other themes, a procedure which was developed much further in the *Pastoral Symphony*. The themes whisk by with much less bustle than in the first movement; the whole scene is softer and more nebulous. In the trio the composer who advocated that musicians should draw their inspiration from life around them calls upon cockney mouth-organists to inspire him. The passage in which the orchestra is called upon to evoke the sound of the street barrel-organ shows scoring of the most imaginative order. The restatement is shorter and firmer than the beginning, and the coda is reflective.

The impassioned cry that opens the finale soon leads to a solemn, Parryesque march. Discipline and solemnity seek now to impose order on the exuberance and variety of the first three movements. The march, repeated with different scoring as if for emphasis, leads into a hectic Allegro which presages the dance of Death, Famine and Pestilence in *Job* without being nearly so macabre in its effect. The style here is sometimes curious; there is an odd, and not wholly satisfactory, blend of chromatic filling-out with modal and pentatonic melodies when the music finally builds up to a majestic Brucknerian climax after the restatement. But, as in the *Sea Symphony*, the last word is a quietly spoken epilogue and not a grandiose peroration. The chimes of Big Ben are heard again; this time they do not build up to a big crash but die into a reflective ending, similar to the introduction to the first movement, though leading away this time into nothing, instead of building up our expectation; there is no nostalgic brooding over what has gone before. The grandiose element thus predominates for once in the finale—yet even there, when the excitement is at its peak, the ceremonial brilliance must vanish, though not into the light of common day, but into the mists out of which it rose.

The *Pastoral Symphony* has always been a stumbling-block for many listeners. It has been criticized for overstepping the border between consistency and monotony, for being so English that foreigners cannot appreciate it, for being 'like a cow looking over a gate'. It is quite the most difficult of Vaughan Williams's symphonies to come to terms with. (Hence the extensive 'cueing', so that it may be performed by a normal-sized orchestra.) The *Sea Symphony* raised its huge curtain with a swift and rhetorical gesture; in the *London Symphony* the mist clears haltingly but definitely to reveal the busy activity of the great city; here the veil is lifted gently and unobtrusively. It is this work which consistently displays Vaughan Williams's mature characteristic style for the first time in a symphonic work. Even when the scoring is airy and brilliant—as it is, for example, in the coda of the scherzo—it does not glitter; the atmosphere it creates is somewhat uncanny and very mysterious. Moreover, the rhythmic clashes in the parts do not generate movement; the parts simply collide and go pensively on their way. It is an interesting fact that the full orchestra, for all its size, is not used once in the first two movements; the first time that all the players are employed together is five bars after letter E in the third movement.

In most modern music, and in the fourth Symphony, semitonal dissonances are 'rubbed in', as it were, as a result of the scoring, the rhythm or the dynamics. In classical symphonies they were usually either dramatic in effect or else a passing chord between two concords. Here they are neither. Quietly, unostentatiously, almost absent-mindedly, they slip into and out of the texture, taking one another nonchalantly for granted. An example of this is the A♮ in the horn solo at the beginning of the second movement against the A♭ in the F minor chord held by the strings. The work is a combination of fresco and impressionism, executed as it were in pastel colours. At about the same time as it was written, Rilke was writing his *Sonnets to Orpheus*, in which the lines occur:

> O Orpheus singt!
> O hoher Baum im Ohr!

Vaughan Williams is exactly fulfilling the role of Rilke's Orpheus in this work.

The themes sprout from one another ('unfold' would perhaps be a better word) in a manner which shows how much further Vaughan Williams had now progressed in developing a new method of sym-phonic construction from his own idiom. Not only the themes, indeed, but the tone-colour strands too. An example of this occurs at the very beginning with the change in the flowing opening chords from flutes to clarinets. Later on in the movement (round about letter Q) these chords form the bass of the harmony for the first time. No theme, no phrase even, has a dominant function; each in turn makes its appearance and then slips quietly in among its neighbours. This is not rhetorical music, but meditative; and a meditative first movement in a symphony scored for a large orchestra was something quite new. The opening theme:

expands, during the course of the movement to:

and is allowed to say the last word in a movement where the themes are more like gentle tributaries to a large river than characters in a dramatic action. All the same the themes are stated, developed and restated.

The quietly undulating themes of the slow movement are subtly differentiated on their various appearances by varying the harmonies behind them. There are two main instances of this; when the first theme of the movement is heard on the horn it is backed simply by a chord of F minor; when, however, it recurs, the texture is like this:

The most arresting feature of this movement is the pair of cadenzas for natural trumpet and natural horn respectively. The first time, on the trumpet in E♭, it is marked *pp*, and swells up into a passage on the strings which has the effect of a bound giant trying to escape. The second time, *p* on the horn, at the end of the movement, it is one melodic thread with a counterpoint (a variant of the main theme) on the clarinet, which flows independently round it, the background being provided by a very slow-motion progression of common chords in a whole-tone scale—F, E♭, D♭, C♭—on the strings. This dies away, leaving the horn exposed on a high C♮—a typical 'fourth Symphony' dissonance, only we do not notice it as such—which dissolves into a flowing chordal passage on the violins. As with the first movement, the end is a dwindling *pianissimo*.

Constant Lambert once remarked that Vaughan Williams's *Sea Symphony* was about human reactions to the sea, rather than being a seascape itself. It is possible that human figures appear on the landscape in the third movement of the *Pastoral Symphony*, but more likely that the cosmic remoteness of the earlier movements takes more urgent rhythmic shape; surely this is a dance of the elements rather than of human figures. These are not Beethoven's peasants making merry, nor even their English cousins. Only the trumpet tune in what corresponds to the trio section seems to have something human about

it. And what are we to make of the Arielesque coda? After the
wordless unbarred melisma of the soprano voice at the beginning of
the finale there seems to be an attempt to gather the various strands
together, but it is the soprano's theme which forms the material for the
most impassioned climax of the movement—declaimed in octaves by
most of the orchestra with no accompaniment—and it is the same
theme which closes the movement, this time, not over a distant drum
roll, but beneath a high sustained violin A. There is more conven,
tional excitement in this movement—tremolos, agitated phrases like
birds calling to their mates before a storm—but the excitement is
again not rhetorical, nor does it lead to a dramatic climax. It is merely
a ruffling of the surface of a vast panorama.

Some enterprising film producer, acting on a suggestion of Vaughan
Williams's which has already been quoted, might well build a film
round the music of the *Pastoral Symphony* one day. The last of the
named symphonies, the *Sinfonia antartica*, was first performed thirty
years later than the *Pastoral*, and was developed out of music originally
written for a film which portrayed human heroism set against an
inhuman natural background. If the *Pastoral* is landscape without
figures, then this is landscape versus figures. And the landscape, the
death-force, as it were, overcomes the figures.

Like the *Pastoral*, the work is scored for a very large orchestra,
including xylophone, glockenspiel, harp, piano, vibraphone, gongs
and organ. There is also a wind-machine, which aroused some unfavourable comment from critics. Prigs who object to Beethoven
making a clarinet imitate a cuckoo in a symphonic slow movement
would also no doubt object to Vaughan Williams's onomatopoeia
here. There is more *Malerei* in this work, more motion, activity and
more light relief; a version of Peter Warlock's fatuous remark about
the *Pastoral* being like a cow looking over a gate would be less out of
place here, simply because whales and penguins (or at any rate the
music associated with them in the film) are to be found in this symphony. As with the Antarctic itself, the most important part of the
work is its centre—the huge, inhuman sonority of the third movement,
—'Landscape'. Here the remoteness which pervaded so much of the
Pastoral Symphony becomes not merely impersonal but hostile; the

infinite weight of this music has no parallel, except possibly Holst's Saturn, the Bringer of Old Age. It is a weight which crushes and numbs, not one which sweeps the listener off his feet. The core of this movement is the fearsome crash of the organ—as at that moment in *Job* when the hero rounds on his God and curses the day he was born.

The slow movement is flanked by two lighter ones—a scherzo, complete with penguins and whales—and an intermezzo. The themes of the two outermost movements are to some extent interrelated. Each movement is headed by a quotation, and none of them is in orthodox sonata form. The Prelude, prefaced by a quotation from Shelley's *Prometheus Unbound*, is programmatic and pictorial; as in a tonepoem, most of the themes have some extramusical association. The main theme was originally the title music to the film; the four subsidiary themes which form the middle section of the movement represent the howling wilderness, the ice, fog and the unknown respectively. A feature of the movement is the imaginative use of sonorities, whether of the voices or of the instruments. At the appearance of the ice, for example, the piano plays broken chords, the celesta has runs, and the glockenspiel and vibraphone add chords. Both in this symphony and its successor Vaughan Williams was stimulated by remarkable new tonecolours available to the composer with the development of new percussion instruments, and at the age of nearly eighty he experimented successfully with them. Yet in a symphony it is the development of the themes, the total design of the complete work, which are the important factors, not the new sonorities the composer invents.

The first movement displays the backcloth; the second brings not a scenic, but a living element into the picture. It is prefaced by a quotation from Psalm 104, and its mood is that of playful wonderment; the details are simple to follow, and the music mostly light in character; it dies away in a mysterious chord formed of an amalgam of the common chords of B♭ minor and F♯ minor. The third movement is an extension of the procedure adopted by Holst in *Neptune* and by Vaughan Williams himself in the finale of the E minor Symphony— an attempt to portray the infinitely remote in terms of orchestral sonority. Added to it we have the overpowering sense of oppressive and insuperable difficulty, the more terrifying because it is cold and passively immobile. Music cannot be immobile, since it moves through time, but this music has the effect of portraying frozen time as well as frozen space. The themes in the *Pastoral Symphony* move but slowly; but they do move, however gentle their motion and ponderous their gait. Here nothing moves at all; we are in a timeless world, not the serene timelessness of the *Heiliger Dankgesang*, but a leaden, lifeless timelessness. The aimlessness of any attempt to overcome it is shown by the organ crash already mentioned—emphasizing the hopelessness of challenging Nature in her own domain.

The fourth movement, by contrast, is warmer and lyrical, tinged a little with regret and longing—which is unusual in Vaughan Williams. The heading is from Donne:

> Love, all alike, no season knows, or clime,
> Nor hours, days, months, which are the rags of time.

After the chill numbness of the 'Landscape' movement, the warmth of human devotion and unselfishness (some of the music was originally written for Oates's departure scene in the film) come as a welcome relief. This movement is less remote, and more orthodox in character than the others. The last movement is the tragic outcome of all its predecessors; we know what the end will be, since we have already seen the power of the passive adversary and the tragedy is that heroism and warmth must succumb to passive lifelessness. Yet the challenge is made, and to the tune of a resolute march the hero joins battle with his enemy, after the preliminary fanfare is thrown across the remarkable tremolo for almost the entire orchestra—including the piano. The theme of the march is derived from the main theme of the Prelude; from time to time it is interrupted, and eventually it is overcome by a ponderous triplet figure (in the film this music represented the blizzard that finally destroyed the Scott expedition). After this the march is resumed, merging into the atmospheric music of the Prelude, and finally dissolving into its original shape as the opening theme of that movement. From then onwards the cruel forces of Nature—portrayed by the wordless voices and wind-machine—dominate the score, and the music dies away to an E♭, and then silence.

The four symphonies discussed here are not programmatic in the strict sense of the term, except for the *Antartica*; they aim at creating a mood rather than a picture with details. Such details as may be pictorial or programmatic are usually a starting-point for musical dis-cussion rather than a musical end in themselves (again the *Antartica* is an exception). Yet the differences between them are enormous; the varying use to which Vaughan Williams puts the *pianissimo* epilogues which close all four would alone show this. Only in one case—the *Antartica*—is this epilogue disquieting; it is so deliberately, because the outcome of the work is not merely remote but also cruel. It does not peer into unknown regions; it is as flat and featureless as the dead landscape which inspired the whole symphony. In the other cases the function of the epilogue is to sum up and at the same time to point forward. The *Pastoral* could not possibly end in any other way, and the ending has the inevitability of a Racine denouement. In the *London Symphony* and the *Sea Symphony* the epilogues show the originality of the composer's mind in being able to conclude a large work by summarizing it and yet pointing beyond it at the same time. That power is even more evident in those symphonies which bear no titles but the keys in which they are said to be written.

CHAPTER XIV

THE SYMPHONIES WITH NUMBERS

VAUGHAN WILLIAMS himself did not number his symphonies; he simply designated them by a name or with a key-signature. Since, however, two of them are in the same key—E minor—it is convenient to refer to them by the numbers which critics have attached to them.

The Symphony in F minor—the fourth—was the first of the series not to have a descriptive title attached to it. It was also the first not to contain any passages for solo violin. It was the first which did not end with a *pianissimo* epilogue. Coming as it did after the *Pastoral*, its brusqueness was even more of a shock. Yet on closer inspection there are points of similarity which indicate that both works are recognizably from the same artist. Whereas in the *Pastoral* every move is slow and ponderous, in the fourth the giant strides are relentless and swift. What is common to both, however, is the unmistakable size of the stride. The *Pastoral* ruminates calmly and in remote mystery over huge issues; the fourth impatiently hurls all obstacles out of the way, but in neither case is there any doubt of the scale of things. Moreover, the torrent of rage which bursts forth in the later work is just as much a cosmic rage as the calm of the earlier is a cosmic calm. This is no personal, subjective anguish, yet the utterance of it is unmistakably individual. In the *Pastoral* very little 'happens' in the conventional sense; in the fourth, things 'happen' all the time—they never stop happening—yet, as in the one case the themes blossom and interchange and regroup themselves, so in the other, each explosion hurls forth, not a mass of dead fragments, but a chain reaction of themes, each closely related to the others. This is one of the tightest musical arguments of all time—and it goes right round in a circle; the net result is 'This is where I came in.'

Almost every significant theme in the work can be traced to one or other of the two formulas: and one of which chases its own tail while the other shoots up like a rocket. The first of the two is in itself a by-product of the very first theme of the work; and this theme itself is played in canon at a bar's interval. As in the *Sea Symphony*, what is worth saying once is worth saying twice—but the manner of speech is tauter and more intensive, less expansive and spacious. The flow of the themes is uneven. Very short ones expand, run up against some obstacle, try to push their way round and then bludgeon through. This goes on until a series of throbbing chords on the horns introduce a passionate lyrical theme which is an expanded variant of the precipitant first theme of all. This long-limbed melody descends into the bass and eventually collapses into its own first three notes, which form into an ostinato background to a very grim theme which is as near horizontal in shape as a theme can be, a bitter blossom from the stem of our first example tugging away in an attempt to break loose from the F# on which it starts. It is punctuated from time to time by a motif on the brass which derives from the first three notes of the lyrical theme. The scoring of much of this symphony is so laid out that the listener gets the impression that there is nothing in the orchestra save brass and strings—though in fact it is scored for the usual full orchestra with triple wood-wind and four percussion players. There are no harps. There is hardly any respite in the volcanic outpouring of vehement music until the beginning of what 'the official analyst' (a favourite butt of Vaughan Williams's scorn) would call the working-out, when the strings start up a tense and mysterious tremolo based on the motif which chases its own tail. It swells up into a galumphing dialogue. Shortly afterwards the piled-up fourths of the other guiding motif lead back to the reprise; the impact of the storm is doubled by the formal treatment—the lyrical theme appears in canon with itself. The great surprise, however, occurs when the very grim theme reappears, quietly whispered—though this is an exhausted rather than a serene calm.

The wood-wind, who have been hard at work in the first movement, but not able to show off their characteristic timbres, are allowed to do so in the second, which begins with more piled-up fourths, out of which a figure is generated; it turns out to be an important part of the main theme of the movement, and is used in augmentation in the basses as a kind of ostinato phrase: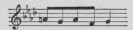

The scoring is hereabouts very bare; there is a great gap between the mournful tune and the *pizzicato* accompaniment. That accompaniment is very important—it is one of Vaughan Williams's striding basses, a terrible perversion of the strong and confident bass of such a tune as *Sine Nomine*. Though the nature of this movement is considerably less brusque than that of the first, it is still dominated by a relentless tension, which culminates in yet another piling-up of fourths on the heavy brass, against which a phrase taken from the

second main theme of the movement:

batters in the strings. Such moments of repose as there are are relegated to cadence themes, imitative passages or the gradual dissolution of the music towards the end of the movement, held together only by our first example on the heavy brass, in a menacing whisper, and as a group of long-held chords.

The scherzo bursts like a bomb on the startled hearer. The upward leap of the theme is oddly similar to the sinister opening theme of the third movement of Beethoven's fifth, but it is plainly a variant of the second of our basic formulas. In no time it has thrust its way through two and a half octaves before its irresistible force meets an immovable object in the shape of No. 1, which immediately works itself up into an ostinato against which the scherzo-theme hurls itself in varying guises. Finding itself blocked, it kicks out with a figure whose

rhythm: is to become important

later, and a new theme asserts itself, starting like a distant cousin to one of the themes in *Till Eulenspiegel* but soon developing a will of its own, complete with syncopations and suspensions. The atmosphere, now less tense, becomes grotesque with the trio—an angular fugato with a theme derived ultimately from No. 2. As it lurches upward through the orchestra, its grotesqueness subsides into a comic caper on the piccolo, with violin accompaniment. This does not last long, and the scherzo explodes on us again with very little warning. Soon the rhythm quoted above is heard in the timpani and string basses, and No. 1 is noted lurking in the background. There is a quick *crescendo*, the rhythm is intensified, and the finale is upon us—a strident march, whose main theme is, according to the composer, a reincarnation of a lyrical cadence-theme from the second movement.

All the main themes in the finale are cousins to one or other of the motto-motives—a prominent feature of each is either a dropping semitone or a jump of a fourth. The second subject sounds like a perverted folk-tune; Frank Howes aptly describes it as 'a swaggering, aggressive tune, such as some simple-hearted pirate might hiss between his teeth'.[1] The climax of the movement, however (formally easy to follow; it is a regular sonata movement), is once again a quiet passage, somewhat like the coda of the first movement. Here, in fact, is what ought to be the usual visionary coda, but it is curtly dismissed. The tension is stepped up in the restatement, and reaches its peak in the electrifying epilogue, which begins as a fugato on No. 1 and throws both the main themes of the finale in as counter-subjects for good measure, casting a new and even more sinister light on them. When the tension has become almost intolerable, the final *coup de grâce* is delivered by a completely unexpected reference to the opening of the first movement. We have just time to realize that all that has gone before can be directly related to that cataclysm, when the music simply stops. 'There,' Vaughan Williams seems to say: 'that's all I have to say about that. Take it or leave it.'

Just over eight years separated the first performance of the F minor Symphony from the D major, and once again the climate is quite different. What is it about horns with a string background that sounds so magically serene? Brahms's second, Bruckner's fourth and Vaughan Williams's fifth all open in a radiant calm which is the direct result of this manner of scoring. This symphony borrows themes from *The Pilgrim's Progress*, it is true, but it develops them according to the composer's symphonic formula. It is scored for a much smaller orchestra than any of the earlier ones (double wood-wind, only two

---

[1] *The Music of Ralph Vaughan Williams* (1954), p. 39.

horns, no tuba, no percussion and no harps), and seems at a first hearing to hark back to the *Pastoral*. At a first hearing, let us repeat, for a closer inspection shows it to be quite different.

The very opening is one of Vaughan Williams's most striking examples of a new meaning given to an old device. The C of the cellos and basses proves to be a flattened seventh, when the horns enter with a theme definitely in D major. 'The music seems', Scott Goddard appositely writes, 'to have been going on underground beforehand.' The effect is magical, so arresting that we tend to overlook the fact that the three constituents of the first subject, out of which the whole movement blossoms, are presented practically simultaneously. Most of the opening *moderato* section of this movement grows gently and

organically from the opening horn-call: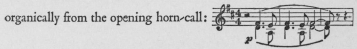

from the cello and bass background to it:

and from the violins' answer:

Later on, the music drops a semitone in pitch and a major third in tonality—the serenity becomes clouded over, as it were. After a little this happens again, and once the Allegro starts, the main theme of which is related to the cello figure, this device becomes

the germ of a theme: It is possible that

this simple but effective formula was consciously or unconsciously 'cribbed' from the opening of the working-out section of Beethoven's ninth Symphony. A feature of this whole movement is the effective use of juxtaposed keys to throw light or darkness on to a passage. Here, instead of placing chords against one another, the composer places whole blocks of music. Within the framework of his medium-sized orchestra he achieves considerable subtleties of texture but reserves the most agitated part of the Allegro for a passage in octaves on the strings. Then the introduction reappears, and mounts to a final climax very like the 'Alleluia' from the tune *Sine Nomine*, not only in thematic outline, but in the underlying harmony as well:

Fifth Symphony:

Sine Nomine:

As we have now grown to expect, the majestic climax, complete with winding, glowing inner parts *à la* Parry or Elgar, yet in some peculiar way less opulent than either, dies away to a quiet close.

The scherzo flits past us like some ghostly vision. It opens with the muted strings passing one another a theme based on rising fourths, but the motif is used in a much more delicate manner than it was in the fourth Symphony; there are a number of themes of varying shape and length (implied rather than stated, for this is a rather mysterious movement), which follow one another in rapid succession, and a considerable amount of cross-rhythm, 3-4 and 3-2 being inter-changed. The strings remain muted until the section which would correspond to the trio, and the scoring is throughout much more in the Franco-Russian tradition of delicate brilliance than is often the case in Vaughan Williams's symphonic movements. Indeed, Ravel might well have envied the scoring that his pupil produced here; most of the instruments are kept busy, yet the spacing and the part-writing ensure that the texture is feathery and buoyant. The trio consists of a kind of chorale in the brass, interspersed with champings in the strings, and there is a bipartite coda, where a little phrase of

one of the scherzo themes:

is altered and expanded into a theme in its own right:

before the original metre and themes are resumed and the movement vanishes like a will-o'-the-wisp.

There are some movements in music which give the listener the sense that time has ceased to exist and which seem to hover in space without any reference to life on earth. Their serenity and profound clarity mark out their composers as belonging to the few transcendently great masters of all time. The Romanza from this symphony is one of them; if ever music deserved the epithet 'heavenly' this does. As in the *London Symphony*, there is an introductory phrase of long, slow chords on the strings, spread over an immense span, against which is projected a cor anglais tune. The combination of an expressive melody and a simple yet subtle background of carefully juxtaposed triads (C major, A major, G minor, A major), the spaciousness and depth of the texture, each constituent element adds something to the effect of this wonderful music. It is not merely the opening that strikes the listener but the manner in which the movement unfolds, working up to an eloquent climax and containing noble solo passages for the oboe and the solo violin. This movement is like the *Lohengrin* prelude; but instead of the Holy Grail descending before our eyes we are ourselves transported to its lodging place. Of the function of its themes in *The Pilgrim's Progress* this is not the place to speak, and in any case it does not materially assist the enjoyment of this symphony to know which themes derive from that work, since the working-out here is conditioned, not by Bunyan's allegory, but by pure musical form.

The fourth movement is a passacaglia; not a passionate and energetic outpouring, such as the finale of Brahms's E minor Symphony, but a calm yet joyous meditation. An interesting formal feature is the quiet filling-in by the violins of the drop of a third in the opening bar of the ground bass when the mode is about to change from major to minor, thus transforming: [musical notation] into: [musical notation] which is in turn an important feature of the counter-melody which fits the ground (but not too conventionally closely; there is a series of consecutive sevenths). The central section of the movement quickens the tempo and enlivens the atmosphere; there is much imitation—one is reminded of a great cathedral choir lifting up their voices in happy exultation. The ending of the movement contains a reference to the opening of the symphony—this time not strange and placid but fervent and close at hand. Just as Beethoven, in the restatement of the first movement of the ninth Symphony, achieved a cataclysmic effect by repeating *ff* and in the major what had first been heard *pp* and indeterminate, so Vaughan Williams reveals the consuming power of a celestial vision instead of its distant glory. The vision fades, and we are left with a calm, glowing coda, based on the main themes of the finale.

If the spiritual climate of the fifth Symphony may be said to be akin to that of the grandiose and devout conceptions of Anton Bruckner, what are we to say of its successor? Here, at the age of seventy-five, was yet once more something utterly new. The violence of the fourth Symphony and the visionary quality of the fifth are here wedded, and the result is one of the most disquieting works in the symphonic repertory. Frank Howes relates it to war, and says that he received a sharp reproof from the composer for doing so.[1] In an earlier chapter I have pointed out similarities between it and Holst's *Planets*—particularly 'Mars' and 'Neptune'. It is difficult to discount the idea that some extra-musical idea was in the composer's mind while the work was germinating, yet its power and originality are in no way dependent

[1] Op. cit., p. 53.

on an external programme. It is a meditation,[1] not a musical Cook's tour of a battlefield.

The opening flourish has all the impatience of a squadron of cavalry champing at the bit, and the orchestra finally stampedes rather than settles down into the first main theme, an angular affair similar in outline to one of the themes in the first movement of the F minor symphony. There is a sudden abrupt change, and a curious fragmentary figure appears over an 'oom-pah' bass:

which is (temporarily) filled out by the violins into a sort of jolting

melody,  and then tries

itself over—with little confidence—in a more lyrical and more extended form:

nagging away at everyone until it blares forth on the trumpets and heavy brass, complete with Scotch snap. After this a very short and concentrated recapitulation of the first theme—in *stretto*, and without the opening flourishes—comes and goes, and we hear the second theme in the shape it has been seeking all through the movement. This is one of those moments of sudden revelation which are as difficult to describe as they are thrilling to experience. It is as if the listener has been climbing a vast mountain slope towards a distant and only intermittently visible peak, when suddenly the clouds are lifted and the summit is revealed in all its power and grandeur. The vision grows in strength, lifting itself up into the opening flourish almost casually, and the movement collapses on to a valedictory growl from the cellos and basses.

[1] For an exhaustive and penetrating analysis of this work *see* Deryck Cooke, *The Language of Music*, pp. 252–70.

As with Tchaikovsky's sixth Symphony, so with Vaughan Williams's; the second movement is not the slow movement proper, which is the finale. The main theme of this movement, Moderato, cannot make up its mind where its main stress should fall, nor can it decide whether C♭ or C♮ is the correct inflection in the key of B flat minor. The leap of an augmented fourth from the tonic of the first movement to that of the second (all the movements are connected to one another) is merely the first of a series of shocks which this move-ment is to inflict on us. The prominent rhythmic kick of the main theme is never quite sure whether it begins with its quaver: ♪♫ or with its semiquavers: ♫♩ The continual cross-rhythms give the effect of an insecure 3–4 rather than the nominal 4–4, a feature which this movement has in common with the first. The central feature of this movement is the passage where the trumpets and drums insistently repeat the latter version of this rhythm. In the Romanza from the fifth Symphony it seemed as though the music was eternal beyond space and time; here eternity appears as time everlasting. It seems interminable—and it is meant to. In his essay on Beethoven's Choral Symphony Vaughan Williams draws our attention to a remarkable passage in the coda of the first movement in these words:

But the light soon dies away. The theme is taken up by the strings in four octaves in the minor, first softly, then louder, while the wind continues a little semiquaver figure. As the strings get louder the wind figure gets drowned, but as they die down again it is found that the wind is still persistently playing its part—a wonderfully poetical conception which is, I am sure, intentional.[1]

One of his most effective 'cribs' occurs in this movement, where he does exactly the same thing. The strings, which have been playing an eerie, swirling figure in octaves, related to the main theme but without its little rhythmic kick, disappear behind the relentless trumpet and drum figure which is that kick itself. The trumpet fades a little, and we find with a sense of shock that the strings are actually restating the main theme, and that the trumpets' figure now fits into its place as part

[1] Op. cit., p. 25.

of that theme. The restatement is menacing and uneasy, and with a wail from the cor anglais, following a number of interrupted climaxes, leads into the scherzo.

The key relationship between the first movement and the Moderato was that of two keys an augmented fourth apart. The augmented fourth now becomes the main feature of the third movement's main theme, as can be seen from a quotation of it:

This theme is constructed simply by piling up an interval—a device we noted in the fourth Symphony. There, however, the piled-up fourths tended to congeal; here they shoot off into erratic motion the moment they are heard. The scoring is as congested and coarse as that of the fifth's scherzo was airy and delicate; the atmosphere is hysterical, and there is an undercurrent of somewhat swaggering vulgarity about much of the material. Not a 'nice' movement at all; but then this is not a 'nice' symphony. There is much activity in this movement, but it leads nowhere very inspiring, and the climax—a grandiose statement of a theme first heard on a saxophone—is as mocking and truculent as the theme heard at the end of the first movement is noble and dignified. After this little jabs of tone and a few snarls from the bass clarinet fade the scherzo into the finale.

This is an epilogue, the longest movement in the symphony and the unexpected yet inevitable solution to the problems set by the first three movements. It is *pianissimo* throughout—yet it is not peaceful. It is quiet without being serene, austere and full of eerie tension. The texture is attenuated, though the very large orchestra is kept quite active. Full chords are not rare in this movement, yet it gives the impression of being starved of them. All in all, it is a remarkable *tour de force*; a fugue without a theme, in which the composer broods over a limitless waste, so bleak and featureless that its impression is all the more profound on the thoughtful listener. This is not the numb, cold, polar landscape of the *Antartica*, but is rather comparable to a broad plain, strewn, as it were, with wreckage, dimly recognizable

161

yet never quite in focus. And it ends with a Vaughan Williams mannerism placed in a context which makes it quite remarkably fresh in its impact. Two chords, E minor and E♭ major, are sighed over and over again by the strings after all pretence at thematic treatment has vanished; the E♭ (= D♯, the leading note in the scale of E) is thus treated as the tonic of its own scale, not as the third of a dominant chord. And so we come to the end.

The eighth Symphony, in D minor, is the lightest and most charming of the nine. Vaughan Williams had already shown, in the *Antartica*, that tone-colour was a subject of absorbing interest to him, even when he was nearly eighty. The eighth, which was first performed in 1956, was written when he was over eighty-three, and is probably the most cleverly scored of all his symphonies. A certain amount of criticism has been levelled at the vigorous and noisy finale, yet if the composer's own direction Moderato maestoso is obeyed and the exuberance of the music is not allowed to get out of hand, it is shown to be a perfect foil to the other three movements. Unfortunately, with music as good-humoured and full-blooded as this, such a requirement is difficult for the conductor and his players to fulfil, and it is not their fault if they cannot manage it, but the composer's. There is something of *Hodie* in this work, in its jollity, but much else besides.

The opening movement is said by the composer to consist of 'Seven Variations in search of a Theme'. It can also—by dint of a little loose definition of terms—be analysed in terms of a sonata movement. It is the longest of the four movements of the work, and musically the most substantial. This reverses the process of the sixth Symphony (where, paradoxically, the most substantial movement—the finale—is thematically the most tenuous) and modifies that of the *Antartica*, which culminates in the slow movement, the third. It breaks new ground in its form and its sonorities. Vincent d'Indy had written his *Istar* in the form of variations culminating in the statement of a theme, and Vaughan Williams himself had incorporated an adaptation of this idea in the first movement of the sixth. Now he carries it a stage further; we never hear the theme at all, but a series of motifs which are used as the basis for variations. If Vaughan Williams had lived in late nineteenth-century Vienna he would have called down the wrath of the ill-mannered Wagnerians and the ill-mannered Brahmins on his head for submitting Wagnerian motifs to Brahmsian treatment.

The whole tone of this movement is light and a little whimsical; the scoring of the opening, with its vibraphone, trumpet and celesta, is deliciously cool. The three fragments of music which constitute the basis of the movement turn up in any number of guises, and are, as the second fragment indicates, 'sisters under the skin', like the

Colonel's Lady and Judy O'Grady. Thus this:

appears later as this:

and this:

The gently swaying secondary motif:

appears as this:

and this:

and the more opulent third motif:

turns up under this guise:

and this:

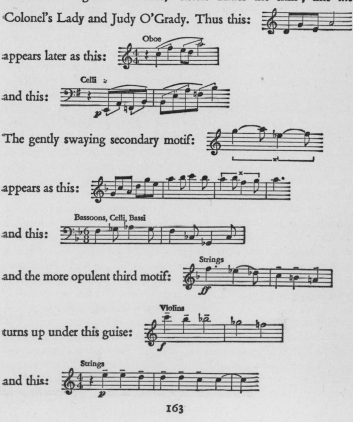

Tempo, mood and scoring all show a remarkable versatility, and if the movement does not expand in the accepted sense, it is intriguing to hear the composer fit his little fragments together in one of the most attractive musical mosaics he ever wrote. The movement ends quietly, after a grandiose climax, like a snake biting its own tail, with a reference to the opening bars.

The tiny scherzo, for wind instruments only, gives the impression of a Salvation Army group holding an un-temperance meeting. It is a witty, Prokofiev-like march, slightly raucous, mischievous and perhaps a little 'under the influence'. The bassoons have much to do, both in the main part of the movement and in the rather sly, lugubrious trio. Formally, the movement is interesting in that the recapitulation of the main music is telescoped into a short *stretto*, with themes piled one on top of each other (a procedure rather like that adopted in the epilogue of the fourth Symphony, but with immensely different results), and the movement bursts like a tiny balloon being popped. It is remarkable that a composer so venerable could write music so very young in spirit.

The cavatina which follows is for strings alone, and the scoring is not so remarkable. This movement, the most lyrical and melodic of the four, is at the same time the least interesting, simply because it tells us little that Vaughan Williams had not told us before in other works. It is more serious than its fellows, but is no more out of place than, for example, 'Nimrod' among the *Enigma* variations, for it is on the same miniature scale as the rest of them. For once in a way Vaughan Williams is not writing 'big' music; he is simply enjoying himself—perhaps looking back ruminatively over a happy life. The writing is grateful and the music agreeable to listen to, but it does not develop any new potentialities of string-writing; it is as if, having ventured into new regions in the first two movements, the composer celebrates his return by an account of more familiar surroundings. The solo violin, for example, has a cadenza-like passage which would fit into Elihu's dance in *Job*, or even into *The Lark Ascending*. As in a Haydn symphony, this slow movement adds grace, weight and charm to wit and fun.

The finale, Toccata, 'commandeers all the available hitting instruments which can make definite notes'. Whereas in the first movement these instruments had been used with subtlety to provide a cool, shimmering tone-colour, here they are used to add to the general air of rumbustious festivity. This is certainly no visionary epilogue, and it makes no attempt to sum up what has gone before. It is a rondo of sorts, and maintains its high spirits throughout, up

till the final flourish. The figure:

occurs

in most of the themes, and is actually heard both as the first element of the movement and in its closing passage. The composer does not mind whether the F is natural or sharp; that is all part of the good-natured, easy-going, rather solid bravura of this movement.

The ninth Symphony—in E minor, like the sixth—was composed in 1956-7, mostly in London, but partly in Majorca and at the home of the Finzis in Newbury. The gait is recognizably slower than in the others; the movements are Allegro moderato, Andante sostenuto, Allegro pesante and Andante tranquillo. The better part of fifty years, therefore, separates its composition from the *Sea Symphony*, and even so late in life the composer is still experimenting with orchestral sonorities. The new instruments which he introduced were the flügelhorn and three saxophones. The latter take their place sedately among the other instruments except in the scherzo, when they enjoy a kind of Teddy boys' picnic; the former, with its silvery tone, gives out the theme of the second movement, unaccompanied.

The ninth Symphony is sombre, and yet it is not as substantial as the fourth or the fifth; the menacing introduction to the first movement gives place to a rather more lyrical mood, and touches sublimity when the second theme is given to the solo violin and taken up by the orchestral violins against a flute accompaniment. The second movement alternates a lyrical theme with a rather barbaric march (a little reminiscent of the march movement of *Flos Campi*) with which it resolves in counterpoint. A feature of this movement is a lyrical episode on the strings of remote and lonely beauty, but any possibility that this is to endure is soon dispelled by the scherzo, which is by Vanity Fair out of Satan's Dance of Triumph, with a hint of Holst's *Uranus*. The humour of this movement is acid, and there is a wickedly witty episode when a lachrymose chorale is played with a glittering accompaniment against interpolations on the saxophones. The movement dissolves and dies away into the sharp side-drum rhythm from which it sprang. Perhaps none of this is new—and yet it is a new rearrangement of elements which we have noted before in Vaughan Williams's music. The finale opens with a long cantilena rather like that in the sixth Symphony, but the texture is thicker and the mood warmer. It is thus no surprise when a lovely theme appears on the horn, accompanied by wood-wind arpeggios. The movement builds up to a gigantic climax, interrupted by soft saxophones, which is repeated, and ends on a big *fortissimo* chord which melts away into silence.

Unlike the sixth and fourth Symphonies, to which it bears most resemblance, this work is lyrical and pensive; there is not the hectic hurry which characterizes those two works, nor is there the same concentration. Even so late in life the veteran composer shows his ability to surprise; the opening is laid out like a typical spacious Vaughan Williams slow movement. 'Aha,' we think, 'there's a serene wood-wind solo coming up.' Instead a threatening brass passage emerges balefully from the vast spread string chords. It is in its scoring that the ninth Symphony impresses immediately—in that, and in its variegated congruity of mood. It is the work, not of a tired old man, but of a very experienced one, and though it is perhaps not the greatest of his symphonies, we may safely say that its musical content offers the contrast that Beethoven's fourth does to the *Eroica*. And that is no mean compliment to it.

CHAPTER XV

WORKS WITH SOLO INSTRUMENTS AND CHAMBER MUSIC

NONE of the works which Vaughan Williams wrote in which a solo instrument is given a prominent part bears any relation to the display concerto of the eighteenth and nineteenth centuries. This is not to say that some of them do not involve the soloist in considerable technical difficulties, but it is certainly noticeable that the dramatic interplay of soloist and orchestra which is a feature of most solo concertos and similar works from the time of Mozart onwards is rarely to be found in Vaughan Williams's works of this kind. This is only to be expected; sheer display and technical brilliance were always suspect to him. In nearly all the works with a *concertante* soloist he is there to lead—or, in some cases, to comment somewhat sardonically on—what is really a discussion, not a duel or dialogue. If we include *Flos Campi* and the *Fantasia on the Old 104th*, there are nine works of this category—four full-sized concertos, all on a small scale, a suite, two short rhapsodic works, and the two works involving the use of a chorus, which differ from the others less than they differ from his larger choral works. Among the concertos there is one for tuba; among the shorter works the *Romance* for harmonica and orchestra, one of the works commissioned for that instrument by Larry Adler, who has done so much to prove that it has potentialities beyond those simply of a music-hall or public-house entertainment. This group of works spans a period of some forty years, and their range is as wide, though probably not as deep, as that of Vaughan Williams's works in any sphere.

The Lark Ascending, written just before the First World War, and revised after it, is a kind of English equivalent of a work like Smetana's *From Bohemia's Woods and Fields*, yet the intention of the work is not strictly programmatic. It is as if the lark in his flight flew over a

landscape as varied as that of the Cotswolds among which the composer revised the work. Mild and gentle, it depicts an atmosphere
where man is reduced to his true proportions; indeed, in the middle
2–4 section, it seems almost as if the lark is flying over some village
fair, viewing the doings of the human beings on the ground from his
height, and the ending gives the impression that he flies off and
upward into the remoteness of the sunset. The form is simple—but the
manner in which the initial melisma on the violin over the chord
softly hummed by the orchestra develops and sends forth shoots as if
it were trying itself over, like a lark trilling though it may be, is still
noticeably another example of what can perhaps be called Vaughan
Williams's 'expanding' melodic technique.

The neo-classicism of the violin concerto is not of the kind that
tinkers about with classical melodic lines and textures by adding
clusters of irrelevant notes; it is rather a development of formulae first
used in the *Pastoral Symphony* within the limits of a smaller design but
a livelier melodic scheme. Like Stravinsky's neo-classicism, it is synthetic; unlike his, the synthesis is of elements of the composer's own
style, not of other people's.

The first movement sets out from the simple text—what is a fifth?
The interval appears both in the melody and the harmonies, and the
first theme has both upward and downward fifths in prominent
places. The economy of structure—the main theme of the 3–4 section
is actually a disguised variant of the diminished version of the second
strain of the principal theme—and the layout remind one of Bach, but
the mood and the modality are pure Vaughan Williams. This is not
the kind of pastiche that adds moustaches on to classical madonnas,
but, as always with Vaughan Williams, a grafting of new stock on to
old stems. The second movement is once more a development from a
Bach-like pattern, but once more the themes are only superficially
Bach-like. Bach's slow movements of this kind often start out with a
very simple tune over which, as a harmonic background, the soloist
weaves lyrical arabesques which constitute the real melodic material
of the movement. Here the main theme is shared between the solo
violin and a solo cello, and is taken up by the orchestral violins.
When, after a second, less elaborate theme has been heard, the first

theme returns after a cadenza, the parts are exactly inverted, the solo violin playing a high *pianissimo* inverted pedal note, the orchestral violins and the solo cello playing the main theme in consecutive full chords as if it had strayed from the *Pastoral Symphony*, and the quasi-ostinato which was originally heard on the violins down in the *tutti* cellos and basses. Throughout the movement the texture is rich and luminous, but clear.

After a kind of 'on your marks, get set' from the orchestra, the solo violin sets the finale in motion with a theme which catapults a reminis-cence of *Hugh the Drover* into the scene. Every time it recurs this theme has a slightly different outline, and the jig-like energy of the move-ment is thrown into high relief by a *cantabile* counter-theme on the violas which would fit well into the scherzo of the *Pastoral Symphony*. Yet the work's playfulness is deceptive; the manner in which the movement simply fades away, and the veiled mystery of such passages as this (from the first movement):

indicate that this is not merely the robustly merry little work that it seems to be at first hearing. In this concerto the thoughtfulness of the *Tallis Fantasia*, the freshness of *Hugh the Drover* and the brooding power of the *Pastoral Symphony* are all fused into a concise summary of Vaughan Williams's stylistic development up till the time (1925) when he composed it.

Flos Campi, which preceded the violin Concerto by some three weeks to its first performance, is usually counted as a choral work; the voices, however, which sing wordless parts, are treated as instruments in that they, together with the small orchestra, form a background against which the solo viola plays. The work is a kind of lyric viola concerto-suite in six movements, each of which bears a quotation from the Song of Solomon. If each heading is assumed to be a kind of guiding thought to the emotions expressed in the music, we have the following scheme:

(1) *Sicut lilium inter spinas, sic amica mea inter filias.* . . . *Fulcite me floribus, stipate me malis, quia amore langueo*—longing—

(2) *Jam enim hiems transiit: imber abiit et recessit: flores apparuerunt in terra nostra, tempus putationis advenit: vox turturis audita est in terra nostra*—

the stirring of Nature, and with it the awakening of desire, followed by an unsuccessful attempt to find an object of satisfaction in

(3) *Quaesivi quem diligit anima mea: quaesivi illum et non inveni* . . .

where the tension builds up in the accompaniment, bursts into a climax and leaves the solo instrument alone and forsaken. A depiction of the martial character of the beloved, his strength and virility follows in

(4) *En lectulum Salomonis sexaginta fortes ambiunt* . . . *omnes tenentes gladios, et ad bella doctissimi*—

the first movement in which the viola has anything approaching pyrotechnics—which is followed by the most intense movement of the six:

(5) *Revertere, revertere Sulamitis! Revertere, revertere ut intueamur te.* . . . *Quam pulchri sunt gressus tui in calceamentis, filia principis.*

A rapturous fulfilment and epilogue follows in

(6) *Pone me ut signaculum super cor tuum.*

Whether or not the love expressed in this superb poem is human and personal, or mystical and symbolic, this work stands somewhat in the same relation to Vaughan Williams's works as *Tristan and Isolde* does to Wagner's. Its passion is not so febrile, so impatient, so erotically narrow-minded; here is no lust dissolving into a shimmering

Liebestod but a sharply etched dissonant, rhapsodic longing finally distilled into realization and fulfilment. Neither nostalgia nor luxury have any place here, nor sumptuous throbbing passion. Yet passion is there—intense and yet ethereal. The viola is—one might somehow expect it—searching once more among the unknown regions in a kind of introverted and personal vision. Here there is no leading upward and onward to deep waters or some remote Heavenly City, but inward into the most intimate introspection. It has the effect of a musing improvisation; it is rich, warm and at the same time remote and strange. The most telling effects derive from its sonorities, which culminate not in the dissolvent richness of a huge Elgar-Strauss climax, but a longing finally satisfied in the glowing finale. The measure of the work is shown by this finale, which unfolds like a Japanese flower opening out in water; it does not surge onward to a *fortissimo* climax sweeping all before it, and it has time for a backward reflective glance at the opening of the work before it dies away.

The emotional scheme is quite consistent, and the stage to which Vaughan Williams had now developed his technique of evolving a long melody out of a short phrase can be seen both in the finale and the second movement, where this:

grows out of this:

widening, as Frank Howes points out, to this:

and reaching its apotheosis in the finale with this:

where instead of starting on the third degree of the mode, it starts on the tonic of a major scale, firmly in D major. This is not a mere paper similarity but part of an organic and logical musical growth. Emotional congruity and musical development go hand in hand.

The second of Vaughan Williams's concertos proper to appear was for piano, which is available in two versions and is the only one of his works of this kind to contain a massive display cadenza in the finale. The range of the work is wide—from the Prokofiev-like opening and the shanty-like theme which develops from it, via the serene slow movement, to the vigour and restlessness of the finale, which in its brassy scoring (e.g. in the *stretto* part of the fugue) seems to foreshadow the fourth Symphony. The last movement seems to be harsher and on a more massive scale than the others, and it is difficult to reconcile it with the dreamy, slightly forlorn atmosphere of the slow movement with its theme centring round one note. In this work Vaughan Williams's habit of moving blocks of chords parallel to the melodic line is pressed into the service of twentieth-century percussive piano-writing, particularly in the opening Toccata, and the concerto, whatever its shortcomings from the pianistic point of view, is undeniably effective.

Nothing could be less like a folksong than the first theme of the Toccata; it simply takes the interval of a tone and repeats it again and again, each time a fourth up; meanwhile the soloist too is busy preaching on the text of a fourth. Folksong or no, this theme is typical of the composer; we have seen how the interval of a fourth is a finger-print of his style. Thus, every alternate note of the first four bars of this theme is a fourth apart:

This theme is certainly an interesting choice for a composer who is usually dismissed by his detractors as a folky homespun. But having discharged this stream of disguised fourths, Vaughan Williams expands his theme at the fifth bar by introducing a new motif which immediately contracts into a *gruppetto* of quavers, and which later on becomes important. Only six years separate the composition of this work from the violin Concerto; yet though the two works are unmistakably characteristic of Vaughan Williams they are utterly different.

The oboe Concerto, written for Léon Goossens, was a product of the war years. It is a gentler work than either the violin or the piano concertos; there is rarely any effect of forcefulness, for most of the work is a kind of *mezza-voce* murmur. The orchestra is kept firmly on the leash; for the most part it tends to nod sagely in agreement every time the soloist says anything particularly wise. This happy give-and-take sets the tone for a genial little work, full of felicitous touches of scoring and poetry—unexpected extensions or foreshortenings of what sound at first hearing like square, straightforward themes. There is even a slight reminiscence—in mood as well as in style—of the finale of *Flos Campi* in the last movement, when the strings have a majestic waltz tune rising against a descending counterpoint from the soloist. The reminiscence is strengthened when the theme is taken up in imitation by the orchestra. There is no real slow movement: the second movement is a minuet which has the tang of the open air rather than the scent of the ballroom, and its return is neatly contrived by allowing the trio section to dissolve into a tripping series of quavers which develop into a counterpoint to the theme of the minuet itself. (Once again, by the way, the interval of the fourth plays an important part, occurring no fewer than six times in the first ten bars of the theme.) After the pastoral first movement and the sprightly little minuet the finale introduces true virtuosity into the work for the first time. The coda is retrospective, recalling themes from earlier movements, but leads us into no unknown regions.

One of the new works introduced by the London Symphony Orchestra for its Golden Jubilee in 1954 was a Concerto for tuba and orchestra written by Vaughan Williams for Philip Catelinet, the tuba player of the orchestra. There is something faintly perverse about this work; the jokes seem somehow to fall flat, and the lyricism of the Romance does not seem to make up for the dullness of the outer movements. This is sad, for the technical difficulties of writing an effective concerto for an instrument whose compass lies even lower than that of the cello or the bassoon were a stimulating challenge to the composer, and the layout of the work is evidence of the fact that he clearly enjoyed overcoming them. But even Vaughan Williams had off-days, and the tuba Concerto is evidence of them. Technically it is quite a success, for the composer skilfully reconciles the somewhat ponderous solo instrument with his own lively and intimate concerto form (particularly by the use of cross-rhythms in the first movement), but thematically it is dull.

The Suite for viola and orchestra, written for Lionel Tertis and first performed by him on 12th November 1934, consists of eight short movements, arranged in three groups—three Christmas pieces, two 'character' pieces and three dance movements. The orchestra involved is small, and not all of it is used in every movement. The large number of movements invites variety; their shortness prevents monotony of tone and texture. The music is easy to listen to and requires a true virtuoso soloist, and the work stands in relation to Vaughan Williams's more impressive compositions as Beethoven's *Bagatelles* do to his; that is to say, its small scale indicates a great mind relaxing rather than a little mind saying elegant nothings. Indeed, the 'Carol' movement, with its haunting tune and its simple yet subtle treatment (particularly in the fourth verse), is one of his most moving pieces.

The *Romance*, written for Larry Adler, is a similar kind of thing. First performed by Adler in 1952, it has become a Saturday-night 'Prom' favourite on account of its melodic charm, attractive scoring (divided strings and 'piano continuo', as it were) and combination of the unusual with the unspectacular. The same combination can be found in the *Fantasia on the Old 104th Psalm Tune*, which consists of a series of variations for soloist, chorus and orchestra on Ravenscroft's stately melody. Here the work is more earnest, and there is more—not always successful—experimentation. In the fourth variation, for example, the piano joins with the voices in a fugato; in the fifth, it has the field to itself. As in Dohnányi's *Variations on a Nursery Song*, the theme is foreshadowed in an introduction before the piano states it (though here the piano itself works up the tune) and before the seven variations get under way. The work ends with a brilliant, somewhat opaque climax.

Vaughan Williams's chamber works—like his operas—are, with one exception, somewhat unjustly neglected, and it is rather difficult to see why. Each of his two string quartets parallels one of his symphonies. The first (written after his return from the visit to Ravel) has some of the shortcomings—and much of the charm—of the *London Symphony*; the second, 'For Jean on Her Birthday', a more successful work, partakes of the noble serenity of the fifth Symphony, as has often been pointed out. It is typical of Vaughan Williams at any time that a work ostensibly in G minor—as the first quartet is—should have, as its first full chord, one of F major. But there is rarely anything unworldly about this happy—in places boisterous—work; the first movement is cast in fairly orthodox sonata form, and the partnership between the instruments is throughout that of a civilized discussion. The ending, in a sort of G major, shows that a work which is happy can also be mysterious, as the parts interweave and arch upwards to a final cadence where the first violin holds a very high D nearly three octaves above its nearest companion, and the other instruments breathe a sequence of full chords—E major, F major, G major—underneath. The minuet and trio—particularly the opening of the former—sound rather as if Haydn was wearing his best English peasant's smock, with the robust opening in octaves and the persistent flat seventh. The Romance is a simple ternary design rather like a folksong rhapsody, and the final Rondo capriccioso contains a number of colour effects and some display writing for each instrument.

The Quartet in A minor ('For Jean on her Birthday') contains themes (the principal one in the scherzo, for example, and that of the final epilogue) borrowed from film music, but it is certainly neither trivial nor scrappy. Miss Jean Stewart, the violist of the Menges Quartet, for whom the work was written, was permitted the first statement of the theme in each movement (the viola opens the proceedings in the G minor Quartet, too; not at all surprising, when we remember that Vaughan Williams was the violist of the Cowley Street Wobblers, and retained a particular liking for the viola all his life). The first movement, Prelude, is rather restless at the outset, expanding swiftly from its initial melisma, and broadening out to a quiet close after a terse and somewhat intense course. The Romance is more leisurely—a calm, partly contrapuntal, partly chordal meditation on a cool and rather aloof theme which unwinds waywardly, changing its shape as each instrument takes it up. The atmosphere has something of the timelessness of the opening orchestral passage of Part II of *The Dream of Gerontius*. The texture thickens and the mood becomes more agitated in the central section, so that the music works naturally up to a climax before the movement dies away, leaving the viola to brood alone. In the scherzo the viola is made to stand out from the other instruments at the outset by being unmuted, whereas they play a tremolando in octaves, with mutes on. Like the scherzo of the fifth Symphony, this movement combined speed, power and lightness. There is no trio section except for fourteen bars which contrast with the rest, and the restatement is compact, leading, via a short coda, to a warm and lovely Epilogue lifted from the music to a projected film on Joan of Arc. The music is akin to the end of *Flos Campi*, or of the fifth Symphony, musing gently and nobly, with the utmost simplicity and easy flow, on a theme which drifts confidently yet imperceptibly to the gentle close.

In Vaughan Williams's other large chamber works the quartet is joined by a fifth instrument, and in the song-cycle *On Wenlock Edge* by a tenor voice as well. The *Phantasy Quintet* has an extra viola. The music of the first three sections—Prelude, Scherzo and Alla Sarabanda—is all thematically related and the emotional scheme seems to aim at a juxtaposition of meditation and brusqueness. The last movement, Burlesca, is a rather more sardonic cousin of the 'March Past of the Kitchen Utensils' from the music to *The Wasps*, and for the most part gives us an excellent early example of the pungent wit which was to come to full flowering later on—notably in the second movement of the eighth Symphony. Only here it is much more ponderously expressed than in that dapper little movement.

On Wenlock Edge combines a vocal line that is like folksong—e.g. in 'Is My Team Ploughing?' 'Oh when I was in Love with You', and 'Bredon Hill'—with an elaborate and atmospheric accompaniment. This is particularly so in the third song of the cycle, 'Is My Team Ploughing?' where the voice of the dead youth, asking his plaintive questions over a remote and timeless chord of D minor in the string quartet, receives his answer in terms of an agitated chromatic wail. A comparison of the accompaniment in these songs with that in the two cycles of Stevenson settings shows how much progress Vaughan Williams had made in technique. Perhaps Ravel's tuition was in part responsible; but it is noticeable that the handling of purely melodic features is much freer and more characteristic than before. Stylistic mannerisms—consecutive chords, for example—associated with Vaughan Williams's mature works are here found cheek by jowl with chromaticism (used rather less resourcefully than in his later music). And there is an ear for the momentary colour effect, such as when the violin and the piano combine in 'Bredon Hill' to sound a dirge on a low G. Word-painting of this kind is not so common in Vaughan Williams's song accompaniments. Indeed, one might perhaps cite this setting as an example in various ways of rendering church bells in a chamber-music combination. One cannot help feeling that the composer transcends Housman's texts in his setting, just as Schubert transcended the maudlin clichés of many of the *Winterreise* poems. The work seems to act on so many different planes at once; the vocal line is firm yet free, while the essentially indoor combination of piano and string quartet evokes an atmosphere that is in part outdoor and pictorial (intentionally so; one can see the trees swaying under the impact of the storm in the first song) and yet in part symbolic of an inner restlessness in the soul of the singer. And when the final calm of death is achieved in 'Clun', we find that the music has strayed into a mood remote from Housman's elegantly ironic melancholy, for it foreshadows the peace that passeth all understanding of so many of Vaughan Williams's later works. One cannot explain the strange fascination of this work by pointing out 'how it is done' any more than one can explain away the bitter vehemence of the F minor Symphony by examining the structure. The total of the music is simply far more than the sum of its not particularly original parts, and although it is not such a perfect work of art as the *Fantasia on a Theme by Thomas Tallis*, which received its first performance just a little later, it is perhaps a more protean one.

The violin Sonata of 1956 reserves most of its surprises for the finale. The opening Fantasia is an attractive lyrical movement whose theme, like so many of Vaughan Williams's themes, develops from its context: two fragments of phrase into which a third fragment is jammed. It is a placid movement, rather solemn and brooding. The scherzo which follows is insistent to the point of obstinacy—a real spitfire. The pianist is kept busy all the time, and there are many fierce displaced accents. The finale, Tema con variationi, opens with a texture and therefore an atmosphere that is possibly unique in violin sonatas. The violin plays inside the top two lines of the piano part, which is laid out in double octaves with a gap of at times three octaves between the left hand and the right. The first variation threads the theme with rich embroidery in the piano part; the second announces it in two modes at once in fairly strict imitation at four bars' interval; each time one version starts on F♯ and the other on D. The third is rather in the vein of *Famous Men*, and the fourth is both technically interesting (the theme is inverted in the violin part and played against itself augmented and the right way up in the accompaniment) and mysterious in atmosphere. With the fifth (in a kind of E major with C♮ and D♮) we are once again on familiar territory—warm, serene, lyrical music; the final variation brings us back to earth again with lively syncopations in the piano part, and the coda recalls the accompanying gestures of the Fantasia, squared up into 4–4 time.

The only other work for a duo-sonata combination is the *Six Studies in English Folk Song* for cello and piano; the other chamber works consist of the *Household Music on Welsh Hymn Tunes* (workaday music devoid of subtleties but pleasant to listen to and not technically difficult), some Chaucer settings for voice and string trio and a Suite for pipes. The Chaucer settings (*Merciles Beauty*) are quaint; the Suite affable and easy on the ear.

It is often thought that Vaughan Williams's range is not very wide nor his technique very subtle. Certainly his music does not impress the listener at first with any dazzling effects. But it is the greatest possible mistake to imagine that because the manner of his music is not glib the mind that created it was that of a homespun. No homespun could have given expression to what he felt with such inspired simplicity. His music is often full of mannerisms, yet on many an occasion a mannerism occurs in a fresh context; it is full of similar moods, yet every mood varies subtly from every other one. His type of greatness does not lie so much in saying things that have never been said before, but rather in simply seeing familiar things in a new way. That is Vaughan Williams's originality and his strength. Just as the man himself enjoyed to the full a rich and varied life, so the music he wrote explored many facets of the experience he enjoyed. It is sometimes found that a composer with a mean character and a selfish outlook towards his fellows can none the less write lofty and ennobling music. In the case of Vaughan Williams man and music were indissolubly one; a simple, profound visionary who was—quite unashamedly—a good man. Whether or not the music is 'English', though important, is only secondary; the primary consideration is that it is the product of a mind that was fearless, honest, balanced and, above all, positive in its outlook. For those who can respond to it it offers an experience both unique and lasting.

APPENDIX A

(Figures in brackets denote the age at which the person mentioned died)

Year	Age	Life	Contemporary Musicians
1872		Ralph Vaughan Williams born, Oct. 12, at Down Ampney, Gloucestershire, son of the Rev. Arthur Vaughan Williams, vicar of Down Ampney.	Alfvén born, May 1; Graener born, Jan. 11; Juon born, March 8; Perosi born, Dec. 20; Sekles born, June 20; Scriabin born, Jan. 6; Moniuszko (53) dies, June 2. Albeniz aged 12; d'Albert 8; Alkan 59; Arensky 11; Balakirev 36; Bantock 4; Benedict 68; Bennett 56; Bizet 34; Boito 30; Bordes 9; Borodin 48; Bossi 11; Brahms 39; Bréville 11; Bruch 34; Bruckner 48; Bruneau 13; Busoni 6; Chabrier 31; Charpentier 12; Chausson 17; Cornelius 48; Cowen 20; Cui 37; Davies (Walford) 3; Debussy 10; Delibes 36; Delius 10; Dukas 7; Duparc 24; Dvořák 31; Elgar 15; Fauré 27; Franck 50; Franz 57; Gade 55; German 10; Glazounov 7; Goldmark 42; Goetz 32; Gounod 54; Granados 5; Grieg 29; Heller 57; Henselt 58; Hiller 61; Humperdinck 18; d'Indy 21; Jensen 35; Lalo 49; Lekeu 2; Leoncavallo 14; Liadov 17; Liszt

Year	Age	Life	Contemporary Musicians
			61; Loeffler 11; MacDowell 11; McEwen 4; Mackenzie 25; Mahler 27; Martucci 16; Mascagni 9; Massenet 30; Mussorgsky 33; Nielsen 7; Novák 2; Offenbach 53; Parry 25; Pedrell 31; Pfitzner 3; Pierné 9; Ponchielli 38; Puccini 14; Raff 50; Reinecke 48; Rheinberger 33; Rimsky-Korsakov 28; Ropartz 8; Roussel 3; Rubinstein 42; Saint-Saëns 37; Satie 6; Schillings 4; Schmitt (Florent) 2; Sgambati 31; Sibelius 7; Sinigaglia 4; Smetana 48; Smyth (Ethel) 14; Somervell 9; Stainer 32; Stanford 20; Strauss (R.) 8; Sullivan 30; Taneiev 16; Tchaikovsky 32; Thomas (A.) 61; Thuille 11; Verdi 59; Wagner 59; Wesley (S. S.) 62; Wolf 12.
1873	1		Rachmaninov born, April 1; Reger born, March 19; Séverac born, July 20.
1874	2		Cornelius (50) dies, Oct. 26; Holst born, Sept. 21; Schönberg born, Sept. 13; Suk born, Jan. 4.
1875	3		Bennett (58) dies, Feb. 1; Bizet (36) dies, June 3; Coleridge-Taylor born, Aug. 15; Montemezzi born, May 31; Ravel born, March 7; Roger-Ducasse born, April 18.
1876	4		Falla born, Nov. 23; Goetz

Year	Age	Life	Contemporary Musicians
			(35) dies, Dec. 3; Wesley (S. S.) (65) dies, April 19; Wolf-Ferrari born, Jan. 12.
1877	5		Dohnányi born, July 27; Dunhill born, Feb. 1; Quilter born, Nov. 1.
1878	6	Has music lessons from his aunt, Sophie Wedgwood.	Boughton born, Jan. 23; Holbrooke born, July 6; Palmgren born, Feb. 16; Schreker born, March 23.
1879	7	Begins to learn the violin.	Bridge (Frank) born, Feb. 26; Ireland born, Aug. 13; Jensen (42) dies, Jan. 23; Karg-Elert born, Nov. 21; Respighi born, July 9; Scott (Cyril) born, Sept. 27.
1880	8	Takes a correspondence course in musical theory and passes examinations.	Bloch born, July 24; Medtner born, Jan. 5; Offenbach (61) dies, Oct. 4; Pizzetti born, Sept. 20.
1881	9		Bartók born, March 25; Enesco born, Aug. 19; Miaskovsky born, April 20; Mussorgsky (42) dies, March 28.
1882	10		Kodály born, Dec. 16; Malipiero born, March 18; Raff (60) dies, June 24-5; Stravinsky born, June 17; Szymanowski born, Oct. 6; Turina born, Dec. 9.
1883	11		Bax born, Nov. 6; Berners born, Sept. 18; Casella born, July 25; Wagner (69) dies, Feb. 13; Webern born, Dec. 3; Zandonai born, May 28.
1884	12		van Dieren born, Dec. 27; Smetana (60) dies, May 12.

Year	Age	Life	Contemporary Musicians
1885	13		Benedict (80) dies, June 5; Berg born, Feb. 7; Butterworth born, July 12; Hiller (73) dies, May 10; Wellesz born, Oct. 21.
1886	14		Kaminski born, July 4; Liszt (74) dies, July 31; Ponchielli (51) dies, Jan. 16.
1887	15	Enters Charterhouse School, where he plays violin and later viola in the orchestra.	Atterberg born, Dec. 12; Borodin (53) dies, Feb. 27; Toch born, Dec. 7; Villa-Lobos born, March 5.
1888	16	Gives a joint concert at school of composition by himself and his friend H. Vivian Hamilton.	Alkan (74) dies, March 29; Durey born, May 27; Heller (73) dies, Jan. 14.
1889	17		Henselt (75) dies, Oct. 10; Shaporin born, Nov. 8.
1890	18	Visits Munich and hears *Die Walküre*. Enters the Royal College of Music, where he studies harmony with F. E. Gladstone, composition with Parry and organ with Parratt.	Franck (67) dies, Nov. 8; Gade (73) dies, Dec. 21; Ibert born, Aug. 15; Martinů born, Dec. 8.
1891	19		Bliss born, Aug. 2; Delibes (54) dies, Jan. 16; Prokofiev born, April 23; Roland-Manuel born, March 22.
1892	20	Enters Trinity College, Cambridge. Studies composition with Charles Wood and organ with Alan Gray. Meets H. P. Allen (organ scholar of Christ's College).	Franz (77) dies, Oct. 24; Honegger born, March 10; Howells born, Oct. 17; Jarnach born, July 26; Kilpinen born, Feb. 4; Lalo (69) dies, April 22; Milhaud born, Sept. 4.
1893	21	Takes an active part in university music.	Absil born, Oct. 23; Goossens born, May 26; Gounod (75) dies, Oct. 18; Hába born,

Year	Age	Life	Contemporary Musicians
			June 21; Tchaikovsky (53) dies, Nov. 6.
1894	22	Takes Mus.B. degree, Cambridge.	Chabrier (53) dies, Sept. 13; Lekeu (24) dies, Jan. 21; Moeran born, Dec. 31; Pijper born, Sept. 8; Rubinstein (63) dies, Nov. 20; Warlock born, Oct. 30.
1895	23	Takes B.A. degree, Cambridge. Re-enters the Royal College of Music, where he studies composition with Stanford. Meets Gustav Holst, a fellow student. Becomes organist at St Barnabas, South Lambeth.	Castelnuovo-Tedesco born, April 3; Hindemith born, Nov. 16; Orff born, July 10; Sowerby born, May 1.
1896	24	Visits Bayreuth.	Bruckner (72) dies, Oct. 11; Sessions born, Dec. 28; Thomas (A.) (84) dies, Feb. 12.
1897	25	Marriage to Adeline Fisher, Oct. 9. Studies with Max Bruch in Berlin, where he hears a great variety of music.	Brahms (63) dies, April 3; Korngold born, May 29.
1898	26		Gershwin born, Sept. 25; Harris (R.) born, Feb. 12; Rieti born, Jan. 28.
1899	27		Auric born, Feb. 15; Chausson (44) dies, June 10; Poulenc born, Jan. 7; Strauss (J. ii) (73) dies, June 3.
1900	28	Meets Cecil Sharp.	Antheil born, July 9; Bush born, Dec. 22; Copland born, Nov. 14; Křenek born, Aug. 23; Sullivan (58) dies, Nov. 22.
1901	29	Takes Mus.D. degree, Cambridge.	Finzi born, July 14; Rheinberger (62) dies, Nov. 25;

Year	Age	Life	Contemporary Musicians
			Rubbra born, May 23; Stainer (60) dies, March 31; Verdi (87) dies, Jan. 27.
1902	30	*Bucolic Suite* performed at Bournemouth. Begins to give University Extension lectures and to write articles for the *Vocalist.*	Walton born, March 29.
1903	31	Begins to collect folksongs. Writes articles on 'Conducting' and 'Fugue' for Grove's *Dictionary. Willow Wood* composed.	Berkeley born, May 12; Blacher born, Jan. 3; Khachaturian born, June 6; Wolf (42) dies, Feb. 22.
1904	32	Begins work as music editor of the *English Hymnal. In the Fen Country* (Symphonic Impression) composed.	Dallapiccola born, Feb. 3; Dvořák (62) dies, May 1.
1905	33	*Toward the Unknown Region* composed. Begins work on *A Sea Symphony.* Edits Purcell's *Welcome Songs* (Part I) for the Purcell Society.	Lambert born, Aug. 23; Rawsthorne born, May 2; Tippett born, Jan. 2; Matyas Seiber born, 4th May.
1906	34	*Norfolk Rhapsody* No. 1 composed.	Arensky (44) dies, Feb. 25; Cartan born, Dec. 1; Frankel born, Jan. 31; Lutyens born, July 9; Shostakovich born, Sept. 25.
1907	35	*Toward the Unknown Region* performed at the Leeds Festival.	Grieg (64) dies, Sept. 4; Maconchy born, March 19; Thuille (45) dies, Feb. 5.
1908	36	Studies with Ravel in Paris. String Quartet No. 1, G minor, composed.	Ferguson born, Oct. 21; MacDowell (46) dies, Jan. 23; Messiaen born, Dec. 10; Rimsky-Korsakov (64) dies, June 21.
1909	37	*On Wenlock Edge* (song cycle) composed. Incidental music for Aristophanes' *The Wasps*	Albéniz (48) dies, May 18; Bordes (46) dies, Nov. 8; Martucci (53) dies, June 1.

Year	Age	Life	Contemporary Musicians
		performed at Cambridge. *Willow Wood* performed at Liverpool (Musical League Festival).	
1910	38	*A Sea Symphony* performed at the Leeds Festival. *Fantasia on a Theme by Tallis* performed at the Gloucester Festival. Edits Purcell's *Welcome Songs* (Part II) for the Purcell Society.	Balakirev (73) dies, May 29; Barber born, March 9; Reinecke (85) dies, March 10; Schuman born, Aug. 4.
1911	39	*Five Mystical Songs* performed at the Worcester Festival. Begins work on *Hugh the Drover*.	Mahler (50) dies, May 18; Menotti born, July 7.
1912	40	*Fantasia on Christmas Carols* performed at the Hereford Festival.	Coleridge-Taylor (37) dies, Sept 1; Massenet (70) dies, Aug. 13.
1913	41		Britten born, Nov. 22.
1914	42	Enlists as a private in the R.A.M.C. *A London Symphony* performed in London. *The Lark Ascending* composed.	Liadov (59) dies, Aug. 28; Sgambati (73) dies, Dec. 14.
1915	43		Goldmark (84) dies, Jan 2; Scriabin (43) dies, April 27; Taneiev (58) dies, June 19.
1916	44	Posted to France with the R.A.M.C. and subsequently to Salonika.	Butterworth (31) dies, Aug. 5; Granados (48) dies, March 24; Roger (42) dies, May 11.
1917	45	Commissioned as a lieutenant in the R.G.A.	
1918	46	Serves in France with the R.G.A. Appointed Director of Music, First Army, B.E.F.	Boito (76) dies, June 10; Cui (83) dies, March 24; Debussy (55) dies, March 25; Parry (70) dies, Oct. 7.
1919	47	Appointed professor of composition at the Royal College of Music. Hon. D.Mus., Oxford.	Leoncavallo (61) dies, Aug. 9.

Year	Age	Life	Contemporary Musicians
1920	48	Revised version of *A London Symphony* performed in London, May 4. *Four Hymns* (composed 1914) performed at the Worcester Festival.	Bruch (82) dies, Oct. 2; Fricker (P. R.) born, Sept. 5.
1921	49	Appointed conductor of the Bach Choir. *The Lark Ascending* performed in London, June 14.	Humperdinck (67) dies, Sept. 27; Saint-Saëns (86) dies, Dec. 16; Séverac (47) dies, March 24.
1922	50	*Pastoral Symphony* performed in London, Jan. 26. *The Shepherds of the Delectable Mountains* performed at the Royal College of Music, July 11. Visits America to conduct the *Pastoral Symphony* at Norfolk (Conn.)	Pedrell (81) dies, Aug. 19.
1923	51	*Old King Cole* performed at Cambridge. Mass in G minor performed at Birmingham.	
1924	52	*Hugh the Drover* performed at the Royal College of Music (July 4) and by the British National Opera Company (July 14).	Busoni (58) dies, July 27; Fauré (79) dies, Nov. 4; Puccini (65) dies, Nov. 29; Stanford (71) dies, March 29.
1925	53	*Flos Campi* and violin concerto (*Concerto accademico*) performed in London, Oct. 19 and Nov. 6.	Bossi (63) dies, Feb. 20; Satie (59) dies, July 1.
1926	54	*On Christmas Night* performed at Chicago. *Sancta Civitas* performed at Oxford, May 7.	Boulez born, March 25.
1928	56	Resigns conductorship of the Bach Choir. *Te Deum*, G major, performed at the enthronement of the Archbishop of Canterbury. Moves from London to Dorking.	Stockhausen born, Aug. 22.

Year	Age	Life	Contemporary Musicians
1929	57	*Sir John in Love* performed at the Royal College of Music, March 21.	
1930	58	Concert performance of *Job* at the Norwich Festival, Oct. 23. *Benedicite, Three Choral Hymns* and *The Hundredth Psalm* performed at the Leith Hill Festival.	Warlock (36) dies, Dec. 17.
1931	59	*Job* staged at the Cambridge Theatre, London, July 5.	d'Indy (80) dies, Dec. 2; Nielsen (66) dies, Oct. 2.
1932	60	*Magnificat* performed at the Worcester Festival. Lectures on 'National Music' at Bryn Mawr College (Penn.). Elected president of the English Folk Dance and Song Society.	d'Albert (67) dies, March 3; Cartan (25) dies, March 26.
1933	61	Piano Concerto performed in London, Feb. 1.	Duparc (85) dies, Feb. 13; Karg-Elert (55) dies, April 9.
1934	62	Suite for viola performed in London, Nov. 12.	Bruneau (77) dies, June 15; Delius (72) dies, June 10; Elgar (76) dies, Feb. 23; Holst (59) dies, May 25; Schreker (55) dies, March 21; Sekles (62) dies, Dec. 15.
1935	63	Symphony, F minor (No. 4), performed in London, April 10. Created O.M.	Berg (50) dies, Dec. 24; Cowen (83) dies, Oct. 6; Dukas (69) dies, May 18; Loeffler (74) dies, May 19; Mackenzie (87) dies, April 28; Suk (61) dies, May 29.
1936	64	*The Poisoned Kiss* performed at Cambridge, May 12. *Dona nobis pacem* performed at Huddersfield, Oct. 2. *Five Tudor Portraits* performed at the Norwich Festival.	van Dieren (51) dies, April 24; German (74) dies, Nov. 11; Glazounov (70) dies, March 21; Respighi (56) dies, April 18.
1937	65	*Festival Te Deum*, F. major,	Gershwin (38) dies, July 11;

Year	Age	Life	Contemporary Musicians
		for the coronation of George VI, performed at Westminster Abbey. *Flourish for a Coronation* performed in London, April 1. *Riders to the Sea* performed at the Royal College of Music, Nov. 30.	Pierné (73) dies, July 17; Ravel (62) dies, Dec. 28; Roussel (68) dies, Aug. 23; Somervell (73) dies, May 2; Szymanowski (54) dies, March 29.
1938	66	*Serenade to Music* performed in London, Oct. 5.	
1939	67	*Five Variants of 'Dives and Lazarus'* performed in New York, June.	
1940	68	Music for the film *Forty-ninth Parallel* composed.	Juon (68) dies, Aug. 21.
1941	69		Bridge (Frank) (61) dies, Jan. 10; Davies (Walford) (71) dies, March 11.
1942	70	*Household Music* composed. Music for the film *Coastal Command* composed.	
1943	71	Symphony, D major (No. 5), performed in London, June 25. Music for the films *The People's Land* and *The Story of a Flemish Farm* composed.	Rachmaninov (69) dies, March 28; Schillings (75) dies, July 23.
1944	72	Oboe Concerto performed in London, Sept. 30.	Graener (72) dies, Nov. 13; Singaglia (75) dies, May 16; Zandonai (61) dies, June 12.
1945	73	*Thanksgiving for Victory* performed in London. String Quartet No. 2, A minor, composed. Music for the film *Stricken Peninsula* composed.	Bartók (64) dies, Sept. 26; Mascagni (81) dies, Aug. 2; Webern (61) dies, Sept. 15.
1946	74	*Introduction and Fugue* for two pianos composed. Concerto for two pianos (arr. from piano Concerto) performed in London, Nov. 22.	Bantock (78) dies, Oct. 16; Dunhill (69) dies, March 13; Falla (69) dies, Nov. 14; Kaminski (60) dies, June 14; Smyth (Ethel) (86) dies, May 9.

Year	Age	Life	Contemporary Musicians
1947	75	*The Souls of the Righteous* performed in Westminster Abbey. *The Voice out of the Whirlwind* performed at St Cecilia's Day service in London. Music for the film *The Loves of Joanna Godden* composed.	Casella (63) dies, March 5; Pijper (52) dies, March 19.
1948	76	Symphony, E minor (No. 6), performed in London, April 21. *Partita* for double string orchestra performed in London. Music for the film *Scott of the Antarctic* composed. Re-starts work on *The Pilgrim's Progress.*	McEwen (80) dies, June 14; Wolf-Ferrari (72) dies, Jan. 21.
1949	77		Bréville (88) dies, Sept. 24; Novák (78) dies, July 18; Pfitzner (80) dies, May 22; Strauss (R.) (85) dies, Sept. 8; Turina (66) dies, Jan 14.
1950	78	*Folk Songs of the Four Seasons* performed in London, *Fantasia on the 'Old Hundredth' Psalm Tune* performed at the Gloucester Festival. *Concerto grosso* for strings performed in London, Nov. 18.	Berners (66) dies, April 19; Miaskovsky (69) dies, Aug 9; Moeran (55) dies, Dec. 1.
1951	79	*The Pilgrim's Progress* performed at Covent Garden, April 26. *The Sons of Light* performed in London, May 6. Begins work on the *Sinfonia antartica* (based on material from the music for the film *Scott of the Antarctic*). Adeline Vaughan Williams (*née* Fisher) dies, May 10.	Lambert (44) dies, Aug. 21; Medtner (71) dies, Nov. 13; Palmgren (73) dies, Dec. 13; Schönberg (76) dies, July 13.
1952	80	*Romance* for harmonica and	Montemezzi (76) dies, May 15.

Year	Age	Life	Contemporary Musicians
		orchestra performed in New York, May 3, 1952. *An Oxford Elegy* performed at Oxford, June 19.	
1953	81	*Sinfonia antartica* performed at Manchester, Jan 14. Marriage to Ursula Wood (widow of Lt-Col. J. M. J. Forrester Wood), Feb. 7.	Bax (69) dies, Oct. 3; Prokofiev (61) dies, March 4; Quilter (75) dies, Sept. 21.
1954	82	Tuba Concerto performed in London, June 13. *Hodie* performed at the Worcester Festival. Visiting professor at Cornell University, where he lectures on 'The Making of Music'. Lectures at the Royal Conservatory of Music, Toronto, University of Michigan, Indiana University, University of California, Los Angeles, Yale University. Conducts *A London Symphony* with the Buffalo Philharmonic Orchestra.	Roger-Ducasse (81) dies, July 20.
1955	83	Violin Sonata, A minor, performed in London, Dec. 20.	Enesco (73) dies, May 4; Honegger (63) dies, Nov. 28; Ropartz (91) dies, Nov. 22.
1956	84	Symphony, D minor (No. 8), performed in London, May 14. *A Vision of Aeroplanes* performed in London, June 4. Begins work on Symphony in E minor (No. 9).	Charpentier (95) dies, Feb. 18; Finzi (55) dies, Sept. 27; Perosi (83) dies, Oct. 12.
1957	85		Korngold (60) dies; Sibelius (91) dies, Sept. 20.
1958	86	Symphony, E minor (No. 9), performed in London, April 2.	Holbrooke (80) dies, Aug. 5; Schmitt (Florent) (87) dies, Aug. 17.

Year	Age	*Life*	*Contemporary Musicians*
		Vaughan Williams dies in London, Aug. 26.	Absil 65; Alfvén 86; Antheil 58; Atterberg 71; Auric 59; Barber 48; Berkeley 55; Blacher 55; Bliss 67; Bloch 78; Boughton 80; Boulez 33; Britten 45; Bush 58; Castel-nuovo-Tedesco 63; Copland 58; Dallapiccola 54; Durey 70; Ferguson 50; Frankel 52; Fricker (P. R.) 38; Goossens 65; Hába 65; Harris 60; Hindemith 63; Howells 66; Ibert 68; Ireland 79; Jarnach 66; Khachaturian 55; Kil-pinen 66; Kodály 76; Křenek 58; Lutyens 52; Maconchy 51; Malipiero 76; Martinů 68; Menotti 47; Messiaen 50; Milhaud 66; Orff 63; Pizzetti 78; Poulenc 59; Rawsthorne 53; Rieti 60; Roland-Manuel 67; Rubbra 57; Schuman 48; Scott (Cyril) 79; Sessions 62; Shaporin 69; Shostakovich 52; Sowerby 63; Stockhausen 30; Stravinsky 76; Tippett 53; Toch 71; Villa-Lobos 71; Walton 56; Wellesz 73.

APPENDIX B

CATALOGUE OF WORKS

SYMPHONIES

A Sea Symphony (Walt Whitman), for soprano and baritone soli, chorus and orchestra (1910).
A London Symphony (1920; revised 1953).
Pastoral Symphony, for soprano or tenor solo and orchestra (1922; revised 1955).
Symphony [No. 4], F minor (1935).
Symphony [No. 5], D major (1943).
Symphony [No. 6], E minor (1948).
Sinfonia antartica (1953).
Symphony [No. 8], D minor (1956).
Symphony [No. 9], E minor (1958).

MISCELLANEOUS ORCHESTRAL WORKS

(a) For the Stage, Films, etc.

Music to Aristophanes' *The Wasps* (1909).
Old King Cole, ballet (1924).
On Christmas Night, folk ballet (1925–6; published 1952).
Job: a Masque for Dancing (1930).
The Running Set, folk dances (1936; published 1952).
Music for films:
  Forty-ninth Parallel (1940).
  Coastal Command (1942).
  The People's Land (1943).
  The Story of a Flemish Farm (1943).
  Stricken Peninsula (1945).
  The Loves of Joanna Godden (1947).
  Scott of the Antarctic (1949).
  The Vision of William Blake (1958).

194

Appendix B—Catalogue of Works

Music for radio and television:
> The Mayor of Casterbridge (1951).
> Epithalamion (1953; published as The Bridal Day, 1956).

(b) For other Purposes

Norfolk Rhapsody, No. 1, E minor (1905; published 1925).
In the Fen Country (1905; revised version published 1937).
Fantasia on a Theme by Thomas Tallis, for string quartet and double string orchestra (1910; revised 1923).
English Folk Song Suite (originally for military band, 1923).
Toccata marziale, for military band (1924).
Two Hymn-tune Preludes, for small orchestra (MS.).
Five Variants of 'Dives and Lazarus' (1939).
Partita, for double string orchestra (1948).
Concerto grosso, for strings (1950).
Variations for brass band (1957).

Solo Instruments and Orchestra

The Lark Ascending, for violin and small orchestra (1914).
Concerto accademico, D minor, for violin and strings (1925).
Flos Campi, for viola, chorus and small orchestra (1926).
Piano Concerto (1933; re-arranged for two pianos and orchestra, 1946).
Suite for viola and small orchestra (1934).
Concerto for oboe and strings (1944).
Fantasia on the Old 104th, for piano, chorus and orchestra (1950).
Romance, for harmonica and strings (1953).
Tuba Concerto (1954).

Operas

The Shepherds of the Delectable Mountains (1922).
Hugh the Drover (1924). *Excerpts*
Sir John in Love (1929).
Riders to the Sea (1931).
The Poisoned Kiss (1936).
The Pilgrim's Progress (incorporating most of The Shepherds of the Delectable Mountains, 1951).

Vaughan Williams

LARGE-SCALE CHORAL WORKS
(for chorus and orchestra, unless otherwise indicated)

Willow Wood (D. G. Rossetti), for baritone solo, women's chorus and orchestra (1903; published 1909).

Toward the Unknown Region (Walt Whitman) (1905; published 1907; revised 1918).

A Sea Symphony (*see* 'Symphonies').

Five Mystical Songs (*see* 'Solo Songs').

Fantasia on Christmas Carols, for baritone solo, chorus and orchestra (1912).

Mass in G minor, for soli and chorus unaccompanied (1922; Anglican version, 1923).

Sancta Civitas, oratorio for tenor and baritone soli, semi-chorus, chorus and orchestra (1925).

Flos Campi (*see* 'Solo Instruments and Orchestra').

The Hundredth Psalm (1929).

Benedicite, for soprano solo, chorus and orchestra (1930).

Three Choral Hymns (Coverdale) (1930).

In Windsor Forest (adapted from *Sir John in Love*, 1931).

Magnificat, for contralto solo, women's chorus and orchestra (1932).

Five Tudor Portraits, for contralto and baritone soli, chorus and orchestra (1936).

Dona nobis pacem, for soprano and baritone soli, chorus and orchestra (1936).

Flourish for a Coronation (1937).

Festival Te Deum, F major (1937).

Serenade to Music, for 16 solo voices and orchestra; also arranged for chorus, semi-chorus and orchestra (1938).

Thanksgiving for Victory, for soprano solo, speaker, chorus and orchestra (1945; later revised as *A Song of Thanksgiving*).

Fanatsia on the Old 104th (*see* 'Solo Instruments and Orchestra').

Folk Songs of the Four Seasons, for women's chorus and orchestra (1950).

The Sons of Light (1951).

An Oxford Elegy, for speaker, chorus and orchestra (1952).

A Cotswold Romance, for soprano and tenor soli, chorus and orchestra (adapted by Maurice Jacobson from *Hugh the Drover*; 1953).

Hodie (*This Day*), for soprano, tenor and baritone soli, chorus, organ and orchestra (1954).

Appendix B—Catalogue of Works

(a) Part-songs
(unaccompanied unless otherwise indicated)

Three Elizabethan Part-songs, S.A.T.B.
1. *Sweet Day* (Herbert) (c. 1896).
2. *The Willow Song* (Shakespeare) (c. 1891).
3. *O Mistress Mine* (Shakespeare) (c. 1891; published 1913).

Sound Sleep (Christina Rossetti), S.S.A., with piano (1903).

Rest (Christina Rossetti), S.S.A.T.B. (1905).

Ring Out, ye Bells (Sidney), S.S.A.T.B. (1905).

Fain would I Change that Note (anon.), S.A.T.B. (1907; arranged for T.T.B.B., 1927).

Come Away, Death (Shakespeare), S.S.A.T.B. (1909).

Love is a Sickness (S. Daniel), S.A.T.B. (1918).

It was a Lover (Shakespeare), S.A., with piano (1921).

Dirge for Fidele (Shakespeare), S.A.T.B. (1921).

Where is Home for Me? (Euripides, trans. Gilbert Murray), 2 parts with piano (1921).

England, my England (Henley), S.A.T.B. (1941).

Three Shakespeare Songs, S.A.T.B. (1951).
1. *Full Fathom Five.*
2. *The Cloud-capp'd Towers.*
3. *Over Hill, Over Dale.*

Silence and Music (Ursula Wood), S.A.T.B. (1953).

Heart's Music (Campion), S.A.T.B. (1955).

Songs for a Spring Festival (Ursula Vaughan Williams), mostly for voices in unison with accompaniment (1955).

(b) Arrangements
(unaccompanied unless otherwise indicated)

I. Mixed voices:

Full Fathom Five (Purcell) (1913).

✓*Five English Folk Songs* (1913):
  ✓1. *The Dark-eyed Sailor.*
  2. *The Springtime of the Year.*
  3. *Just as the Tide was Flowing.*
  4. *The Lover's Ghost.*
  5. *Wassail Song.*

Our Love Goes Out (1920).
The Lass that Loves a Sailor (1921).
Heart of Oak (1921).
The Mermaid (1921).
Loch Lomond (1921).
✓*Linden Lea* (1921).
A Farmer's Son so Sweet (1923).
✓*Bushes and Briars* (1924).
Alister McAlpine's Lament (1924).
✓*Ca' the Yowes* (1924).
Mannin Veen (1924).
The Turtle Dove (1924).
I'll Never Love thee More (1934).
✓*John Dory* (1934).
Almighty Word (Tallis's III mode melody) (1953).
✓*The Old Hundredth*, for choir, congregation, organ and orchestra (1953).

II. Male voices:

✓*Bushes and Briars* (1908).
The Jolly Ploughboy (1908).
The Winter is Gone (1912).
Down Among the Dead Men (1912).
✓*Ward, the Pirate* (1912).
✓*The Turtle Dove* (1912).
Heart of Oak (1921).
The Farmer's Boy (1921).
✓*Loch Lomond*, baritone solo, T.T.B.B. (1921).
The Old Folks at Home (S. Foster), baritone solo, T.T.B.B. (1921).
Mannin Veen (1921).
A Farmer's Son so Sweet (1923).
✓*The Seeds of Love* (1923).
High Germany (1923).
Ca' the Yowes (1925).
✓*An Acre of Land* (1934).
The Ploughman (1934).
The World it Went Well with Me then (1934).
Nine Carols (1942).
The New Commonwealth (1948).

Appendix B—Catalogue of Works

(c) Anthems, etc.

(unaccompanied unless otherwise indicated)

Three Motets:

    1. *O Praise the Lord*, triple chorus (1920).

    2. *O Clap your Hands*, double chorus, brass and organ (1920).

    3. *Lord, Thou hast been our Refuge*, chorus, semi-chorus and orchestra (1921).

O vos omnes, alto solo and 8-part chorus (1922).

Magnificat and Nunc Dimittis, C major, unison voices and organ (1925).

Te Deum, G major, S.A.T.B. and organ (1928).

The Pilgrim Pavement, chorus and organ (1934).

O How Amiable, S.A.T.B. and organ (1934; published 1939).

Morning, Communion and Evening Service, D minor, unison voices, S.A.T.B. and organ (1939).

A Hymn of Freedom (G. W. Briggs), unison voices with accompaniment (1939).

Six Choral Songs to be sung in time of war (Shelley), unison voices with orchestra (1940).

Valiant-for-Truth, S.A.T.B. and organ (1941).

The Airmen's Hymn (Lord Lytton), unison voices and accompaniment (1942).

Two Carols (1945):

    1. *Come Love we God.*

    2. *There is a Flower.*

The Souls of the Righteous, treble, tenor and baritone soli, chorus S.A.T.B. (1947).

My Soul, Praise the Lord, S.A.T.B. (1947).

Prayer to the Father of Heaven (Skelton), S.A.T.B. (1948).

The Voice out of the Whirlwind (Book of Job), S.A.T.B. (1947).

O Taste and See, S.A.T.B. (1953).

A Choral Flourish (Psalm 32), S.A.T.B. (1956).

A Vision of Aeroplanes (Ezekiel), S.A.T.B. and organ (1956).

The First Nowell, soli, chorus S.A.T.B. and small orchestra (1959).

Vaughan Williams

SOLO SONGS

(with piano accompaniment, unless otherwise indicated)

Whither must I wander? (R. L. Stevenson) *c.* 1894; published 1912).[1]
How Can the Tree but Wither? (Lord Vaux) (*c.* 1896, published 1934).
The Splendour Falls (Tennyson) (*c.* 1896; published 1905).
Claribel (Tennyson) (*c.* 1896; published 1906).
Dreamland (Christina Rossetti) (*c.* 1898; published 1906).
Linden Lea (W. Barnes) (*c.* 1900; published 1912).
Blackmwore by the Stour (W. Barnes) (*c.* 1900; published 1912).[2]
The Winter's Willow (W. Barnes) (*c.* 1903; published 1903).
Adieu (A. E. Ferguson, from the German) (1903).
Tears, Idle Tears (Tennyson) (1903).
When I am Dead (Christina Rossetti) (1903).
Orpheus with his Lute (Shakespeare) (first setting) (1903).
The House of Life (D. G. Rossetti) (1903):
  1. *Lovelight.*   *Love Sight!*
  2. *Silent Noon.*
  3. *Love's Minstrels.*
  4. *Heart's Haven.*
  5. *Death-in-love.*
  6. *Love's Last Gift.*
Songs of Travel (R. L. Stevenson):
  1. *The Vagabond.*[3]
  2. *Let Beauty Awake.*[4]
  3. *The Roadside Fire.*[3]
  4. *Youth and Love.*[4]
  5. *In Dreams.*[4]
  6. *The Infinite Shining Heavens.*[4]
  7. *Whither must I wander?*[5]
  8. *Bright is the Ring of Words.*
  9. *I have Trod the Upward and the Downward Slope.*[6]

---

[1] No. 7 of the original *Songs of Travel* (see below), first published in the *Vocalist* in 1902.

[2] The Barnes songs and *Whither must I wander?* were published by the *Vocalist* in 1902 and 1903.

[3] Published as *Songs of Travel*, first set, 1905.

[4] Published as *Songs of Travel*, second set, 1907.

[5] Published in the *Vocalist*, 1902, and subsequently by Boosey & Hawkes in 1912 (see above).

[6] Found among the composer's manuscripts after his death and first performed in a broadcast recital, 20th May 1960.

Appendix B—Catalogue of Works

Cradle Song (Coleridge) (1905).

Buonaparte (Hardy) (1909).

The Sky above the Roof (Mabel Dearmer, after Verlaine) (1909).

Five Mystical Songs (George Herbert), with optional chorus and organ or orchestra (1911):
1. *Easter.*
2. *I Got me Flowers.*
3. *Love Bade me Welcome.*
4. *The Call.*
5. *Antiphon.*

On Wenlock Edge (A. E. Housman), for tenor, piano and string quartet (*ad lib*) (1911):
1. *On Wenlock Edge.*
2. *From Far, from Eve and Morning.*
3. *Is my Team Ploughing?*
4. *Oh, when I was in Love with You.*
5. *Bredon Hill.*
6. *Clun.*

Four Hymns, for tenor, piano and viola obbligato (1914; published 1920):
1. *Lord, Come Away* (Jeremy Taylor).
2. *Who is that Fair One?* (Isaac Watts).
3. *Come Love, Come Lord* (Richard Crashaw).
4. *Evening Hymn* (Robert Bridges, from the Greek) (also with orchestra).

Merciles Beauty (Chaucer), 3 rondels, with accompaniment for two violins and cello (1922).

Three Poems by Walt Whitman (1925):
1. *Nocturne.*
2. *A Clear Midnight.*
3. *Joy, Shipmate, Joy.*

Four Poems by Fredegond Shove (1925):
1. *Motion and Stillness.*
2. *Four Nights.*
3. *The New Ghost.*
4. *The Water Mill.*

Two Poems by Seumas O'Sullivan, with optional piano accompaniment (1925):
1. *The Twilight People*
2. *A Piper.*

Vaughan Williams

Nine Songs for Voice and Violin (A. E. Housman) (c. 1925; published 1954):
1. We'll to the Woods no More.
2. Along the Field.
3. The Half-moon Westers Low.
4. The Soldier.
5. Goodbye.
6. In the Morning.
7. The Sigh that Leaves the Grasses.
8. Fancy's Knell.
9. With Rue my Heart is Laden.

Three Songs from Shakespeare (1925):
1. Orpheus with his Lute (second setting).
2. Take, O take those Lips Away.
3. When Icicles Hang by the Wall.

In the Spring (W. Barnes) (1952).

Seven Songs from 'The Pilgrim's Progress' (Bunyan) (1952):
1. Watchful's Song.
2. The Song of the Pilgrim.
3. The Pilgrim's Psalm.
4. The Song of the Leaves of Life and the Waters of Life.
5. The Song of Vanity Fair.
6. The Woodcutter's Song.
7. The Bird's Song.

Ten Songs for Voice and Oboe (Blake) (1958):
1. Infant Joy.
2. A Poison True.
3. The Piper.
4. London.
5. The Lamb.
6. The Shepherd.
7. Ah! Sunflower.
8. Cruelty has a Human Heart.
9. The Divine Image.
10. Eternity.

Three Vocalises for Soprano and Clarinet (1960).

Four Last Songs (Ursula Vaughan Williams) (1960):
1. Procris.

2. *Tired.*
3. *Hands, Eyes and Heart.*
4. *Menelaus.*

UNISON SONGS

Let us Now Praise Famous Men (Ecclesiasticus) (1923).
Darest thou Now, O Soul (Walt Whitman) (1925).
Three Songs from Shakespeare (*see* 'Solo Songs').
Three Songs for a Children's Spring Festival (Frances M. Farrer) (1930).
Nothing is Here for Tears (Milton) (1936).
A Hymn of Freedom (*see* 'Shorter Choral Works, (*c*) Anthems, etc.').
Six Choral Songs to be sung in time of war (*see* 'Shorter Choral Works, (*c*) Anthems, etc.').
The Airmen's Hymn (*see* 'Shorter Choral Works, (*c*) Anthems, etc.').
The New Commonwealth (Harold Child) (1943).
Land of our Birth (Kipling) (from *A Song of Thanksgiving*, 1945).
Almighty Word (1953).
A Vision of Aeroplanes (Ezekiel) (1956).

ARRANGEMENTS
(for unison voices or solo voice)

L'amour de moy and *Réveillez-vous, Piccarz* (1907).
Folk Songs from the Eastern Counties (1908).
Folk Songs from Sussex (1912).
Folk Songs for Schools (1912).
Spanish Ladies (1912).
Five English Folk Songs (1913).
The Turtle Dove (1919).
Eight English Traditional Carols (1919).
On Christmas Night (1919).
And All in the Morning (1919).
Down in Yon Forest (1919).
The Dark-eyed Sailor (1919).
Just as the Tide was Flowing (1919).
The Angel Gabriel (1919).
Dives and Lazarus (1919).
The Motherland Song Book, Vols. III and IV; *Sea Songs and Shanties* (1919).
Twelve Traditional Carols from Herefordshire (1920).

Our Love Goes Out (1920).
The Lass that Loves a Sailor (1921).
Heart of Oak (1921).
The Mermaid (1921).
She's Like the Swallow (from Newfoundland) (1934).
Six English Folk Songs (1935):
    1. *Robin Hood and the Pedlar.*
    2. *The Ploughman.*
    3. *One Man, Two Men.*
    4. *The Brewer.*
    5. *Rolling in the Dew.*
    6. *King William.*
Two English Folk Songs, for voice and violin (1936):
    1. *Searching for Lambs.*
    2. *The Lawyer.*
Two French Folk Songs (1937):
    1. *Chanson de quête.*
    2. *La Ballade de Jésus-Christ.*
Two Old German Folk Songs (trans. by Walter Ford) (1937):
    1. *Entlaubet ist der Walde.*
    2. *Wanderlied.*
The Penguin Book of English Folk Songs (with A. L. Lloyd) (1959).

CHAMBER MUSIC

Phantasy Quintet, for strings (1921).
Romance and Pastorale, for violin and piano (1923).
String Quartet [No. 1], G minor (1924).
Six Studies in English Folk Song, for cello (or violin, or viola, or clarinet) and
    piano (1927).
Household Music: Three Preludes on Welsh Hymn Tunes (1944).
String Quartet [No. 2], A minor ('For Jean on her Birthday') (1945).
Suite for pipes (1947).
Sonata for violin and piano, A minor (1956).

PIANO

Suite of six short pieces (1921; arranged for strings as the *Charterhouse Suite*)
Hymn-tune Prelude on Gibbons's Song 13 (1930).

Canon and Two-part Invention (1934).
2 Two-part Inventions (1934).
Valse lente and Nocturne (1934).
The Lake in the Mountains (from the music to *Forty-ninth Parallel,* 1947).

Two Pianos

Introduction and Fugue (1946).

Organ

Three Preludes on Welsh Hymn Tunes (1920).
Prelude and Fugue, C minor (1921).

Instrumental Arrangements

Perhaps the most famous arrangement is the 'Greensleeves' music from *Sir John in Love.* Apart from its original form in the opera there are also arrangements (incorporating a middle section based on the Norfolk folksong *Lovely Joan,* collected by Vaughan Williams in 1908) for small orchestra, piano duet, violin and piano, organ, and viola or cello with piano, as well as the well-known versions for string orchestra with harp and for piano solo. These arrangements are by various hands, as are a number of instrumental arrangements of other works by Vaughan Williams.

Editions

Purcell's *Welcome Songs,* ed. for the Purcell Society in two volumes (XV and XVIII) (1905 and 1910).
Music of *The English Hymnal* (1906; 2nd ed., 1933).
Music of *Songs of Praise* (with Martin Shaw) (1925; 2nd ed., 1931).
Music of *The Oxford Book of Carols* (with Martin Shaw) (1928).

Literary Works

National Music (1934).
Some Thoughts on Beethoven's Choral Symphony and Other Writings (1953).
The Making of Music (1955).

Some of the earlier essays, as well as his correspondence with Gustav Holst, are published in *Heirs and Rebels,* ed. by Ursula Vaughan Williams and Imogen Holst (1959). An adaptation of Bach's B minor Mass for the English liturgy remains unpublished.

APPENDIX C

Adler, Larry (born 1914), self-taught American harmonica virtuoso for whom Vaughan Williams wrote the *Romance* for harmonica and strings. After his first success in a C. B. Cochran revue in 1934 he quickly gained an international reputation and has done much to interest serious composers in the possibilities of his instrument.

Allen, Hugh P. (1869–1946), organist, conductor and educationist. A superb choir-master who was Vaughan Williams's predecessor as conductor of the Bach Choir, he became a fellow of New College in 1908 and professor of music at Oxford in 1918 on Parry's death. The same year he was appointed director of the Royal College of Music and was responsible for appointing Vaughan Williams and Holst to the teaching staff there.

d'Aranyi, Jelly (born 1895), Hungarian-born violinist who settled in London in 1923 after having studied at the Budapest Conservatoire under Hubay. She greatly impressed Vaughan Williams by her musical gifts and gave the first performance of his violin Concerto, as well as appearing many times as a soloist at the Leith Hill Festival.

Barbirolli, John (born 1899), English conductor of Italian extraction who studied at the Royal Academy of Music, formed his own chamber orchestra, and was for a time conductor of the Scottish Orchestra before going to New York in 1936 to take over the Philharmonic Symphony Orchestra from Toscanini; in 1943 he returned to England to re-form and revitalize the Hallé Orchestra and has remained in charge of it since.

Bax, Arnold (1883–1953), British composer and friend of Vaughan Williams, who dedicated his fourth Symphony to him. A prolific writer, he composed seven symphonies, a number of tone poems and much chamber music and keyboard music, richly Romantic and mainly lyrical in idiom.

Boult, Adrian (born 1889), English conductor who studied under Nikisch and at Oxford. In 1924 he became conductor of the City of Birmingham Orchestra, and director of music and chief conductor of the B.B.C. Symphony Orchestra in 1930, training it to such a pitch that it became one of the best in the world. After retiring from the B.B.C. in 1950 he accepted the post of musical director of the London Philharmonic Orchestra.

Broadwood, Lucy (1859–1929), the first hon. secretary of the Folk Song Society and one of the first systematic collectors of English folksong. Together with J. A. Fuller-Maitland she was responsible for the publication, in 1893, of *English County Songs*.

Butterworth, George S. K. (1885–1916), composer, critic and folksong collector. Vaughan Williams made his acquaintance after he had gone down from Oxford, where he had been president of the University Music Club. A sensitive and gifted musician who, like Vaughan Williams, felt that English folksong fertilized his own idiom. It was on his suggestion that Vaughan Williams wrote the *London Symphony*, and he provided programme notes for its first performance.

Child, Harold (1869–1945), author and journalist who became secretary to the Royal Society of Painters, Etchers and Engravers in 1902, Assistant editor of the *Academy* in 1905, and dramatic critic of the *Observer* in 1912. He was the librettist of Vaughan Williams's ballad opera *Hugh the Drover* and also wrote the words of the song *The New Commonwealth*.

Cobbett, Walter W. (1847–1937), amateur violinist, musical patron and lexicographer, who instituted and endowed prizes for chamber music and its performances at the Royal College of Music and elsewhere. A great lover of chamber music and of string instruments, he also collected and constructed violins. Vaughan Williams won one of the Cobbett prizes with his *Phantasy Quintet*, the fantasy being a form that Cobbett particularly admired. He was also responsible for the encyclopaedic *Survey of Chamber Music* which bears his name.

Cohen, Harriet, leading exponent of modern English piano music and friend of many English composers, including Elgar, Bax, Ireland and Vaughan Williams, who dedicated his piano Concerto to her.

Davison, Archibald T. (born 1883), American scholar, professor of music at Harvard from 1940 onwards, whose interests lie particularly in the field of choral music.

Dearmer, Percy (1867–1936), Anglican clergyman, scholar, art connoisseur and sociologist who persuaded Vaughan Williams to become musical editor of *The English Hymnal*. His great interest in the place of the arts in religious worship and his profound knowledge of liturgics greatly influenced the shape of the book, and he later collaborated with Vaughan Williams on *Songs of Praise* and the *Oxford Book of Carols*.

Desmond, Astra (born 1898), English contralto singer for whom Vaughan Williams wrote the solo part in the *Magnificat*. Her versatility is shown by the fact that she also gave the first performance of the solo part in *Five Tudor Portraits*.

Douglas, Roy (born 1907), English composer and arranger who, in addition to becoming a member of the Committee for the Promotion of New Music, of which Vaughan Williams was president, has written much music for film and the B.B.C. Towards the end of Vaughan Williams's life Douglas was his trusted copyist.

Elwes, Gervase (1866–1921), English tenor singer. He served from 1891 to 1895 in the British diplomatic service. A great interpreter of English religious compositions, such as Vaughan Williams's *Five Mystical Songs*.

Epstein, Jacob (1880–1959), English sculptor, originally of American nationality, who (at his own request) did the well-known bronze head of the composer.

Falkner, Keith (born 1900), English bass-baritone singer who lived for several years in the United States and did much to develop interest in Vaughan Williams's music in that country. Director of the Royal College of Music since 1960.

Fuller-Maitland, John A. (1856–1936), English scholar, composer and pioneer of the folksong revival in England, translator of Spitta's *Bach* and music critic of *The Times* from 1889 till 1911. He collaborated with Lucy Broadwood on *English County Songs* and, together with William Barclay Squire, edited the *Fitzwilliam Virginal Book* in 1899. He also served on the editorial committee of the Purcell Society.

Gladstone, Francis Edward (1845–1928), English organist, teacher and composer who was responsible for Vaughan Williams's first instruction at the Royal College of Music. He was a prolific composer of organ music, songs, part-songs, choral and church music, professor of harmony at the Royal College of Music, a celebrated cathedral organist and choirmaster and a first cousin of William Ewart Gladstone.

Gray, Alan (1855–1935), English organist and composer, conductor of the Cambridge Univsersity Musical Society from 1892 till 1912 and organist of Trinity College from 1892 till 1930. He originally studied to be a lawyer before turning to music after taking two degrees in his original subject.

Appendix C—Personalia

Gurney, Ivor (1890–1937), English composer who was also a talented lyric poet. He studied under Stanford and Vaughan Williams and showed great promise as a song-writer. He enlisted in the 2/5 Gloucester Regiment in 1914 as a private, was gassed and shell-shocked, staged a partial recovery after the First World War but became permanently mentally disabled in 1922.

Haig Brown, William (1823–1907), headmaster of Charterhouse, who took a double first at Cambridge (classics and mathematics), became a fellow of Pembroke College and took Holy Orders in 1852. After being head-master of a school in Kensington he was chosen as headmaster of Charter-house in 1863. It was under his direction that the school emigrated from Smithfield to Godalming, and it was for this that he became known as the school's second founder.

Holst, Gustav (1874–1934), English composer and teacher who studied at the Royal College of Music under Stanford, where he met Vaughan Williams. His experience as an orchestral player and teacher, his breadth of interests and his fearless criticism were invaluable to his friend. There is no need here to mention his many fine compositions, since they are still regularly performed, but Vaughan Williams's most extended tribute to him occurs in the *Dictionary of National Biography*, and his life has been described by his daughter Imogen.

Howells, Herbert (born 1892), English composer and scholar, professor of composition at the Royal College of Music and King Edward Professor of Music in the University of London. Vaughan Williams dedicated *Hodie* to him.

Hull, Arthur Eaglefield (1876–1928), English organist, writer on music, composer, teacher and patron. After settling in Huddersfield, where he did much to stimulate musical teaching and activity, he founded the British Music Society in 1918, which aimed at bringing forward interest-ing contemporary British works for performance. He wrote a number of books, including studies of Scriabin and Cyril Scott.

Irving, Ernest (1878–1953), English conductor who worked mainly in the theatre and the film studio, becoming musical director for Ealing Films Ltd in 1935, a post he held till his death. Vaughan Williams's *Sinfonia antartica* is dedicated to him, and he was in charge of the orchestra for the film *Scott of the Antarctic*, from the music of which the symphony originated.

Jacob, Gordon (born 1895), English composer, pupil of Vaughan Williams. He taught at Birkbeck and Morley Colleges and joined the staff of the

209

Royal College of Music in 1926. He was Collard Fellow of the Worshipful Company of Musicians from 1943 to 1946. His music is notable for impeccable craftsmanship and superb orchestration.

Keynes, Geoffrey (born 1887), English scholar and surgeon whose enormously varied interests include a wide and profound knowledge of literature. House surgeon at St Bartholomew's Hospital from 1913, he was chief assistant there in 1920, and Hunterian Professor at the Royal College of Surgeons in 1923, 1929 and 1945. He has edited the writings of Blake, Sir Thomas Browne and Izaak Walton, and compiled bibliographies of writers ranging from the seventeenth-century naturalist John Ray to Rupert Brooke. He was knighted in 1955.

Lambert, Constant (1905–51), English composer, critic and conductor; one-time pupil of Vaughan Williams at the Royal College of Music, where he had won a scholarship from Christ's Hospital. Besides writing a number of highly original compositions, he also arranged the score of Vaughan Williams's *Job* for its first stage performance, and his work as a ballet conductor was in considerable measure responsible for expanding the appreciation of ballet in this country. His *Music Ho!* remains one of the most brilliant and stimulating critical accounts of modern trends in music yet written.

Maconchy, Elizabeth (born 1907), English composer and pupil of Vaughan Williams. She studied at the Royal College of Music and in Prague. Although she is known mainly for her chamber music, her opera *The Sofa*, to a libretto by Vaughan Williams's widow, was well received on its first performance.

Mathieson, Muir (born 1911), Scottish conductor who won the Boult and Leverhulme conducting scholarships at the Royal College of Music and later specialized in conducting for the film studio. He has been musical director to the J. Arthur Rank Organisation since 1945 and has been responsible for persuading many eminent composers (among them Vaughan Williams) to write scores for feature films.

Morris, R. O. (1886–1948), English composer and scholar who married Vaughan Williams's sister-in-law. He was professor of counterpoint at the Royal College of Music and wrote many standard textbooks on that subject.

Mukle, May (born 1880), English cellist, active both as a soloist and as a chamber-music player, for whom Vaughan Williams wrote his only extended work featuring the instrument (apart from a *Fantasia* on Sussex folksongs for Casals, afterwards destroyed).

Mullinar, Michael (born 1895), pianist and composer who studied composition under Vaughan Williams at the Royal College of Music and later became his copyist. The sixth Symphony is dedicated to him, and the piano part in the *Fantasia on the Old 104th* was written for him.

O'Sullivan, Seumas (1879–1958), Irish poet; editor of the *Dublin Magazine*.

Parratt, Walter (1841–1924), organist, teacher and composer who held a long list of distinguished posts culminating in that of Master of the King's Musick from 1893 till his death. He also succeeded Parry as professor of music at Oxford in 1908 and was the first professor of the organ at the Royal College of Music. His interest in counterpoint induced him to draw attention to works by composers like Reger who were virtually unknown at that time in England.

Parry, C. Hubert H. (1848–1918), English composer, scholar and philosopher. Among the first musicians in England to develop an interest in the later works of Wagner, he had been trained as accountant (despite early evidence of his musical gifts.) A many-sided man whose gifts ranged from athletics to great administrative ability, he composed voluminously as well as holding the posts of director of the Royal College of Music (from 1894), professor of music at Oxford (1900–8) and teacher of advanced composition at the Royal College of Music.

Sargent, Malcolm (born 1895), English conductor who is also a brilliant pianist; first appeared as a professional conductor in the 1920's, although he had already conducted Gilbert and Sullivan operettas with amateur casts as a boy. Chief conductor of the Liverpool Philharmonic Orchestra from 1942. He has conducted the Henry Wood Promenade Concerts since 1947, and was principal conductor of the B.B.C. Symphony Orchestra from 1951 to 1958.

Sedley Taylor, Charles (1834–1920), distinguished mathematician and expert on acoustics who became sixteenth Wrangler in 1859 and a fellow of Trinity College, Cambridge. He was one-time president both of the Cambridge University Musical Society and of the University Music Club, and wrote books on such subjects as *Science and Music*.

Sharp, Cecil J. (1859–1924), the most famous of the pioneers in the rediscovery of English folksong, an inspired teacher, and a tireless worker on behalf of the subject to which he dedicated his studies. He was educated at Uppingham and Clare College, Cambridge, and after spending some time in Australia, where he was assistant organist of Adelaide Cathedral from 1889 to 1891, returned to Britain, where he taught music in schools.

It was in 1899 that he first realized the beauties of traditional song, and from then onwards he travelled far and wide—even to the Appalachian Mountains of the United States—in search of material. A vigorous and forceful personality, he always regarded scholarship as a means to an aesthetic and educational end.

Shaw, Martin (1876–1958), English composer and scholar who collaborated with Vaughan Williams on *Songs of Praise* and the *Oxford Book of Carols*. His songs are perhaps the most successful of his compositions, but he also wrote two musical plays for children, much church music and an oratorio *The Redeemer*.

Shove, Fredegond (1889–1949), Georgian poet, the wife of G. F. Shove, Reader in Economics at Cambridge, whom she married in 1915.

Stanford, Charles V. (1852–1924), Irish composer, teacher and scholar, who was a choral scholar at Queens' College, Cambridge, organist of Trinity College, conductor of the University Music Society and the Bach Choir in London, musical director of the Leeds Festival, professor of music at Cambridge from 1887 to 1924 and professor of composition at the Royal College of Music from its inception. A superb teacher and a gifted though derivative composer, he wrote seven symphonies, several operas and a large number of songs, choral and chamber works, but is now best known as the teacher of such composers as Vaughan Williams, Bliss, Ireland and Benjamin.

Stewart, Jean (born 1914), English violist who played in the Menges Quartet and the Richards Piano Quintet and often appeared at the Leith Hill Festival.

Stoeckel, Carl (1858–1925), American philanthropist who was active in founding and financing music festivals and societies in his native region, one of which, the Norfolk Music Festival, became internationally famous.

Toye, Geoffrey (1889–1942), English conductor who devoted much attention during his career to the popularization of contemporary English works. An interest in the stage—thanks to his experience with the D'Oyly Carte Opera Company—is shown in his compositions.

Waddington, Sidney P. (1869–1953), English composer and teacher who studied at the Royal College of Music, in Frankfurt and in Vienna, worked as *maestro al pianoforte* at Covent Garden, taught harmony and counterpoint at the Royal College of Music and became master of the opera class there. His compositions include a setting of *John Gilpin*, a piano concerto and a body of chamber music.

Appendix C—Personalia

Walthew, Richard (1872–1951), English composer who studied with Vaughan Williams as a pupil of Parry and Stanford.

Wood, Charles (1866–1926), Irish-born teacher and composer who was one of the first scholars of the Royal College of Music, where he studied with Parry and Stanford, later becoming organist scholar of Selwyn College, Cambridge, and organist at Caius College, where he was elected to a fellowship in 1894. On Stanford's death in 1924 he became professor of music at Cambridge. He was a prolific composer.

Wood, Henry J. (1869–1944), English conductor who founded and directed the famous Promenade Concerts at the Queen's Hall (and latterly at the Royal Albert Hall) which bear his name. A stalwart protagonist of contemporary music, and particularly of contemporary British music.

APPENDIX D

BIBLIOGRAPHY

Blom, Eric, 'Vaughan Williams,' in *The Book of Modern Composers*. (New York, 1942.)

Dickinson, A. E. F., 'An Introduction to the Music of Vaughan Williams.' (London, 1928.)

——, 'The Legacy of Vaughan Williams: a Retrospect.' (*Music Review*, XIX, 1958, pp. 290–304.)

——, 'Toward the Unknown Region.' (*Music Review*, IX, 1948, pp. 275 ff.)

——, *Vaughan Williams* (Faber & Faber, 1963).

Foss, Hubert, 'Ralph Vaughan Williams: a Study.' (London, 1950.)

Fox Strangways, A. H., 'Ralph Vaughan Williams.' (*Music & Letters*, I, 1920, pp. 78–86).

Hawthorne, Robin, 'A Note on the Music of Ralph Vaughan Williams.' (*Music Review*, IX, 1948, pp. 269 ff.)

Howells, Herbert, 'Vaughan Williams's "Pastoral" Symphony.' (*Music & Letters*, III, 1922, pp. 122–32.)

Howes, Frank, 'The Dramatic Works of Ralph Vaughan Williams.' (London, 1937.)

——, 'The Later Works of Ralph Vaughan Williams.' (London, 1937.)

——, 'The Music of Ralph Vaughan Williams.' (London, 1954.)

Kimmel, William, 'Vaughan Williams's Choice of Words.' (*Music & Letters*, XIX, 1938, pp. 132–42).

Murrill, Herbert, 'Vaughan Williams's Pilgrim.' (*Music & Letters*, XXXII, 1951, pp. 324–7.)

Pakenham, Simona, 'Vaughan Williams: a Discovery of his Music.' (London, 1957.)

Pannain, Guido, 'Ralph Vaughan Williams,' in *Modern Composers*. (London, 1932.)

Rubbra, Edmund, 'The Later Vaughan Williams.' (*Music & Letters*, XVIII, 1937, pp. 1–8.)

Tovey, *Donald Francis,* 'Vaughan Williams: "Concerto Accademico", "Pastoral Symphony" and "Overture to The Wasps",' in *Some English Symphonists* (London, 1941). Reprinted from *Essays in Musical Analysis,* II and IV. (London, 1935–6.)

Young, Percy M., 'Vaughan Williams.' (London, 1953.)

There are also articles and sections on aspects of Vaughan Williams's work in the following Pelican books:

'British Music in our Time' (1946): article by Scott Goddard, pp. 83–98.

'Chamber Music' (1957): article by David Cox, pp. 338–40.

'The Concerto' (1952): article by William Mann, pp. 422–30.

'The Symphony' (1949): article by Scott Goddard, pp. 395–429.

For a list of writings by Vaughan Williams (including his published correspondence) see under Appendix B, p. 205.

INDEX

INDEX

Index

226